D0899193

RETREAT FROM REFORM

Nagai Ryūtarō
(1881–1944)

RETREAT FROM REFORM

*Patterns of Political Behavior
in Interwar Japan*

SHARON MINICHIELLO

UNIVERSITY OF HAWAII PRESS
Honolulu

First printing 1984
Second printing 1986
©1984 UNIVERSITY OF HAWAII PRESS
ALL RIGHTS RESERVED
MANUFACTURED IN THE UNITED STATES OF AMERICA

Library of Congress Cataloging in Publication Data

Minichiello, Sharon, 1939–
    Retreat from reform.

    Bibliography: p.
    Includes index.
    1. Nagai, Ryūtarō, 1881–1944. 2. Japan—Politics
and government—1912–1945. I. Title.
DS885.5.N26M56 1984   952.03   84–8535
ISBN 0–8248–0778–2

Frontispiece photograph of Nagai Ryūtarō courtesy of Nagai Michio

To My Parents

Contents

Preface

IN his provocative essay "Values and Social Change in Modern Japan" Robert Bellah addresses the matter of problematique. He makes the point that each of us comes to a problem with a sense of it that is not dictated by objective reality. We are predisposed (in part, at least) by the situation in which we find ourselves—including the ideological dimensions of that situation. As Bellah sees it, the problems of modern Japanese history take focus around the date August 15, 1945, when Japan's defeat was declared by the emperor. Bellah contends that "any attempt to understand the last hundred years has to be able to cope with that fact."*

I came to my study of Japanese history with a belief that there are certain universal values that transcend the particularities of culture and circumstance. It is not surprising, then, that early in my studies I became intrigued with the problem of how Japanese who seemed so attracted to Western liberal ideals and systems in the 1910s and 1920s, could in the 1930s turn their backs on that same Western liberalism and opt for more totalitarian models, both in the national and international spheres. The political historian Maruyama Masao posed the question as follows:

What were the *internal* factors which drove Japan into her disastrous war? How was it that Japanese intellectuals, who for decades past had been absorbing Western scholarship and techniques and ways of life, who were more familiar—or at least believed themselves more familiar—with Western than with Japanese or Asian traditions, proved in the end so willing to accept, or at least so impotent to halt, the onrush of a blindly nationalistic militarism inspired by the crudest beliefs in the mythology of a uniquely Japanese "Imperial Way"?†

Maruyama's focus here was the intellectuals, but I was concerned also with Japanese leadership, both those who could work through

* Bellah, "Values and Social Change," pp. 42–44.
† Maruyama, *Thought and Behaviour*, p. xii.

formal channels to make and influence policy and those who had the
ability and means to affect Japanese public opinion in other ways—
through the power of the spoken and written word and through the
direction they provided in Japanese movements. An essay on Nagai
Ryūtarō by Peter Duus* suggested to me that a larger study on this
political reformer might facilitate deeper understanding of prewar
Japan. An educator, politician, and governmental official, Nagai
Ryūtarō (1881–1944) was a man intimately involved with his times.
Because he drew so intensively on the life around him, his experience
had the potential to reveal much about the zeitgeist of those years.

All of these factors have led to this book. What follows is an
attempt to illuminate in some way the sociopolitical dynamics of
Japan's interwar period, especially the complex relationship between
the two periods that comprised those years, the era of "Taishō
democracy" and the more authoritarian early Shōwa period. I have
adopted a hypothetical behavior pattern, which I have labeled the
"reformist" pattern, and a case study, that of Nagai Ryūtarō, to
examine the problem. My overall aims are to provide additional
insight into the nature of Japan's problems as it moved into the mat-
uration stage of its modernization process, and, through Nagai's
experience, to understand (if not entirely appreciate) how some Japanese came to choose the tragic options they did as the 1930s progressed.

This is not an attempt to present a neatly packaged explanation of
interwar Japan, but rather a consideration of alternatives to the
"Taishō democracy–Shōwa fascism" dichotomy that has provided
the conceptual framework for so much of the study of early
twentieth-century Japan since 1945. I have adopted instead the term
"reformism." This seems both a viable concept with which to analyze
interwar Japan from a more Japanese-oriented perspective and a
means to see that same period as part of an ongoing pattern of
response to the major challenges Japan has faced since the mid-
nineteenth century.

Many people and organizations provided the assistance necessary
to complete this work. I am greatly indebted to my dissertation advisor, George Akita, who stimulated and supported my commitment to
the study of Japanese history; to Professor Satō Seizaburō, who initially suggested the viability of this research; and to Professor Peter
Duus, who was instrumental in getting the project started. All three

---

* Duus, "Nagai Ryūtarō: Tactical Dilemmas," pp. 399–424.

have been a source of inspiration and ideas, as have other of my colleagues and teachers who read the manuscript at various stages of completion: Professors Gordon Berger, Thomas Burkman, Marius Jansen, Harry Lamley, and Patricia Steinhoff.
Nagai Michio arranged for me to meet in Tokyo and Kanazawa with family and acquaintances of his father, Nagai Ryūtarō, the case study in this research. He also made available the latter's personal library, important since most of Ryūtarō's papers were burned in bombing raids during the war. Katayama Tetsu, Matsumoto Shigeharu, and Yatsugi Kazuo were obliging with their time for interviews. Among the many others who have contributed in numerous ways, I wish to acknowledge Arai Kōtarō, Itō Takashi, Kamikawa Rikuzō, Kimbara Samon, Kimura Ki, Kitaoka Shin'ichi, Matsumoto Sannosuke, Matsuo Takayoshi, Mikuriya Takashi, Mitani Taichirō, Murayama Kingo, Ian Nish, and Sakai Yukichi.
I received generous financial assistance for this study from the American Council of Learned Societies, American Association of University Women Educational Foundation, Crown Prince Akihito Scholarship Committee, East-West Center, Hatakeyama Cultural Foundation, Japan Gift to the University of Hawaii for Japanese Studies, Loyola Marymount University, and the Yoshida International Education Foundation. The International House of Japan and Maryknoll (Japan) provided invaluable moral support along the way. I am very grateful to Iris Wiley for her work in processing the manuscript and to Patricia Crosby for her editorial expertise and insightful suggestions.
To all of the above and to the many others who helped in less direct ways, I express my appreciation.

RETREAT FROM REFORM

Introduction

On August 18, 1919, a group of young Japanese formed the Kaizō dōmei (Reconstruction League), their purpose being to change Japan along the lines of the world democratic trends that had emerged after World War I. Many of the members—some, talented up-and-coming journalists, and others, "amateur" politicians—had been in Paris at the time of the peace conference and had been incensed at the incompetence of the Japanese bureaucratic representatives at the meeting. They were indignant, too, at the Anglo-American frustration of Japanese claims. For these and other reasons Paris was, in a sense, the birthplace of Japan's "reconstruction" movement.[1]

One of the forty-five who formed the Kaizō dōmei was Nagai Ryūtarō, a journalist and former professor at Waseda University. Upon his return to Japan from the Paris conference, he published a book entitled *Kaizō no risō* (The idea of reconstruction), in which he outlined Japan's problems. He declared that although the current trend was for politics to focus more and more on the people, certain obstacles lay in the path of reconstruction in Japan.

In our country, to what extent do politicians and educators understand the spirit of the times, and how far are they prepared to adapt to those hopes? Not only do they underrate things like individual rights and freedom of conscience, but in maintaining feudalistic traditions and past customs, they have no scruples about oppressing the life of the individual and in trampling underfoot the individual character.[2]

The reason for the continued control of the Diet by a privileged few and the failure of a new Japan to evolve, Nagai continued, was that the Japanese people lacked the fervor to discover a new self. They simply had not made the necessary effort to manifest their rights.[3]

Suzuki Umeshirō, another Kaizō dōmei member, reflected the emotions of these returnees from Paris—their anxiety over the setbacks Japan had suffered there and the pressing need they felt for national unity to support the country's future international position and rights. At Versailles, so it seemed, Japan had been humiliated with the rejection of its proposed racial equality clause, and the Anglo-American powers had succeeded in maintaining the status quo that buttressed their interests. Like Nagai, Kita Ikki, Nakano Seigō, and others who had been present at the proceedings, Suzuki lashed out at Japan's ruling bureaucracy as those responsible for the country's diplomatic weakness.[4]

These same uninspired bureaucratic policies had resulted, he charged, in domestic problems of crisis proportions wherein the masses of the people—"the treasure of the Imperial House"—had fallen into acute suffering. The rice riots of 1918 bore witness to this fact. He pointed to the present sad condition of the people and questioned how Japan would survive in the twentieth century. The challenge was clear to him.

England and the United States talk of the horrors of war and advocate a League of Nations based on the ideal of peace among different peoples. Yet, they will not give at all on commercial imperialism and aggressive capitalist policies. . . . The instances of their self-centeredness are innumerable. They are all for limiting armaments on the one hand, but, on the other, for maintaining their territories, rights, and colonies as they originally were. One does not need to be a great politician or statesman to guess how the future of world peace to be secured by this League of Nations will go. There is no way to counter economic power and resources except with economic power and resources.[5]

Japan's first step to meet the challenge should be major reforms in national social policies. He called this "social reformism" and added that unlike some commentators, he saw no reason for this to clash with Japan's efforts at economic international competition. "Rather, I believe the two share an interdependent relationship and act in unison toward the fulfillment of each other."[6] Only through the necessary social reforms could Japan compete and survive in the postwar world.

The Kaizō dōmei was typical of Taishō-democracy groups, but the goals of this group took a more concrete form than those of other societies. One might say those goals expressed the greatest number of public commitments to the aims of the Taishō-democracy movements.[7] As listed in the league platform, they were:

1. realization of universal suffrage
2. abolition of the distinction between the peerage and the common people
3. ending bureaucratic diplomacy

4. establishing democratic politics
5. official recognition of labor unions
6. guaranteeing the livelihood of the people
7. socialistic reform of the tax system
8. liberation of formalistic education
9. reform of rule in the new territories
10. ridding the Imperial Household of corruption.[8]

These, along with the general aim of reconstructing the existing political parties, constituted the work these men set out for themselves. The platform, in fact, represented some of the central issues around which activity for political and social reform revolved for the rest of the Taishō period. The issues were not new ones. They had been demanding attention in varying degrees as problems resulting from imbalances within the Meiji system became increasingly evident. The very political, economic, social, and military distortions and strains resulting from the Meiji program of modernization, in fact, had shaped the dominant Taishō trends.

It was in reaction to these problems that social reformers and politicians like Nagai Ryūtarō appeared. He was not so prominent a figure as Itō Hirobumi, Yamagata Aritomo, Hara Takashi, Katō Takaaki, or Ōkuma Shigenobu (though he was often called a "little Ōkuma" by his contemporaries).[9] But if Taishō democracy may be described as a significant reform movement predicated on democratic principles, then an analysis of the thought and action of one of the most visible participants of that movement may be conducive to a clearer understanding of the Taishō period as a whole.[10]

As a reformer and politician Nagai had many unique experiences, and in attempting to cope with Japan's problems, he did not follow the same route as more well-known figures of the period, such as Yoshino Sakuzō, Nakano Seigō, or Ōyama Ikuo. In a sense he was more mainstream in that concern for his own political advancement deterred him from behavior unsuited to that goal. (Indeed, he became a cabinet minister three times.) Being more in line with the major trends of thought and action of the times, he could not help but share the sentiments of a greater number of his countrymen. He was also representative of a composite political type active in the Taishō–early Shōwa period of Japanese history, a type that shaded into people on either side of the political fence but that nevertheless embodied large areas of agreement symbolized by such concepts as "Japan," "nation," "emperor," and "the West."

I use the term "reformist" *(kakushin ha)* for Nagai as one of this group, as distinct from the more general term "reformer." The Japanese historian Itō Takashi has developed this reformist concept, suggesting the following thesis regarding the makeup of the group and its pattern of development during the interwar period.[11] Reformists were generally people in their twenties and thirties who appeared in the public arena about 1918–1919 with the goal of liberating their fellow Japanese from the established political system. The means was to renovate and reconstruct that system so as to build a new era for Japan both nationally and internationally. The Kaizō dōmei had a reformist cast to its membership, as did the Shinjinkai (New Man's Society), the Reimeikai (Dawn Society), the Minjin dōmeikai (People's League), the Kensetsusha dōmei (Reconstruction League), the Rōsōkai (Old and Young Society), the Rikken seinentō (Constitutional Young Men's party), the Kitakazekai (North Wind Society), and the Yūzonsha.[12]

As Itō points out, reformists covered the broad spectrum from left to right. Among these groups and individuals were undeniable differences in ideological positions, political affiliations, and the means they envisioned and adopted to achieve their renovationist goals. The freethinking Rōsōkai, for example, reflected the more radical side of the reformists—and the Taishō era.[13] The Reimeikai, an organization of intellectuals and journalists founded in December 1918 by Yoshino Sakuzō and Fukuda Tokuzō, and the Shinjinkai, formed at Tokyo Imperial University about the same time under Yoshino's guidance, were dedicated to the general goals of internationalism, democracy, and social reform. They lacked, however, the concrete proposals of the Kaizō dōmei. Moreover, the Shinjinkai eventually became more involved with labor, syndicalism, and Marxism than with the general suffrage movement, a situation somewhat different from the causes adopted by another of these groups, the Rikken seinentō.

Still, notable similarities among reformists cut across these differences. An original major objective had been the overthrow of established political power bases in Japan, but tandem to their attack was an attempt to use the bases of that power to gain authority for themselves. Another similarity was the reformists' tendency to take a strong foreign policy stand. They had had a general lack of faith in the new international order set up at the Versailles and Washington conferences—although they were willing to cooperate with it in the 1920s, resigning themselves to protect Japan's interests insofar as was possible within its framework. When it appeared from the late 1920s that this new order might not guarantee and enhance those national interests, the reformists gradually withdrew their support.

In retrospect, the result of this interplay of forces and objectives is evident. The reformists involved themselves in the various Taishō-democracy movements during the 1920s; but in the wake of internal and external crises during the early Shōwa period, many were absorbed into the Shintaisei (New Political Order) symbolized by the Taisei yokusankai (Imperial Rule Assistance Association, or IRAA). Accordingly, some say that the flower of democracy blossomed for a short while, only to wither and be supplanted by militarism. If so, why and in what way had it left behind a soil so fertile for its substitution by a more authoritarian system? What can we say of reformists like Nagai who seemed to abandon their former ideals in the thirties to jump on the bandwagon of one-party government? Part of the answer to these questions lies in the recognition that the story is really not so much one of good or bad as it is one of movement along a spectrum ranging from relatively more to less parliamentary.

Itō illustrates this in his analysis of changes within the reformist camp. He sees two factions: the "progressive-reformists" (including socialists, communists, and liberals close to these two) and the "restoration-reformists" (which may be defined broadly as the right wing).[14] During the late 1920s and early 1930s, the progressive-reformists came under governmental pressure and were largely eliminated by 1935. There were progressives who, despite imprisonment, either did not recant on former beliefs or who remained active without their former organizational affiliations. Many progressives, however, realigned with the restoration-reformists, thereby creating the combination that was to represent the reformists from that point on and that gained ascendance within the power structure. Once within the structure, reformists became part of a developing confrontation within the rightist ranks—namely, between the "reform right" and the "spiritual right," whose general positions were evident by 1940.[15]

Vanguard cliques from the core of the reformists tended to join with the reform right, which included, for example, the Tō-A kensetsu kokumin renmei (People's League for the Building of East Asia), sympathizers with the Tōsei-ha (Control faction) of the army, reform bureaucrats (including Cabinet Planning Board people), and core members of the Shōwa kenkyūkai (Shōwa Research Association). Aiming at a so-called New Political Order and a New Order in East Asia, they favored a controlled economy, the Tripartite Pact, the

push south, and, by extension if necessary, war with the United
States. The spiritual right was nationalistic more in the tradition of
the Kokuryūkai (Black Dragon Society) and the Genyōsha (Dark
Ocean Society), advocating the "true" national polity and claiming
that they represented the genuine imperial will. At this time, they
called for a speedy settlement of the China Incident, regarded a
southern advance as dangerous, and launched an attack on the New
Political Order. They tended to oppose (or at least did not encourage)
the Tripartite Pact, a controlled economy, and war with the United
States. And although their rivals in the reform right gained predominance, this spiritual right offered constant resistance.

Hypothesizing in terms of Itō's theory, one could say that Nagai
Ryūtarō walked the usual path of the reformists. He too appeared on
the public scene during the Taishō era with the goal of liberal social
and political reform. Initially a progressive-reformist, he moved into
the restoration-reformist camp in the mid-thirties. As one of the
power elite during the late thirties and Pacific War years (and as an
important member of the IRAA), he worked with some of the reform
right. He was committed to Japan's new orders at home and in East
Asia, and can be counted among those reformists who initially
wanted to change Japan along the lines of the West, but who later
helped lead their nation into war with Western nations.

Having outlined the reformist paradigm, a caveat seems war-
ranted. This work deals with Nagai not solely in terms of that paradigm. His life was too rich and unique for that. Nevertheless, each
individual reflects to some extent his time and station, and one cannot slight the impact of reformist thought and activity on both
interwar Japan and Nagai. To understand the Nagai experience (and
by extension that of other Japanese who followed a similar course) is
also to understand somewhat better the zeitgeist of that era, the relationship between the Taishō and early Shōwa periods, and the meaning of the interwar years for the course of modern Japanese history.
Such topics make up the chapters that follow.

The basic premise of the background chapter, "Taishō Democracy," is that the term is not an empty one. The period was a time of
social, political, and economic ferment in which some Japanese were
attempting to become world citizens in line with universal post–
World War I democratic trends.[16] In Japan this current found
expression in two ways: the *spirit* of democracy, as was manifest in the
liberalistic mobilization of the people through various democratic
movements; and the *structure* of democracy through establishment of

party cabinets and recognition thereby of the parties as a major constituent of political power. Although brief, the period from 1924 to 1932 became known as that of *kensei no jōdō,* or "constitutional government as the normal way of running the state." A second thesis of this background chapter is that the formula *wakon yōsai* (Japanese ethics and Western knowledge), which the Japanese scholar Sakuma Shōzan had advocated in the latter years of the Tokugawa period, retained import in Taishō Japan. Sakuma had pushed for this policy to cope with the Western threat of his time, and concerned Taishō Japanese espoused a version of the *wakon yōsai* approach in dealing with Japan's problems in the post–World War I era. The result was the presence of two parallel lines of thought and action. One was that of change, modification, and adaptation—a pragmatic strategy designed to take in from outside that which was necessary for national survival and progression and adjust it to the requirements of the times. In Taishō this would be represented by the democratic reforms and practices that later gave the period its popular name.

The second line was that of continuity—the Japanese tendency toward traditionalism, their nationalism as a people, as well as the emperor system around which that nationalism revolved. This line would be represented by the ideal of restorationism.[17] Just as an awareness of the foreign threat provided a stimulus to those calling for reform and restoration in the mid-nineteenth century, so it was with those demanding a Taishō (and, later, Shōwa) restoration.[18] James Morley once wrote regarding Japanese history, "Scratch a modernizer and find a nationalist." In terms of this study, his statement might be modified to read, "Scratch a reformist and find a nationalist."[19]

The major portion of this work consists of five chapters on Nagai, analyzing his experience in terms of the reformist paradigm. I portray the young Nagai as a liberal and a democrat, drawing at the same time a distinction between the concepts of liberalism and democracy. One of the differences in these two is that liberalism aims at the ideals of plurality and freedom of the individual, and democracy, at broadening the base of the people's participation in politics.[20] This distinction is significant in grasping the role of each in prewar Japan and their influence on people like Nagai. In addition to the sway of democratic trends, definite Western elements were present in Nagai's early development: his conversion to Christianity, close contact with late Meiji socialism, education in private institutions, and broad exposure to the literature and philosophy of individualism. Though disparate forces, they combined to give his world view a liberal dimension even before the era of Taishō democracy.

In choosing to enter politics during Taishō, his professed desire was to become one of the governing class so as to give it a "people's flavor." This goal was to be accomplished by putting an end to the dominant political coalition consisting of the *hambatsu* (government by clan, which for early Meiji meant essentially government by the Satsuma and Chōshū, or Sat-Chō, *han*) and the Seiyūkai (Political Fraternity), and avenging what he saw as affronts to constitutional government. Indeed, Nagai did build a political base, garner the necessary popular and material support, and win election to the Diet. That this relative political amateur was able to do so suggests much about the Taishō milieu.

The remaining three chapters on Nagai cover his political career from 1920, the year he entered the Diet, until his death in 1944. Advancing in that career, he felt frequent frustration at the clash between spirit and politics in trying to effect his goals and ideals. For Nagai, these were the same in Shōwa as in Taishō—that is, as he articulated them. These goals were the reconciliation of class antagonisms within Japanese society and Asian liberation from white domination. To achieve any measure of success, however, he (like others in the Hara tradition) found compromise useful and, at times, necessary. The result was that although Nagai's slogans may have remained constant, the means he worked out to implement them changed dramatically over his quarter century in public life.

The conclusion to this work is an attempt to place Nagai's career in historical perspective and to make suggestions concerning the reformist pattern for modern Japanese history. There are three final introductory comments to be made at this point. First, this is not a biography of Nagai Ryūtarō, but rather the profile of a man whose career reflects a common pattern of thought and action in prewar Japan. Second, although the study spans from late Meiji through early Shōwa, the focus is on Taishō and the traits of the age that contributed to a climate of progressive reform and internationalism. In essence, the Taishō period is the base point for tracing both changes and consistencies in the positions of reformists like Nagai on internal and external problems during the interwar period.

My third point concerns the concept Taishō democracy, which many view with skepticism. In fact, the reformist pattern presented in this study is good reason to question the concept's validity. However, the time factor is one consideration in assessing that validity. There were some notable successes for the Taishō-democracy movements and the reformers who led them, but any substantial change requires time. Japan did not exist in a vacuum, and the tide of reform was affected by forces both from within and without.

The world depression, Japan's involvement in China, the London Disarmament Treaty controversy and resultant attack on Prime Minister Hamaguchi Osachi, the proliferation of Japanese nationalist societies, the Manchurian Incident, the rise of dictators in Europe, the assassination of Prime Minister Inukai Tsuyoshi by the Young Officers, Japan's withdrawal from the League of Nations—one outcome of these and related developments was that many Japanese (the governing and governed alike) became disappointed and frustrated at the limited results of Taishō democracy and at their efforts to become world citizens. In the concomitant search for alternative answers to the country's problems, many solutions sought justification in the emperor system, a reversion to tradition that is hardly surprising under the circumstances.

While one can say that a greater degree of democracy during Taishō was achieved in that the base of popular participation in politics grew considerably, nevertheless liberalism, aiming at plurality and freedom of the individual, was not so successful. The reason for this imbalance can be found in the Taishō-democracy movements' continued allegiance to the emperor system and the sovereignty of that system with respect to the individual. This situation ultimately provided a type of brake to the greater advancement of liberalistic trends underway. It also represented critical dilemmas for Nagai and other public figures in the reformist camp.

Taishō Democracy

MANY have seen parallels in the histories of interwar Germany and Japan, and the comparisons are indeed tempting. One point worth noting is suggested in the observation of historian Peter Gay that "the Weimar spirit . . . was born before the Weimar Republic; so was its nemesis."[1] Similarly, the Taishō spirit was born before 1912 when the Taishō emperor ascended the throne, as was its nemesis. One way to begin to understand the Taishō period and to examine it in historical perspective is to focus on a central theme of that period, what we today call Taishō democracy—the concept and its time frame—and to briefly sketch the career of one of the leading Taishō democrats, Nagai Ryūtarō.

One problem of the Taishō period relates to the Japanese tradition of foreign borrowing and the implantation of Western thought into Japan. The scholar Tsuda Sōkichi has tried to explain the frequent disharmony between what has been adopted and the indigenous Japanese way of life. He sees the basic problem as an inadequate exertion of discrimination in the borrowing process, an insufficiency that he attributes to the Japanese inferiority complex in the face of the perceived superiority of Western culture. Downgrading themselves as a nation, the Japanese often have imitated Western life and institutions without adequate consideration of the fundamental meaning and logic behind what is being imitated. Neither has there been adequate reflection on the presence or absence in Japan of the necessary conditions to complement that meaning and logic. One example would be the unlikely combination of a Western-type parliamentary system and Japan's emperor-centered system.[2]

Disharmony has often occurred, too, because of the difference in attitude between Japan and the West regarding individual rights and duty. Tsuda sees duty in Japan as having moralistic implications, with responsibility toward others holding more importance than individual rights. With the adoption of a Western constitutional system

after 1890 and the ongoing insistence on individual rights and democratic practices (demands of the antiestablishment groups), two problems in particular emerged. One difficulty was a confused morality
in politics, the other, the status of people's rights as compared with
those of the emperor.[3] These were problems for the Taishō propo-
nents of democracy as well. Their position regarding the emperor,
for instance, became somewhat vague as they maintained that matters could probably best be settled according to the traditional moral
relationship between the ruler and the people. Inherent in such
vagueness was an inconsistency that reveals much about the nature
of Taishō democracy.

THE CONCEPT

Two approaches are particularly fruitful in analyzing the expression
Taishō democracy. For one, it may be used to point to the political
phenomena that symbolized the age. One such phenomenon was the
establishment of party cabinets, which signified the legitimacy of the
parties as a major constituent of political power. The Meiji government has resembled other revolutionary governments in its tendency
to be intolerant of political parties, as had been the case after the
Puritan Revolution in England and the American War of Independence. An important aspect of Taishō democracy was its challenge to
the principle of nonparty governments of the Meiji order, thus causing a party system to evolve from the base of the very parliamentary
system that the Meiji Restoration produced.[4] At the same time,
Taishō democracy was not simply the confrontation of party power
and the bureaucratic power of the *hambatsu*. The movement was comprised of many different groups and gradually the function of inte-
grating these diverse elements fell to the parties, which eventually
came to exert control over the bureaucratic line of administration.[5]

A second approach to this concept is to utilize it to represent the
underlying current of the times—that is, the "mobilization of the
people" in providing the motive power for major events and trends
of the period. As such, Taishō democracy followed the "movement
for liberty and people's rights" *(jiyū minken undō)* of early Meiji as the
second cycle in modern Japanese history wherein mass-supported
democratic movements were of sufficient importance to cause vibra-
tions in the political world and to be characterized as constituting the
spirit of the age.[6]

THE TIME FRAME

Scholars do not confine the Taishō-democracy phenomenon to the actual reign of the Taishō emperor, 1912–1926.[7] Rather, they tend to agree that the Russo-Japanese War was an important turning point in ushering in the preconditions for the period. They cite various reasons for establishing the war as the catalyst. First, with Japan's victory in that war, the historical role of the political leaders who had established and sustained the Meiji state ended. Japan had at last become entitled to the status of a major power, and to some extent, the war "buried the anxieties of one generation, and shaped the illusions of the next."[8]

Second, some Japanese intellectuals of the time saw the victory in a dual light. With the privileges as a major power in the community of nations came the responsibility to further the material and spiritual progress of humankind. Such thinkers perceived these years as the ebb tide of the "rich country, strong army" mentality, and a new emphasis on the individual began to gain precedence over that of the nation. This individual came to be associated with the world citizen, who expended himself for the betterment of all humanity in accord with the ideals of "humanism," "personalism," and "culturalism."[9] Hence, the admonitions of Fukuzawa Yukichi in his "Datsu-A ron" (On fleeing Asia) were no longer applicable. To disaffect from the Asian community and to treat other Asians as Westerners treated them may have been necessary for Japan as Fukuzawa perceived the world situation in the mid-Meiji period. For Japanese to do so in the early twentieth century would have been to shirk their newly acquired responsibility.[10]

Nagai was typical of those who espoused the new world citizen attitude in the years following the Russo-Japanese War, as is evident in an early work in which he analyzed contemporary changes by periodizing Japan's history since the Meiji Restoration. The first ten years he characterized as an age of idealism, a time when the energies and resources of the nation were directed toward westernization. Itō Hirobumi most closely typified the age. But, wrote Nagai, the ideals of that time were out of touch with reality and led to a reaction that lasted for about thirty years. The figure and politics of Katsura Tarō personified this new age of realism, during which time Japan became embroiled in the affairs and battles of Asia. The lives of the Japanese people, however, could not be complete nor their hopes fulfilled by living with reality alone. They were a people at the dawn of a new era with hopes for the future—hopes related to the Meiji emperor's professed desire to share governance with his subjects.[11]

Nagai's concern with joint governance suggests a third reason for considering the Russo-Japanese War of significance in preparing the way for Taishō democracy; namely, the advent of the commoners' self-confidence and their greater participation in political affairs.[12] A by-product of increased taxation levied to finance the war was a considerable expansion of the voting population. Having met the tax qualification to receive the franchise, that same population came to feel entitled to a greater voice in public matters. The Hibiya riots of September 1905 protesting the Portsmouth peace settlement ending the war along with the demonstrations against streetcar fare hikes the following March were indicative of new urban trends and were also notable social uprisings constituting the initial stages of Taishō democracy.[13]

Hibiya had still another dimension. While the success of Japanese diplomacy in 1904–1905 stemmed from the oligarchic character of the government, that same character was greatly responsible for the negative domestic consequences of the peace. Hibiya and other demonstrations had occurred because the oligarchs had failed to keep the people properly informed. In the process, they had allowed outside activists (lawyers, journalists, professors, members of nationalist societies, and politicians of the opposition parties, who often resorted to demagogic tactics) to shape and lead public opinion in demands for a harsh settlement.[14] Such activists provided the motivation for the Taishō-democracy movement during its formative stages; the impetus came from diverse bases. In addition to liberals and those socialists who had been pushing for universal suffrage since the third and fourth decades of Meiji, these activists came from the wider range of socialists in general, the nonprivileged bourgeoisie, newspapers, and later the journalistic magazines.

An integral element in this growing political consciousness of the commoners was the combination of changes taking place in the class structure since the Russo-Japanese War. Of particular note was the migration from the countryside and the changed appearance of the labor market.[15] In the years between 1905 and 1918, Japan's economy took on the modern characteristics of growth as the nation shifted from an agricultural to an industrial economy. As Kazushi Ohkawa and Henry Rosovsky explain, a variety of factors favorable to the development of modern industry appeared from about 1905. The Russo-Japanese War stimulated industry connected with the

war effort. Increased imports, inflation, and foreign loans supported
expansion, as did government military expenditures and those for
the nationalization of the railroad trunk lines. This modern industry
began to find an export market in Japan's new empire. At the same
time, the home market was being strengthened because of rising per
capita gains. Then, World War I facilitated the expansion of Japan's
export market at a more rapid rate than the country's growing
import requirements.

One result of these cumulative developments was what Ohkawa
and Rosovsky call the creation of a differential structure. While the
growth rate of the traditional (agricultural) sector was stagnating, the
modern (non-agricultural) sector was accelerating. The gap between
the two created a problem that population changes then aggravated.
The population grew by one-fifth (approximately ten million) during
the period 1903 to 1918. The agricultural population remained
largely constant, and the increase was seen in the growth of the new
commercial and industrial cities like Tokyo, Yokohama, Nagoya,
Osaka, and Kobe. Moreover, by the end of the Meiji period, this
increase in the city population was not so much a result of migration
from the country to the city (though that did continue) as it was a
natural increase of the urban population.

Along with changes in class structure and urbanization were the
concomitant factors of industrialization—the dislocation, alienation,
and other tensions inherent in the modernization process. Exacerbat-
ing the tensions was the dual economic structure that was emerging
during Taishō, when "a highly skewed distribution of economic
power became an ingrained characteristic of the Japanese economy."[16] This widening disparity in income distribution (the oligopo-
lists on the one hand and the factory workers and farmers on the
other) contributed to social unrest and political instability. Between
1914 and 1917, the number of labor disputes accelerated, reaching a
record-breaking 2,388 in 1919.[17]

In the final analysis, it was the emergence of labor unrest that gave urgency
to the new demands for "reconstruction." Neither the new liberals nor the
student enthusiasts would have made much of an impact with their demands
for change had there not been stirrings of political activity among the working classes as well.[18]

Economic unrest and opposition to the governing classes continued
to grow. As early as 1913 public dissatisfaction had taken on new
intensity. Unlike the rather contained effects of the 1905–1906 dem-

onstrations and riots, the people's latent energy exploded this time with the first "movement for safeguarding constitutionalism."

In December 1912, the liberalistic cabinet of Saionji Kimmochi, backed by the Seiyūkai, refused to create two additional army divisions. Under severe army opposition, the cabinet collapsed to be succeeded by the third Katsura Tarō cabinet. The following February 10, at the instigation of certain newspapers and political party leaders, a mass meeting was held in support of "safeguarding the constitution." They denounced the high-handedness of the military and the excessive power of the *han* cliques. Indignation gave way to large-scale demonstrations. Katsura resigned, marking the first time a cabinet had been brought down by mass pressure.

Naturally, slogans like Destroy the *Hambatsu!* and Protect the Constitution! did not have the same meaning for all classes. Precisely because of their generality, however, the slogans proved to be advantageous in concentrating great popular energy against those under attack. One target was the *genrō* (elder statesmen), who formed the base of the *hambatsu*. Another was the military cliques, with their special privileges and powers, and, of course, the bureaucracy, which propped up the whole system.

This growing popular demand for a voice in public affairs was buttressed by the theory of democracy espoused by Yoshino Sakuzō, a professor at Tokyo Imperial University. This theory, widely known as *mimponshugi*, was popularized by Yoshino and his writings in *Chūō kōron*, a prestigious journal of public opinion, but was not his work alone.[19] Professors such as Kawakami Hajime and Sasaki Sōichi of Kyoto University and Ukita Kazutami and Ōyama Ikuo of Waseda also actively promoted the doctrine, though not always in full agreement with Yoshino's interpretation and ideas.

Yoshino's *mimponshugi* contained two basic propositions. One was the universal suffrage argument advocating broad political participatory rights for the general populace. The second was a call for true parliamentarianism, locating the base of politics in the Diet as the representative organ of the people's will. The theory requires further explanation, however, for it actually represented Yoshino's redefinition of democracy, and the points he stressed serve as one significant indicator of the prewar Japanese perception of democratic government.

In his earlier writings Yoshino had advocated "government centered on the people" as the fundamental principle in politics. As he saw it, the aim of sovereign power was to enhance the profit and happiness of the general public. After completing a study tour of Europe in 1913, however, he began to focus on the principle of "government based on the people"—the theory of *mimponshugi*. By this he meant the common people's right to determine the use of sovereign power. In short, he had added the idea of "government by the people" to "government for the people." He did not, however, adopt the principle of "government of the people."[20]

Yoshino's failure to take that final step can be adduced to the distinction he drew between *mimponshugi* and *minshushugi,* the latter meaning "government where sovereignty was legally placed in the people." Kiyoko Takeda has summarized what these distinctions meant for Yoshino:

In Japan, which by its constitution was obviously a monarchy, *minshu-shugi* as he saw it was irrelevant; instead, government was by *mimponshugi,* which did not concern itself with legal questions of the location of sovereign power but made concern for the interests, happiness, and views of the general public the guiding principle in the actual functioning of government institutions.[21]

Thus, by *mimponshugi* Yoshino did not mean popular sovereignty, but rather democracy (or the spirit of democracy) within the framework of a constitutional monarchy, whereby the people had the dual right to select leaders and render judgment over governmental policy.[22]

Like Yoshino, Nagai Ryūtarō's position regarding greater political privileges for the people was well in place by the mid-1910s. Writing in 1914, for example, he argued that the first point of the Meiji emperor's Five-Point Charter Oath had not been fulfilled. The oath provided for the establishment of deliberative assemblies on an extensive scale and pledged that all measures of government would be decided by public opinion. Instead, he insisted, it seemed that major decisions had been opposed to the people's wishes. Likening Japan's National Assembly to that in France before 1789 and England's before 1832, he made an appeal for Japan to move forward, to be part of the coming age in the world community. To accomplish this, a consensus both within the Diet and between the Diet and the people must be achieved.

Therefore, voting rights in our country . . . should not be allocated according to the amount of taxes one pays, but should be given and demanded on the standard of equal political rights—at least for all those who have an education above middle school, who obey the emperor's commands, and who have the common sense and sincerity of heart to be entrusted with deliberation on governmental matters.[23]

Indeed, one of Nagai's goals throughout his career was to raise the general level of education so that more people would be eligible *and* qualified to exercise the franchise.

Still, a close examination of the writings of Nagai, Yoshino, and other liberals of the day reveals that they had a dual view of the greater populace. They recognized the potential of the commoners to progress and eventually make viable judgments through free participation in the political process. Education was a key, but proper leadership was also essential. The pronouncements of liberals like Yoshino and Nagai showed the unmistakable influence of Confucian as well as traditional Japanese principles of government and suggested that this leadership role belonged to an enlightened few.

For Yoshino, this was an intellectual elite who, through wisdom and vision, would help the common people to realize their potential. In Nagai's perception, the enlightened few were the new political amateurs who would oppose the corrupt political professionals and lead the people in ways that would help guarantee their well-being. In fact, many of Nagai's so-called amateurs and Yoshino's intellectuals did come to form a vanguard element in the Taishō-democracy movements and gave impetus to the proletarian party activity that followed. The latter reached its peak between 1922 and 1926, taking the form of a political movement aimed at creating one proletarian party for the whole country. Leaders in the labor and agricultural unions, as well as socialists, urged this movement on.

The Heyday of Taishō Democracy

The late 1910s was a period of considerable upheaval on both the international and Japanese national fronts. The Romanov dynasty had toppled in Russia, ultimately to be replaced by Lenin's government in 1917. Japan participated in the Siberian expedition. World War I ended, and the Paris Peace Conference convened. At home, rice riots broke out in Toyama prefecture during the summer of 1918 and spread throughout the country. That September, after a mass meeting of nationwide newspaper writers, the cabinet of Terauchi Masatake resigned under intense pressure, to be succeeded by a new cabinet under Hara Takashi. And Japan's first major strike occurred at the Ikegai Ironworks.

These foreign and domestic occurrences had a profound effect on the reformists—those young men and women who were active in various reform groups and who appeared on the political scene around 1918–1919. Under the impact of these events, and stimulated further by intellectual leaders advocating renewal in line with postwar international trends, the reformists pushed forward with their goals. They were determined not only to liberate the people from the established political system, but also to renovate that system from within and create the foundation for the emergence of a new era. Moreover, with the relaxation of speech and newspaper laws after the establishment of the Hara cabinet, they were able to express their demands more freely.

In general, the different groups in the Taishō-democracy movements had a degree of uniformity concerning the direction and goals for internal reform. There was less agreement, however, on foreign policy. Yoshino, for instance, saw Wilsonianism as a world trend, but others, including reformists like Nakano Seigō and Nagai, were more cynical. Itō Takashi suggests a reason for such cynicism.

From the time of the *jiyū minken* movement—one might even say from the time of the movement to "revere the emperor and expel the foreigner" of the late Tokugawa period—the mixing together of national rights and people's rights has been an important pillar of movements in Japan. The "strong foreign policy faction" usually supported movements [of this dual nature] before 1918–1919, and the Kaizō and universal suffrage movements of 1918–1919 also were tinged with that coloring.[24]

Despite differences in views on foreign policy and other matters, most groups of the time—including democrats, nationalists, and socialists—found it possible to rally around one central cause. This was the universal suffrage issue, and it, along with the movements related to it, generally set the pattern for the politics of the twenties. Indeed, Nagai Ryūtarō's vanguard position in the campaign for universal suffrage established his reputation as a champion of the people and greatly enhanced his ability to move up in the political world. A sketch of his political career is therefore an appropriate preface to the ensuing chapters.

THE NAGAI PROFILE

The meaning that politics had for Nagai Ryūtarō has been suggested by his son. Nagai Michio wrote in 1964 that his father "had something close to a positive conviction that society was progressing dramatically from the Meiji Restoration and on throughout the *jiyū minken* and universal suffrage movements, and his reason for living was to take part in one bit of that progress."[25] He did play a part in this progression, and a rather visible one. Nagai's fellow traveler in Taishō-Shōwa politics, Miki Bukichi, often referred to him as a politician of the "leading actor" *(shite)* type, one who loved the grand gesture and romance of politics.[26] In the words of another contemporary, "With the power of oratory, Nagai became famous."[27] Armed with and cultivating those gifts of speech and dramaturgy, he rose in the political world and continued to appeal effectively to the general public until his death in 1944.

Several features of his behavior during that political career deserve note. The first pertains to Nagai and socialism. In his earlier years he had received strong socialist influence through his associations with Abe Isoo, Katayama Sen, and Katayama Tetsu, among others. In fact, he attended as standard bearer when the Japan Socialist party (Nihon shakaitō) was formed in 1906.[28] Still, Nagai joined one of the established parties, the Kenseikai (Constitutional Government party). And rather than break his own party ranks in late 1920 to join with the socialists in effecting common goals after the establishment of the Socialist League (Shakaishugi dōmei), Nagai tried to work from within the Kenseikai, encouraging a reformation of the established parties to achieve similar ends.

Nagai's similarity to Yoshino Sakuzō is another notable aspect of his political character. In some ways Nagai resembled Yoshino, who was simultaneously an elitist and a democrat *(mimponshugisha)*. At the same time, however, various influences in Nagai's life led him to become a leading proponent of *heiminshugi* (commonerism), a position once promoted by the prominent Meiji journalist Tokutomi Sohō. Nagai's special focus was the little man, one reason he so strongly endorsed universal suffrage. From the Forty-third to the Forty-fifth Diet, he hammered away on the issue in the House of Representatives,[29] as he did in his outside speeches and writings. An excerpt from his December 1923 article in the journal *Kaizō* amply illustrates his position.

The significance of universal suffrage resembles somewhat the restoration of power to the emperor by Tokugawa Keiki. That was the first step in taking special rights from the privileged classes and giving them to the people. However, the restoration of power to the emperor was only the beginning of the Meiji Restoration and not its entirety. In the same way, the goal of universal suffrage—to take from the present governing class those control privileges and give them to all the people—is only the beginning of the Taishō Restoration and not the completion of what has occurred so far. Still, if Tokugawa Keiki had not returned power to the emperor, the forfeiting of registers by the *han* and the other great reforms would not have been possible. Similarly, without the achievement of universal suffrage, neither will other social reforms by way of parliamentary politics be possible.[30]

This excerpt is more than a sample of Nagai's attachment to universal suffrage. It also reveals a third notable feature of his behavior throughout his career, and one that caused problems for him, namely, the mingling of Western and Japanese ideas and the application of the mixture to a Japanese situation. Thus, in his maiden speech before the House on July 8, 1920, Nagai could in the same breath refer to the need for maintaining the dignity of *bushidō* (the samurai spirit) and for fulfilling one's responsibility as a parliamentary politician—as if the two naturally went together.[31] Earlier, in a 1919 speech, he enumerated Japan's reasons for entering World War I and said, "Japan's theory is that international law is an expresson of international justice, without which it is impossible to establish international peace. . . . Japan stood loyally by her ally to defend international justice and to teach Germany the validity of international law. If *liberty* is a lasting heritage of American democracy, then *loyalty* is the eternal legacy of the Japanese nation."[32] Though the ideals and slogans of Western democratic nations are present throughout Nagai's speeches and writings, they are generally accompanied by Japanese explanations and justifications.

A fourth and final note in this sketch of Nagai concerns the course of his career. Depending on what value judgments one associates with the word, one could say his political career was a personal "success." Overcoming the drawbacks of an extremely poor childhood, he rose to the rank of cabinet minister and chief secretary of the Minseitō (Democratic party, formerly the Kenseikai). Despite his early conviction of the necessity of a parliamentary system for Japan, however, he became dissatisfied with the actual functioning of that system in his country. By 1935 he was suggesting openly that a one-party system might be the most effective way to rid the current multi-party system of the vice and graft that were seriously impairing its effectiveness in directing and controlling national policy.[33]

After participating in three nonparty cabinets during the 1930s, he took more drastic action in July 1940 when he led almost forty members out of the Minseitō. In August he was appointed a member of the Shintaisei Preparatory Commission and was again in the vanguard—this time as a leading figure in the IRAA and as a proponent of the "Holy War."

It is tempting to explain Nagai's thought and action through the concept of *tenkō*, abandoning one's former beliefs and convictions. The historian Tsurumi Shunsuke has expressed this view succinctly.

While retaining the appearance of a liberal politician, Nagai slipped into fascism. This very type of smooth movement from the Japanese type of liberalism to the Japanese type of fascism is the mystery of the transfiguration of Japanese liberalism, which almost resembled a bloodless revolution. Nagai is important in that he was a leadoff man in this step-by-step process.[34]

The immediate reaction might be that Tsurumi has come close to the mark. Nevertheless the *tenkō* concept is deficient as an explanation here, as is the Taishō democracy–Shōwa fascism dichotomy.

Any attempt to explain Nagai's course of action in the late thirties and early forties cannot evade the larger question. That question, simply put, asks why those Japanese seemingly so attracted to Western liberal ideals and systems in the 1910s and 1920s began to reject that same liberalism in the 1930s and opt for more totalitarian models, both in the national and international spheres. The choice of Nagai's career as a means to explore this problem necessitates going back to the years before he entered public life—to look first at the people, places, and institutions that gave direction to his future course, and then, to trace the development of his own political consciousness.

Liberal Beginnings

DEMOCRACY and liberalism are terms that denote different political concepts. Nevertheless, the distinction between the two is frequently overlooked. We tend to evaluate democracy and its existence or non-existence from a moral standpoint in which the meanings of the two are mixed. This has been no less the case with Taishō democracy than with democracies in the West. There has been a tendency to assume liberal democracy for democracy, with the result that our understanding of both terms has been distorted or obscured. A corrective to this misassumption has been offered by one Western thinker, Guido de Ruggiero. The theories presented in his book *The History of European Liberalism* can be helpful in dealing with Taishō democracy and in understanding Nagai's experience. R. G. Collingwood, in the preface to his translation of this work, has neatly summarized Ruggiero's thesis on liberalism.

Liberalism . . . begins with the recognition that men, do what we will, are free; that a man's acts are his own, spring from his own personality, and cannot be coerced. But this freedom is not possessed at birth; it is acquired by degrees as a man enters into the self-conscious possession of his personality through a life of discipline and moral progress. The aim of Liberalism is to assist the individual to discipline himself and achieve his own moral progress; renouncing the two opposite errors of forcing upon him a development for which he is inwardly unprepared, and leaving him alone, depriving him of that aid to progress which a political system, wisely designed and wisely administered, can give.[1]

Collingwood then explains the author's views on the relationship of a "Liberal policy," democracy, and authoritarianism. A "Liberal policy"

is not democracy, or the rule of the mere majority; nor is it authoritarianism, or the irresponsible rule of those who, for whatever reason, hold power at a given moment. It is something between the two. Democratic in its respect for human liberty, it is authoritarian in the importance it attaches to the necessity for skilful and practised government. But it is no mere compromise, it has its own principles; . . .[2]

In Ruggiero's view, then, liberal democracy is actually a "higher synthesis" wherein the qualifier "liberal" emphasizes "the demand for specification and differentiation which makes itself felt within the oppressive and deadening uniformity of democratic society."[3]

Relating all of this to Nagai, it was suggested earlier that during the Taishō period he could be considered a liberal in his thought and action; that is, in his espousal of the ideals of plurality and freedom of the individual. He was also a democrat in his belief that the people's participatory base in politics had to be greatly expanded. However, his long-range record of involvement in governmental policy does not show sustained adherence to the "higher synthesis" of liberal democracy. The record does reveal ongoing democratic tendencies, and later in his career, greater stress on more authoritarian policies. The following chapters explore why Nagai's liberalism did not hold up under the pressures of national and international problems.

Finally, it should be noted that a clear underlying cause of Nagai's original preoccupation with liberal democracy was his desire to help balance the greater polity and the individual in effecting a harmonious, productive society. This dilemma was particularly troublesome for him and other Japanese because of their traditional dyadic emphasis on the group and loyalty to the emperor-centered state as opposed to emphasis on the individual and individual rights (as we understand these in the West). So, as Nagai and other Japanese perceived their country's situation with growing alarm in the late 1930s, the need for a unified, harmonious state seemed increasingly urgent. Circumstances thus called for direct action. There was no time, so they thought, to work through the process of trial and error, to experiment with the noncoercive methods inherent in a more liberal democratic approach. In a word, they had difficulty in adhering to principles that transcended the Japanese state and challenged the prevailing particularistic, emperor-centered ethic of their society.

Ultimately, then, Nagai did not adhere to the philosophy intrinsic to the liberal democratic forces that had helped shape his ideas through his formative years. Still, one cannot ignore the nature of these forces or their impact on Nagai.

THE EARLY YEARS

In 1881, the same year the Emperor Meiji issued the imperial rescript promising a national assembly in 1890, Nagai Ryūtarō, a future member of that assembly, was born into the house of a former

samurai family of Kaga Province.[4] Kaga had been the realm of the
wealthy Maeda lords, who sided with the Tokugawa house in the battle of Sekigahara (1600) and consequently enjoyed special status
under the Tokugawa administration (1603–1868). Ryūtarō's grandfather had been a swordsman, zealous in the warrior spirit but
unambitious where his own wealth or fame was concerned. This latter characteristic, coupled with the difficult adjustment experienced
generally by samurai families during the changeover in governmental systems after the Meiji Restoration, resulted in desolate days for
the Nagai family.

Family conditions did improve for a time. Ryūtarō's mother,
Tsuru, became the Nagai heir and was given in marriage to Nishida
Minoru, who came from a family of scholars. Minoru's specialities
were mathematics and *kambun* (Chinese composition), and his teaching necessitated his living apart from the family, which remained in
Kanazawa, Ishikawa Prefecture (formerly Kaga). He also had an
attachment to sake. Ryūtarō thus knew responsibility from an early
age. He was constrained to fulfill family obligations normally carried
out by the household head while at the same time coping with domestic conditions once more bordering on poverty. In later years he
recalled time and again that the rice gruel consisted of considerably
more water than rice.

The family closeness provided by his grandmother, Aiko, and his
mother balanced somewhat the material hardships. Aiko had worked
as wardrobe mistress for the Daishōji clan, and later was greatly
responsible for her own household because of her husband's advancing years. She was enterprising, stouthearted, strong, and a good
manager, and many say that Ryūtarō's personality was inherited
from her. Tsuru had those qualities the Japanese have traditionally
admired in a woman, and both Aiko and Tsuru had the community's
respect. They also had Ryūtarō's lifelong praise. Throughout his
career he worked to raise the status of women and gain them greater
rights, a distinguishing mark that derived partly from the influence
of his early years.[5]

Unlike his later patron, Ōkuma Shigenobu, Nagai applied himself
assiduously to his studies. Again, unlike Ōkuma, who appears to
have been derelict in his training in the military arts,[6] Nagai prided
himself on being one of the "sons of the north country" and labored
to discipline himself in the warrior spirit. Long periods of rising at
3:00 A.M. for kendo practice was one means to this end. This training
also reinforced his unyielding spirit and will to win, earning him the

title of "little general" among his companions. Other classmates went further, referring to him as a megalomaniac. His retort was always, "A man must be a hero to understand a hero."[7]

As Albert Craig has pointed out in discussing the role of personality in Japanese history, success in Japan is for a special few, and those who attain it must exhibit drive to an exceptional degree. Not only are considerable ability and unrelenting effort necessary, but tremendous self-discipline as well.[8] Nagai possessed these traits to an unusual degree, and he never slackened in exercising them. Moreover, they were enhanced by his deep-seated self-confidence. These characteristics were coupled with a fighting spirit, however, which led to his dropping out of school after his second year in middle school. In a winter scuffle with schoolmates, he injured his right leg. The result was long periods of hospitalization, burdensome medical expenses, and permanent disability.

This adolescent accident also altered the direction of his life. The military career that Nagai, his mother, and grandmother had envisioned was declared an impossibility by the doctor. Neither would he be able to enter the national schools. His education would be instead at private schools and colleges, where his rebellious spirit would continue to cause problems and grief for him, his family, and acquaintances. Trouble erupted again only a short time after he resumed his education at Dōshisha Middle School in Kyoto.

By the late 1890s, the family's financial condition had worsened, and Nagai's father decided that they should resettle in Kyoto. Once there, Minoru procured better educational posts, gave up his sake, and moved finally into a high-paying principal's position in the Yamakuni District. Under these circumstances, Nagai entered Dōshisha, the institution founded by the Japanese Christian Niijima Jō. The orientation of the school reflected its founder's spirit, emphasizing religious freedom and *jiyū minken,* both of which had a permanent effect on Nagai's life. He later became a Christian, as well as a leader in the successor movements to *jiyū minken.*

At Dōshisha also, Nagai's schoolmates recognized his leadership qualities. During a school strike in 1898 they asked him to act as student leader before the negotiating committee, a role he accepted and for which he was asked to leave the school. Nagai did so after consulting with Abe Isoo, whose acquaintance he had made at Dōshisha. He had been at the school only a year, and Niijima had already passed away by Nagai's time there. Still, the philosophy on which the school had been founded—individual fulfillment, recognition of human equality, the goal of building a better national society and international community—contributed to a growing liberal consciousness. The strong Christian socialist influence of Abe was also an influence.

At the same time, one must balance these forces against others. Nagai was born only thirteen years after the fall of the Tokugawa regime and the establishment of the Meiji state. Just as exposure to Christianity had an effect on him, so too did Japan's own brand of religiosity, a religiosity with a highly political coloration, wherein the emperor was the ultimate source of morality and political legitimacy. Indeed, an important factor in Nagai's original desire for a military career was the inspiration of the Meiji emperor.[9] In addition to Christianity and Japanese beliefs, there was the influence of Confucianism. This resulted both from the Tokugawa legacy of Confucian ideology and from Nagai's own studies, which included the years of learning *kambun* with his father.

Balancing the transcendent, universalistic values woven into the philosophies of Niijima, Abe, and others, was the intense, particularistic nationalism of Nagai's early milieu. He not only saw his country defeat the onetime overlord of Asia in the Sino-Japanese War of 1894–1895, he also witnessed the Triple Intervention immediately following, which deprived Japan of some of the fruits of victory. Social Darwinism, so influential among Japanese thinkers as the nineteenth century drew to a close, could only have had increased impact in such an environment. Equally, Nagai could hardly have missed the message that so many Japanese derived from Spencer's ideas—that only the fittest societies survive and conquer and that the fulfillment of an individual's potential was the way to help the nation survive and compete. Similar ideas became part of Nagai's rhetoric from that time on, combining with elements of liberalism, Christianity, Confucianism, Meiji nationalism—and socialism.

Late Meiji Socialism and Nagai

From Dōshisha Nagai moved to Kansei Gakuin, a Methodist school with an emphasis on gaining converts. At Kansei, students had to present talks twice a week, and in the church hall in 1899, Nagai delivered his first public speech entitled "Internal medicine for an ailing Japan." External economic relief alone was inadequate for the ills that were plaguing Japanese society, he insisted. The people had to be renewed from within in order to effect social peace and happiness. Ideas such as these, which emphasized the dignity of the individual as one of the necessary conditions for curing social evils, remained a constant theme in his later speeches and writings. His presentation evidently impressed his audience. It resulted in numerous invitations for addresses thereafter, as well as encouragement by Nishikawa Tamanosuke, a wealthy Kobe businessman and sponsor of the school, to become a politician.

Nagai worked diligently at Kansei Gakuin with the encouragement of such teachers as the missionary Reverend S. H. Wainwright (principal of the school), and he considered his private-school education of lifetime value. Nagai Michio later suggested why this was so. The contact with Christianity gave him strength to overcome his physical handicap. It was, furthermore, an environment that offered the opportunity to learn from and to cultivate close relationships with excellent teachers as well as to develop an understanding and appreciation of the meaning of mass politics.[10]

The extended exposure to Christianity, and especially the strong influence of Abe Isoo, resulted in Nagai's own conversion to the Unitarian faith in 1901, a commitment he retained throughout his life. Around 1904–1905, he joined with a group centering on the minister of the Hongō Church, Ebina Danjō. This group, which included the liberal politician Shimada Saburō, as well as younger people like Ōyama Ikuo of Waseda and Uchigasaki Sakusaburō of Tokyo Imperial University, formed the National Renovation Society (Kokumin sakushinkai).[11] In effect, Nagai's commitment to Christianity was intimately related to his evolving public consciousness. For him, the tenets of that faith coincided with and reinforced his own ideals and goals.

In an early book, he devoted several sections to Christianity and Jesus Christ's role in world history. Jesus, in his opposition to those in positions of wealth and power, and in his empathy for the underprivileged, represented for Nagai the archetypal social reformer. "He's our great model, and we must strive courageously to follow in his footsteps."[12] Many other Taishō democrats, including Yoshino Sakuzō, had embraced Christianity during their formative years, and their incorporation of this Western ideology into the rhetoric of the Taishō-democracy movements added a dimension that should be considered when trying to understand the Taishō period as a whole.

In 1901, the year he converted to Christianity, Nagai made another decision that would influence the course of his life. Even if his disabled leg had not hindered his chances for entering a national university, it seems likely that his personal orientation at that point in life would have led Nagai to opt for a private, nonestablishment insti-

tution. In September he entered Tokyo Semmon Gakkō after having
placed first out of nine hundred candidates on the entrance exam.[13]

Tokyo Semmon Gakkō had been founded by Ōkuma Shigenobu in
1882 on the conviction that to establish true constitutional government, you must first foster talent. Furthermore, to guarantee the
independence of a country, you must first insure the independence of
the spirit and thereby the people through learning. As in the case of
the Kaishintō (Progressive party), founded by Ōkuma and others the
same year, the *bête noire* of the school was the establishment *hambatsu;*
and energy within both Tokyo Semmon Gakkō and the Kaishintō
was expended toward ending Sat-Chō domination of the government. Nagai entered in 1901 in the same class with Ōyama Ikuo, and
as the school became Waseda in 1902, they were members of the first
graduating class of that university.

The school's emphasis on parliamentary politics and the ideal of
mass participation in government had a long-lasting effect on Ryūtarō. Once he had come under the influence of Ōkuma and the Waseda
group, politics became his consuming interest for life. Abe Isoo had
joined the staff of the school in 1899 as a professor of social policy,
and it was he and Ōkuma who made the deepest impression on
Nagai.[14] Two other of his teachers also had a profound impact. One
was Ono Azusa. Ono had studied Western political systems in
England and the United States, and had assisted Ōkuma in the
founding of Tokyo Semmon Gakkō. The other, Ukita Kazutami, was
a philosopher and influential commentator on current affairs who
espoused the concept of "ethical imperialism" in his influential 1901
work, *Teikokushugi to kyōiku* (Imperialism and education). Finally
there were the students with whom longtime relations would be
important. Among them were Matsumura Kenzō, Nakano Seigō,
Ishibashi Tanzan, Kazami Akira, Ogata Taketora, and Miki Bukichi. All would be active in political life. Ogata later became editor of
the *Tokyo Asahi,* and Ishibashi a postwar prime minister.

The year 1901 was significant in Nagai's development for other
reasons. Two events in that year added new dimensions to his world
view. Socialists, including Abe Isoo, labor movement activist Katayama Sen, and an antiestablishment radical, Kōtoku Shūsui organized the Shakai minshutō (Social Democratic party). The organization was outlawed by the authorities the same day of its birth.
Another organization was formed by Yano Fumio, a disciple of
Ōkuma, and others to achieve universal suffrage.

By early 1902 a group of university students who would be active later in the universal suffrage movement were becoming involved in a student relief society for the victims of the Ashio copper mine pollution problem. Under the leadership of Tanaka Shōzō, a Christian and Diet member from Tochigi Prefecture, the cause was embraced not only by students and socialists but by many Japanese who recognized the need for social reform. Nagai participated through his lectures, and Kawakami Hajime donated his clothing to aid the farmers and fishermen in the Ashio District whose livelihoods had been destroyed by pollutants emptied into the Watarase River from the mine.[15] The problem was not settled until after extensive riots had occurred in the region in 1907. Still, the Ashio affair had alerted an increasing number of Japanese to the threat to social welfare implicit in the Meiji government's commitment to the goals of national wealth and power.[16]

Nagai's own childhood experiences had made him keenly aware of the effects of human suffering caused by poverty and other forms of privation, and his student days in Tokyo intensified this impression. To pay for school expenses he tutored in mathematics and did German translation work for a language school professor. Returning home late at night, he could see factory workers laboring under abhorrent conditions. It was from that time, he later recalled, that he began his own serious study of social policy on the conviction that speedy measures were necessary to deal with the growing social problem in Japan. But he went a step further, reasoning that one way to alleviate human suffering would be a more equal distribution of wealth, not only on the national level but on the international level as well. Land would be the most important factor, and since the white race had monopolized this crucial resource throughout the world, it must be taken from them and parceled out on a more equitable basis. To his study of social policy he therefore added colonization.[17]

For the Nagai of that time, however, labor was the most pressing problem for the Japanese, and he directed his efforts to its investigation and the search for ways to protect workers. In the meantime, he entered the Universal Suffrage League in late 1903.[18] He also participated actively in the Waseda School Studies Association founded on November 22 of the same year. Discussion focused on socialist ideas, and Nagai served as manager under association president Abe Isoo. Again under Abe's direction, he became immersed in Leo Tolstoy's writings and views on commonerism and pacifism.

It is hardly surprising, then, that he became a supporter of the *Heimin shimbun* (Commoners' news), the first issue of which appeared on November 15, 1903.[19] Under the direction of Kōtoku Shūsui, Sakai Toshihiko, Ishikawa Sanshirō, Nishikawa Kōjirō, and other socialists who had earlier formed the Heiminsha (Commoners' Fraternity), the paper was dedicated to commonerism, pacifism, and socialism. With its clear-cut stand on issues—especially the impending conflict with Russia—it attracted intellectuals as well as students like Nagai. Despite his feelings on white imperialism, he was at that time firmly committed to the pacifist principle. As he perceived the situation, Japan should take care of its problems at home first, sentiments he expressed in a speech on January 30, 1904, at the opening meeting of the Waseda Debating Society.

Russia and Japan had broken relations several days earlier, and most debaters chose themes centering on the problem, especially Japan's weak policy toward Russia. Nagai's speech was conspicuous both for his delivery and his rather singular topic, "Policies for the protection of industry." A first step toward building a new and greater Japan, he said, was the protection of industry, and serious consideration must be given to the ways of effecting that goal. Temporary methods would be inadequate, as would solutions based on the assumption that the problem's cause emanated basically from outside. The answer did not lie in raising tariffs and adopting a harder foreign policy line, but rather in protecting the workers who were the very foundation of industry.

This theme harked back to his earlier speech "Internal medicine for an ailing Japan" and impressed those in attendance, including Ōkuma Shigenobu. That same evening, Ōkuma invited Nagai to visit his home to discuss the labor problem further. When the two met with each other on February 1, Ōkuma, like others, had recognized Nagai's promise, and their mutual concern formed the basis of a long relationship. Ōkuma's support and influence, in fact, became an important factor in the development of Nagai's career.

A WESTERN ORIENTATION IN POLITICAL THEORY

When Tokyo Semmon Gakkō became Waseda University in 1902, Nagai was enrolled in the Department of Politics and Economics. Ōkuma's plan had been to pattern his school on the English model, as opposed to Germany's imperial university system, and Waseda ultimately did become a center of English-style political studies in Japan. One person greatly responsible for this was Ono Azusa, who had resigned an official appointment in the government bureaucracy and entered the popular rights movement as a chief advisor to Ōkuma.[20] Indeed, Nagai's study under Ono was one of the Waseda experiences that contributed to his early liberalism and his development as a future politician.

One factor was Ono's stress on breaking *hambatsu* political power and investing that power instead in the people. Second, he had profound knowledge of Western political practices and legal theory. He had studied in England during Gladstone's first ministry and had become a disciple of the utilitarianism of Bentham and Mill. Third, he impressed his students with his insistence that for the Japanese to benefit from Western ideas, they would have to understand not only Western ideology but the Western methodology of learning as well.[21]

Through his own studies, Nagai came to adopt Gladstone as a model for his own political development. The English statesman became the subject of both his college thesis and a later book.[22] Essentially Nagai incorporated Gladstone's ideas and historical role into his own conception of social reform and national mission. In working for national renovation, for example, Nagai saw a parallel between himself and Gladstone. He later extended this analogy to embrace those he saw frustrating such progressive efforts. Hara Takashi, for example, symbolized for Nagai not only Seiyūkai-*hambatsu* power, but represented Japan's equivalent of Disraeli as well. He saw Hara and Disraeli representing the forces of conservatism while Gladstone and himself stood for liberalism.[23]

Nagai had read widely in Western sources and drew his inspiration and ideas from many of the same writers who had impressed Ono. John Stuart Mill was one, and while a student abroad, Nagai translated and sent sections of "On Social Freedom" to Waseda for publication in the *Waseda gakuhō* (Waseda school news).[24] Again, like Ono, he stressed the need for Japanese to incorporate Western methodology into their own thought and learning processes. A simplistic understanding of Western ideology was not enough. He criticized severely the traditional Japanese practice of accepting without questioning. Westerners, he felt, were far superior to Japanese in their ability to question and analyze. If Japanese could imitate them by developing a more discriminating attitude, perhaps new social and intellectual ideas would result. Only then could Japan contribute to world enlightenment. It was not by accident, he concluded, that Western history boasted of a series of great inventions and extraordinary discoveries.[25]

Despite Nagai's preoccupation with Western learning and theories during his period of formal schooling, his eyes were not turned solely toward the West. While at Waseda, he attended meetings of the East Asia Society (Tō-A-kai) organized by Matsumura Kenzō and others and presided over by Inukai Tsuyoshi. Ōkuma's goal was to have the society focus on problems dealing specifically with China and Korea. Nagai's concern was broader, however, and he stopped attending on the grounds that his commitment to the betterment of the human condition extended to all Asians—and their relation to other peoples as well.

Nagai expressed this ideal in the Waseda yearbook as *keisei saimin,* or "easing the people's suffering through statecraft." At graduation in September 1905, however, he was still unsure about what his role might be in realizing this ideal. He sought a position with Hayashida Kametarō, chief secretary of the lower house, but did not do well on the personnel examination, even though the subject for oral translation was English parliamentary law. To tide him over until something more permanent developed, he assisted a Chinese governmental official studying finance in Japan. Finally in May 1906, through the recommendation of Abe Isoo, he received a Unitarian scholarship to study theology at Oxford University. He chose to attend Manchester College at that institution and in August departed from Kobe for England.

Manchester College was established in the latter half of the seventeenth century mainly to train Unitarian ministers. Despite its theological orientation, the school was small and students were given relative freedom in designing their own programs. After close consultation with E. Carpenter, a teacher and friend at Manchester, Nagai decided to pursue his true interests in social policy and colonization, concentrating much of his work on Gladstone.

Firsthand observation of social conditions and movements in England (and on the Continent) supplemented textbook learning and provided a keen awareness of current trends. The labor movement was on the rise and socialism along with it. Nagai himself attended the Stuttgart meeting of worldwide socialist parties in August 1907. As is evident in his later writings, his reflections on both the labor and socialist movements became an integral part of his world view. So too did his impressions of the effects in Europe of other prevalent isms, such as syndicalism, Marxism, and Veblenism.

Other experiences abroad left a lasting mark. A pacifist at the time of the Russo-Japanese War, Nagai had not participated in the Hibiya riots protesting the peace treaty. By 1907, however, he was writing to Abe Isoo that world conditions were incompatible with pacifist theory. Pacifism, in his view, was inadequate to deal with reality.[26] And though he remained a lifelong admirer of Tolstoy, he later wrote that he could no longer agree with his ideas on nonresistance.[27] This 1907 shift in Nagai's thinking is important for his future course and therefore merits further consideration.

Nagai's about-face on the issue of pacifism has led some who interpret his career in terms of tenkō to see 1907 as the first stage in his reversal on former beliefs.[28] Moreover, Ishikawa Sanshirō, with whom Nagai was associated through the Heimin shimbun, has written that Nagai went out into the world as a "malformed child" of the Heiminsha in that his commitment to pacifism, which ideology the Heiminsha had supported, was incomplete.[29] Regardless of what interpretation might be derived from the change in Nagai's thinking at that time, it seems clear at least that experiences as a Japanese in Europe during the early 1900s do account for some of that change.

He explained in later years how sorely disappointed he had been upon reaching the West. More than mere disappointment in England, he was incensed at what he saw and personally experienced by way of white prejudice. Through his boyhood reading of great writers like Carlyle, Milton, Byron, and Tennyson he had come to believe that the English were generally a broad-minded people capable of appreciating and generating noble ideas. His actual encounters with English life and English students, however, disillusioned him. As an Oriental, he became the target of racist jokes, taunting, water dousing, and other forms of abuse. A Japanese friend tried to mollify Nagai, saying that Nagai's reading of English literature had been too narrow to give him any appreciation of their way of joking; but Nagai was not convinced. He was convinced, however, that these people neither appreciated nor were willing to make the effort to understand Asian culture.

At times his indignation became so great that he went after his adversaries with his cane. He wanted to "pulverize" this white prejudice. He lashed out on the matter at an oratorical gathering at Manchester in December 1906, and discrimination against him in the dormitory abated somewhat. Still, he continued to meet prejudice (as he did later during his travels on the Continent). His conclusion was that while many English people were generous and concerned about humanity, England as a nation was imperialistic. Such

feelings reinforced his growing sense of mission to supress white bias
against Orientals and to help "liberate Asia from white imperialism."[30]

After the October 1906 trouble over exclusion of Japanese children
from San Francisco schools, Nagai sent a piece from England for the
Waseda school paper. In his essay he diagnosed the racial, political,
economic, and social arguments of American scholars in favor of
rejecting Japanese immigrants.[31] He directed his complaints mainly
toward America, but his comments were a general appeal to Western
countries to understand the Asian and, particularly, the Japanese situation.

As often happens, a person's experience abroad results in heightened nationalism rather than in increased international good will. To
some extent this was true for Nagai. His study and travels had been
in Europe, not in the United States. Even so, Americans were part of
the white race, that greater group he saw obstructing the realization
of Asian hopes and needs. Nagai's exclusion essay was a reflection of
his heightened nationalism and race consciousness, and his conclusion to the piece summarized his study until that time concerning
social policy and colonization.

In short, wrote Nagai, at the same time Japan was experiencing a
rapidly growing population, she was plagued with a low per capita
income. The answer to the problem was an economic arena abroad.
Japan needed the opportunity to break open unexploited sources of
wealth. The government, while preparing new plans for such expansion, should not despair over American exclusion policies. Instead,
qualified Japanese should make wholehearted efforts to dispose of
obstacles in the path of such expansion, for, "Japanese, until the end,
embrace the Pacific, and require determination to expand onto both
the American and Asian continents."[32] Nagai was right in line with a
great many Meiji thinkers and patriots. He was also in tune with the
ideas of his former professor Ukita Kazutami, who believed that
expansionism was the only way to maintain Japan's independence
and active participation in world civilization.[33]

Through all of this Nagai retained a certain admiration for England, both as a nation and for its accomplishments as a people. He
expressed that admiration in his "Recollections of the English People," published upon his return to Japan. This work also reflects his
heightened nationalism as a Japanese with respect to English great-
ness. Drawing a comparison between England and Germany, he
likened the former to the "retired master of a great, established

house," and the latter to a "commoner." The self-confidence and nobility of the master is reflected in the dignity of his family (that is, the English people). The commoner, on the other hand, is so concerned with mere livelihood that there is no leeway for reflection on more universal matters. Nagai closed with the idea that Japan, the "England of the Orient," should in no way be ashamed or deficient in front of its Western counterpart.[34] Indeed, to the end of his career he could never break completely away from the English system as a frame of reference. Nor could he abandon the idea that constitutional government and colonial expansion were compatible. England, after all, had both.

RETURN TO WASEDA

Nagai arrived back in Japan in October 1909. In November he was appointed an instructor at Waseda, taking over the lectureship on social policy vacated by Abe Isoo, who was concentrating on research. Added to his lectureship was another chair in colonization. Nagai's special talents and timely appeal qualified him to join Ōyama Ikuo, Kawakami Hajime, and Yoshino Sakuzō as one of that Taishō group of young professors whose popularity rested on their unusual rapport with students.

Matsumura Kenzō wrote in his memoirs that although Nagai had given some famous speehes in the Diet during his career, he was basically a speaker for the masses.[35] His lectures at Waseda, in fact, were more like popular public addresses than regular classroom presentations. The approach was innovative and enthusiastically received, especially since he incorporated into his lectures the latest European developments. Nagai was apprehensive at first about the educational effects of mixing classroom and oratorical techniques, but continued to do so when encouraged by Abe, who thought it would be valuable in the long run for Waseda's Department of Politics.

Young people were a major support group for Nagai during his political career. He built the base of that support at Waseda. Along with Ōkuma, the veteran progressive politician Ozaki Yukio, and others, he supported the Seinen dōshi kurabu (Club of Like-Minded Young Men). The club had been organized at the end of Meiji and became in 1912 the Rikken seinentō (Constitutional Young Men's party). Having been himself a member of the Seinen yūbenkai (Young Men's Oratorical Society) as a student, Nagai served as advisor to the school magazine *Seinen yūben* (Oratory of youth) and also led a special study group on European events. Remembering, too, the kindness of his mentor, Professor E. Carpenter, while in England, Nagai became close with foreign students at Waseda.

Many of his writings and speeches during those years were aimed at inspiring young people, for he was convinced they were Japan's hope for progress and reform. His 1914 book *Zampan* was dedicated to them. He wrote in the preface: "If one young person, by reading this book, derives hints for improving himself and the level of his life, then I have attained my desire in publishing the work."[36] The book hardly reached as large an audience of youth as Abe Jirō's *Santarō no nikki* (Santarō's diary), the first part of which also appeared in 1914. Nevertheless *Zampan* added to Nagai's youthful following. Even after entering the Diet, he remained actively involved with young people's organizations, such as the Sekishunkai of Ibaraki Prefecture, for which group he served as advisor in the 1920s.

True to the Waseda tradition and Ōkuma's educational philosophy, he encouraged students to break away from past, outmoded traditions and standards in their thinking. Drawing a dichotomy between two main streams of thought in Japan at that time, he described one as rooted in the past and in maintenance of the status quo, with little stress on universal values such as human dignity and freedom of conscience. Opposed to that was the thinking of individuals who searched for moral standards within themselves. The Western influence in the latter was strong, Nagai conceded, but he suggested that such an orientation could effect unprecedented changes through an increased awareness of individual rights.[37] In speeches such as "Let youth accomplish their life's work," he drew upon these themes and appealed to young people for support in building a new Japan grounded in democratic values.

New Japan

Nagai's additional duty as editor of Ōkuma's publication *Shin Nippon* (New Japan) was directed to the same goal. With its first edition in April 1911, the journal was dedicated to the enlightenment of thought. More than just dealing with political, economic and foreign issues, Ōkuma intended to elicit debate on idealistic problems as well.[38] In his usual optimistic manner, he explained that Japan had progressed remarkably in the forty years since the Meiji Restoration, and it was time the world knew about it. Granted, those forty years had been a time of preparation. Progress had involved inescapable confusion and unsettlement, but the country was now at the threshold of a new era. Two things were vital for the survival of the new Japan that was evolving: the nurturing of the Japanese as modern citizens in the twentieth-century world, and a greater knowledge of foreign trends and ideas to reach that goal.[39]

Shin Nippon appeared every month for seven years and monopolized much of Ōkuma's and Nagai's time. The two consulted on a regular basis. Ōkuma dictated his ideas to Nagai, who then wrote up the notes in journalistic form and submitted them to his senior for consideration and revision. At times Ōkuma would start dictating at noon, and the two would end their session in the early hours of the next morning.[40] Nagai was also responsible for his own essays, editorials, and book reviews, and that collection of writings reveals a great deal about his sociopolitical thought during early Taishō. In addition to the usual national and international events, many essays concentrated on labor, race, and women's rights. His two longtime concerns, class antagonisms and Asian liberation, were, naturally, woven into many of the writings, and these causes received added impetus through his affiliation with Ōkuma and Waseda.

Ōkuma's political career had been based on opposition to *hambatsu* rule. A second tenet was his faith in the common man. These two reinforced Nagai's own adherence to commonerism as against governance by a privileged elite. Ōkuma's ideas on Asia also influenced Nagai. The former's theory of Pan-Asianism was known already by the turn of the century as the Ōkuma Doctrine, a kind of Oriental analogue to the Monroe Doctrine. He believed that Japan could perform a double service for China by guiding it in the ways of modernization and enlightenment, while at the same time helping to prevent further violations of its sovereignty by Western nations.[41]

Ōkuma's doctrine tied in with his views on expansionism, for he (like Nagai) gave much consideration to Japan's population problem. Population growth did not necessarily mean heightened national power. In fact, it could produce the reverse effect unless accompanied by technological and industrial advances to insure that society could absorb the increase in manpower. Ōkuma argued that a policy for overseas expansion and colonization would also be necessary, backed up by a strong merchant marine.[42]

Given such views on expansion and Japan's relationship with China, it is not surprising that Ōkuma strongly endorsed the Twenty-one Demands presented to China by Katō Takaaki, foreign minister in the second Ōkuma cabinet (1914–1916). Neither is it strange, knowing Nagai's views on Japan's requirements abroad,

that he should have referred to the demands as an "epoch-making
event in the history of Japan's foreign policy" and praised the success
with which they had been carried out.[43] He would voice similar views
again in the 1930s.

In Nagai's article for *Shin Nippon*'s inaugural issue he described the
process by which the entire globe was being drawn into a collision
between imperialists and anti-imperialists. It was natural that governments should concern themselves with the maintenance of sufficient armaments. Realizing the vulnerability of unpreparedness,
they did not wish to subscribe to arms limitations. At the same time,
these governments were plagued with urgent social needs and faced
the critical problem of deciding how national resources, energy, and
funds should be expended—for civilian social needs or military preparation.[44]

This international dilemma was also for Nagai a personal dilemma. By "linking the cause of social democracy to a sense of 'national
mission,' "[45] he was committed on the one hand to alleviating the
social distress that was the natural product of the urbanization and
industrialization accompanying rapid modernization; on the other
hand, he stood behind expansion as one way to mitigate internal
pressure. The contradiction inherent in this dual commitment was
that the very expansion deemed necessary would require increased
hardship for and sacrifice by the Japanese people. It was their labor
and privation that would, after all, support the enlarged military
establishment necessary to acquire, protect, and maintain territory
abroad. Such an endeavor would also exacerbate the problems and
suffering in lands like China, where the Japanese felt eventually they
had to expand.

There is no difficulty in detecting these dilemmas and contradictions in the writings of the more liberal Nagai during his years at
Waseda. They are even more readily apparent later in his political
career when his thought and action took on a more conservative coloring.

THREE

Toward Democratic Reform

In addition to his teaching and journalistic duties at Waseda, Nagai served as a political campaigner. Later he and Nakano Seigō, as Ōkuma's disciples, would become spokesmen for the statesman's views and policies in the Diet.[1] Yet an overview of Nagai's work as editor of *Shin Nippon* indicates that he had been serving that function long before he attained a seat in the House, for his journalistic support was augmented by growing political involvement on his senior's behalf. As one of Ōkuma's biographers wrote,

Ōkuma's magnetism and expansive concerns enabled him to attract remarkably able young men to his following. Not only journalists but young intellectuals with political aspirations found in him a natural leader. It was a role Ōkuma loved well, and he never tired of boasting of his championing of party government. This fostering of a coterie of future statesmen, men of the stature of Inukai and Ozaki, must be deemed one of Ōkuma's political contributions.[2]

Nagai joined Ozaki and others to campaign with Ōkuma in the March 1915 election, and by his speeches in Kanazawa on behalf of Diet candidate Yokoyama Akira, the name of this amateur politician began to stick with those who would later make up his own constituency.[3] Nagai himself had been urged by another Waseda man, Miki Bukichi, to run in the 1915 election as a candidate from Tokyo's Ushigome District. Nagai deliberated on this as a political base and finally decided against the recommendation. He directed his energies instead to working for Miki's own election as well as that of other Ōkuma-backed candidates.

Only two years later, he threw his hat into the political ring as a candidate from Kanazawa. This chapter will focus on two questions related to that action. What lay behind Nagai's decision to enter politics, and how did he achieve the ultimate object of that decision, election to the Diet? A few general observations should be made, however, before proceeding to the answers to these questions.

Nagai Ryūtarō's real talents probably lay in the fields of journalism and teaching rather than in politics. Still, despite the fact that he had been well established at Waseda in two areas where he was conspicuously adept, this amateur embarked on a political career. Other Taishō "new liberals" such as Yoshino Sakuzō and Ōyama Ikuo did not opt for politics, and the nature of their imprint on Japan's history was markedly different.

Also important for an understanding of Taishō is the matter of support for those who did choose to enter politics. Nagai had not graduated from an imperial university, nor had he gone the usual route of those aspiring to a political career. His ideal politician and statesman may have been Gladstone, but just as the critic Komatsu Midori referred to Nagai as the Disraeli of the East, his entrance into the political field did indeed follow more Disraeli's pattern.[4] Both came from families that had experienced severe financial difficulties, and had entered from fields outside the bureaucracy. For Disraeli it had been literature, whereas for Nagai, teaching and journalism. Thus Nagai had to draw mainly on personal talents and popular support to win at the polls, for he lacked even the usual party affiliation. The fact that he had a hope of success implies something about the Taishō–early Shōwa period as a time of tremendous flux. One wonders if Nagai could have risen so quickly and successfully in more stable times.

The Push toward Politics

On March 24, 1914, the cabinet of Admiral Yamamoto Gonnohyōe resigned amidst a bribery scandal involving several naval officers. The *genrō* finally settled on Ōkuma Shigenobu as Yamamoto's successor. There were various reasons for this choice, not the least of which was a power rivalry among the elites. Ōkuma made an attractive candidate because he was from neither Satsuma nor the majority party, the Seiyūkai, both being out of favor with some powerful *genrō* at the time. Moreover, it appeared that he might be won over to Yamagata Aritomo's program for army expansion. Too, Ōkuma had long supported Japan's interests in China. His widespread popular appeal capped the lid of requirements. After some vacillation Ōkuma accepted and on April 16, 1914, became prime minister for a second time.

As Taishō premier, he campaigned widely for the lower-house election held on March 25, 1915, the first Japanese prime minister to do so. From his early party days with the Kaishintō, Ōkuma had adhered to the Meiji oratorical tradition, realizing the power of personal appeal in gaining popular support. Seldom preparing his speeches in advance, he still succeeded in captivating his audiences with his ready wit, self-confidence, and sense of conviction in his cause. This all added greatly to his image as a democratic politician, but earned for him at the same time the disdain of the more elitist Meiji statesmen.[5]

In June 1914, the Ōkuma Supporters Association formed in opposition to Seiyūkai politics and policies, and committed itself to the preservation of the Ōkuma cabinet. Subsequently, nationwide branches of the association opened, and the cumulative result of this activity was that Ōkuma's party won an absolute majority in the Diet in the 1915 election. It marked a turning point in Japanese electioneering practices, both in the magnitude of financial expenditures and in the incorporation of Anglo-American-style campaigning techniques.[6] But the election of 1915 is remembered also for the widespread bribery that occurred to insure a Seiyūkai defeat.[7] This goal was accomplished, and the absolute majority of that party was broken for the first time since 1908. To help insure continued success, opposition partisan forces joined together under the leadership of the Dōshikai (Fellow Thinkers Association) to form the Kenseikai in 1916.

Nevertheless, Katō Takaaki, who had taken over the reins of the Dōshikai upon the death of Katsura Tarō, had earned the ill feeling of Yamagata and the *genrō* while Ōkuma's foreign minister for his handling of Japan's entry into World War I and for the Twenty-one Demands to China. So despite Ōkuma's attempts to insure Katō's succession to the premiership, the *genrō* were determined to have another try at a nonparty cabinet. They chose this time Terauchi Masatake, a protégé of Yamagata. Ōkuma tendered his resignation to the emperor on the grounds of poor health, and Terauchi assumed office on October 9, 1916.

The Kenseikai under Katō formed an opposition bloc to the Terauchi program, and the prime minister found himself relying increasingly on the Seiyūkai and the cooperation (when it could be obtained) of its leader, Hara Takashi. Terauchi then called an election in 1917 to forestall successful passage of a nonconfidence resolution against the cabinet by the Kenseikai. It was in that lower-house election that Nagai became a candidate, giving the following explanation for running against Seiyūkai candidate Nakahashi Tokugorō:

The greatest trouble with politics in our country is the domination of the *hambatsu*. At the same time, there's the shilly-shallying of the Seiyūkai. They call themselves the greatest party in the land but also have come to depend on a type of sustenance from the *hambatsu*. . . . Before we destroy white despotism in order to make the world a world of all races, we must first destroy the despotism of the *hambatsu* in order to make Japan a Japan of the Japanese.[8]

In a speech delivered at a campaign meeting the previous day, he related how as an elementary school student in Kanazawa during the 1892 general election he had been incensed at seeing governmental abuses against members of the opposition. He had resolved then, he said, to avenge such outrages against constitutional government, and he was running now to help continue the renowned history of the people's party in Kanazawa.[9] It is ironic that he should have made such an issue of governmental interference in elections after the 1915 jobbery connected with Ōkuma's campaign, especially since abuses were particularly conspicuous in Kanazawa.[10] A more basic question concerning his speech, however, is why he chose to run in 1917 when he had refused before.

As mentioned earlier, he had made a positive impression in Kanazawa through his campaign speeches for the 1915 election. In particular, his name began to appear among anti-Seiyūkai (and even Seiyūkai) forces as one who possibly could score a victory against that party's entrenched position.[11] Through a combination of factors, one being division among the opposition forces, the Seiyūkai had been able to secure a monopoly on political power in Ishikawa prefecture by the beginning of Taishō. It was a golden age for the party in that area. In 1912, the prefectural assembly comprised 219 Seiyūkai members and 2 from the Kokumintō (National People's party); 5 Diet members came from the Seiyūkai and 1 from the Kokumintō.[12] Despite such odds Nagai accepted the invitation of representatives from Ishikawa who approached him to run.

Evidently, he had strong personal feelings for the region, and his refusal to run in 1914 had not been from doubts as to whether or not he wanted to become a politician. Rather, he was convinced the political base was wrong. The decision to eventually enter politics had been made already. It was a decision brought about through a variety of factors: his inability to enter the military because of his leg injury; his natural political inclinations and talents as orator and writer; and encouragement from outside.

As early as 1906–1907 Nagai was expressing his desire outwardly, beginning with his request to specialize in social policy and colonization instead of theology at Manchester. In July 1907, at the same time that he wrote to Abe Isoo expressing his views on pacifism's unsuitability as an ideology for the times, he sent a letter to his fiancée breaking their engagement. His explanation was that her poor health would be a hindrance to his political aspirations.[13] Shortly thereafter he wrote another to her, telling of meeting Komura Jutarō at the British embassy and Inoue Katsunosuke at the German embassy. In that letter he expressed both his exasperation at the incompetents who represented Japan abroad, and a heightening of his own career aspirations. He wrote that he, himself, would become part of the governing class and give it a popular flavor.[14]

Kanazawa

The area that was to become Nagai's political base centered on Kanazawa in what is now Ishikawa Prefecture on the northern Japan Sea side. As the former capital of Kaga, the fief of the Maeda clan (who had received it from Toyotomi Hideyoshi in the sixteenth century) and the richest feudal domain in Japan, Kanazawa produced an annual rice yield of one million *koku* (approximately five million bushels) and was known as the castle town of one million *koku*. The area came on hard times after the Meiji Restoration, when the samurai class was officially dissolved and lost its privileged economic position (as was the case with Nagai's grandfather). By the end of the Taishō period, however, Kanazawa had gradually regained its prosperity. The principal industries were silk thread production, weaving, and gilding.

Local pride was strong in its history. Since the Nagai family had moved from the area when Ryūtarō was only fifteen, he had misgivings about his acceptance as a native son. In fact, the Seiyūkai argued that he was not a true man of Kanazawa. Another worry for Nagai was finances, especially in light of the resources available to his opponent, Nakahashi Tokugorō (the man against whom Nagai had campaigned in 1915 for the Dōshikai candidate Yokoyama Akira). Nakahashi was born in Kanazawa in 1861, attended local schools and proceeded to Tokyo Imperial University where he graduated in law in 1886. He eventually became a shipping magnate in the Kansai (Kyoto-Osaka) area and served as president of the Osaka Shipping Company.

Despite this comfortable position, he retired as company president in 1915, entered the Seiyūkai, and ran as a candidate for the lower house from Kanazawa. Nakahashi's case is noteworthy in two respects. First, it is an example of Hara Takashi's tactics to improve the quality of Diet and party members by encouraging businessmen to join the Seiyūkai and run for the Diet with party support.[15] Another significant feature of Nakahashi's candidacy is that although Osaka would have been a very strong base, he ran from Kanazawa at Hara's request because of the lack of qualified Seiyūkai talent in the area at the time.[16]

Yokoyama defeated Nakahashi in 1915, but the election was declared invalid after a Seiyūkai lawsuit resulted in an investigation disclosing interference by the prefectural governor. Yokoyama chose not to run in the new election held in November 1916, and Nakahashi defeated the replacement candidate.[17] In 1917, therefore, he was in a rather secure position. He was the incumbent candidate, had strong Seiyūkai backing, personal prestige, and financial resources. Nagai was clearly the underdog. He ran as an independent (although he did receive support from the Kenseikai and other anti-Seiyūkai groups during the election). His funds were so limited that he had to mortgage his home and sell family possessions to finance campaign expenses. His greatest assets were his personal magnetism and his prepotent presence on the platform. In late March 1917, less than a month before the election, he declared his candidacy.[18]

Upon arriving in Kanazawa on April 1, he immediately made two visits, one to the grave site of the Maeda lords, the other to the grave of Shimada Ichirō. Shimada too had been from Ishikawa and was responsible for the assassination in 1878 of Ōkubo Toshimichi, leader of the Satsuma faction. In fact, it had been rumored that one reason Nagai's father, Minoru, had left Kanazawa originally to teach elsewhere was that he was considered a party to the Shimada plot and had to escape the region.[19] Be that as it may, Nagai's point in visiting Shimada's grave was obvious. He, like Shimada, was committed to ending *hambatsu* power.

During the campaign he received backing from the Kenseikai as well as Kanazawa's anti-Seiyūkai organization, groups connected with the city's silk thread industry, the Nagai Supporters Association (formed by young men associated with Waseda), and independent citizens. Among the latter, women counted heavily and formed their own suporting organizations. In addition, well-known figures like Ozaki Yukio, Ōyama Ikuo, Shimada Saburō, Abe Isoo, Ukita Kazutami, the novelist Ozaki Shirō, and scholar Kita Reikichi (younger brother of Kita Ikki) delivered speeches on his behalf. Backing Nakahashi were the Seiyūkai, local industrial leaders, and the Kanazawa Zaigō gunjinkai (Military Reserve Association). The critic Miyake Setsurei and economist-academician Fukuda Tokuzō were among notables who spoke for Nagai's opponent.[20]

It was a high-powered campaign on both sides, and at times hopes ran high in the Nagai camp. When the votes were in, though, Nakahashi had won by a margin of 203 out of 2,435 votes cast. Back in his room at the Genen Inn, Nagai wrote what was to be one of his most famous speeches, one he delivered as an expression of gratitude to his supporters and to the people of Kanazawa in general. Speaking the next day, April 22, to a huge crowd at Kenrokuen, Nagai used a play on the famous words written by Caesar at the time of his victorious campaign in Asia Minor. Caesar had boasted, "I came, I saw, I conquered" (*Kitari, mitari, kachitari*). Nagai said, "I came, I saw, and I was defeated" (*Kitari, mitari, yaburetari*). The people of Kanazawa still talk of that day, and a stone slab with the inscription *Kitari, mitari, yaburetari* now sits on the spot where Nagai spoke. His speech was not strictly political, directed not so much to Nakahashi and the Seiyūkai as to the people of Kanazawa.[21]

Kitari, mitari, yaburetari

Throughout the campaign the opposition had referred to Nagai as a young upstart. His rebuttal that day at Kenrokuen was that age had not been the crucial factor in the election. After all, Alexander had been only twenty-eight at the time he extended his "conquest" into India, and the renowned Sat-Chō *shishi* (loyalists) had been generally about thirty at the time of the restoration. No, he said, it was not age that had defeated him so much as the power of big money. Moreover, his disappointment was less his personal loss than the fact that he would be unable to contribute in the Diet toward achieving true constitutional government. The people had been generous, and he considered the votes cast for him a step toward realizing that constitutional government, not only for Kanazawa and Ishikawa, but for all Japan. At the same time, the election results had made it clear that the country had to have universal suffrage to eliminate the gulf between Japanese inside the Diet and those outside. He closed his speech with a plea for the future support of the people of Kanazawa to achieve his purpose.[22]

As with his speeches in 1915 on Yokoyama's behalf, his message this time left a strong impression. Large crowds saw him off as he left for Tokyo on April twenty-fourth. One group returning from the station got out of hand and stoned the *Hokkoku nippō* (Hokkoku daily news), which supported the Terauchi cabinet, and also the offices of the *Hokkoku shimbun* (Hokkoku news), which had backed Nakahashi. The incident was later recorded in the *Ishikawa ken shi* (History of Ishikawa Prefecture) as follows:

> The violence was spontaneous, but also represented the first movement of the people, who, despite general prosperity resulting from the [world war], were laboring under price rises and calling for a new restoration to meet current times. In the face of these hopes for a new restoration, Nagai offered the route of "universal suffrage" and "party politics" and became democracy's leader in Ishikawa.[23]

One can sense from Nagai's April 30 correspondence to a strong supporter, Ishikawa Hanzan, how deep was the disappointment in losing—disappointment, but not despair as to future possibilities. Still, two major problems were awaiting him upon his return to Tokyo, his heavy campaign debts and disturbances at Waseda. These problems at Waseda severely divided the school, and some would say that the institution never really recovered.

The trouble began with opposition to placing a statue of Ōkuma's wife on the school grounds.[24] The argument was that the statue would contradict the basic democratic principles of the school's founding; Waseda was not Ōkuma's institution alone. From there, demands escalated for more democratization within the school, replacement of certain administrative personnel, and general reform of the school system. Both faculty and student factions joined in the wrangle, and the affair received wide news coverage because of the political as well as academic implications of the problem. The struggle between the Kenseikai (Ōkuma) and Seiyūkai groups both within and outside the school, growing polarization at Waseda over developments in the Russian Revolution, and socialist activity were all involved in the school strike that finally broke out in mid-September 1917.

Nagai's position was particularly difficult.[25] The students approached him to join them, but he declined, explaining his long-standing gratitude to Ōkuma and asking for their understanding. He evidently did try to remain neutral even as he attempted to mediate between different factions in the administration and faculty. In the process he antagonized many, who then complained to Ōkuma that Nagai's interference was only complicating the situation. Ōkuma was not in good health, and his wife and adopted son Nobutsune took umbrage at Nagai's actions. Both apparently also resented Nagai for being called a "little Ōkuma" and even the statesman's "illegitimate child" because of their many resemblances and Ōkuma's favoritism toward him. Now when Nagai tried to see his longtime mentor, he was turned away on the grounds of Ōkuma's illness. Ultimately he (along with others) was dismissed from his professorial duties despite loud student outcry. He also was ousted from his position as *Shin Nippon*'s editor in chief. On October 1 an announcement appeared in the journal that staff changes would be taking place owing to Ōkuma's illness and Nagai's impending travels.

It appeared, therefore, that 1917 had been a hapless year for Nagai. Having married in 1914, he now had two small children—one slightly over two, and the other less than a year. To run in the lower-house election, he had gone into heavy debt and was then dismissed from his positions at Waseda. Especially troublesome was his misunderstanding with Ōkuma and his family. This came in conjunction with outside accusations that he had used his association with Ōkuma for selfish reasons, including plans to move into a political career.

When one surveys the real attraction Nagai had to politics, however, 1917 was advantageous in two ways in particular. First, having actually been an electoral candidate, he had gained valuable campaigning experience, had begun to build a political base, and had the confidence of knowing that he had come very close to victory. Second, having been relieved of his Waseda duties, he was free to pursue alternative interests and to join other Japanese in Paris when the peace meeting ending World War I opened in January 1919.

A Second Trip West

Hearing that Nagai would be dismissed from Waseda, concerned friends Iseri Tsugushi and Noda Utarō suggested that the timing was right for another foreign trip. Nagai was amenable, but money was a problem. Gotō Shimpei, then home minister in the Terauchi cabinet and a friend of Nagai's through their Waseda connection, introduced him to Yamamoto Tadasaburō, who had made a fortune in shipping during the war. Yamamoto agreed to make the necessary funds available, and on June 5, 1918, Nagai left Yokohama for a study tour of the United States and Europe. As with his first journey to the West in 1906–1909, this second trip proved invaluable for his future career and the further development of his political consciousness. A notable difference between the two trips was that earlier, as a student abroad, it was Europeans who had made the deepest impression on him; in 1918–1919, it was contacts with other Japanese that in the long run gave the trip its real meaning.

Both in its motivation and activities, this study tour carried the underlying motif he had introduced in a talk two months earlier. The occasion then had been the establishment of the Kaigai Shokumin Gakkō (School for Foreign Colonization), and Nagai's speech was entitled "The world must be a world for all races."[26] Likewise, when he addressed in English a gathering at the state fair in Sacramento, California, concerning Japan's participation in the war, he asserted that, "The ideal of Japan is a universal emancipation, when all races and nations shall be free under a world democracy, and such an ideal of 'universal emancipation' is essentially contrary to Germany's ambition of a 'universal empire.' It is one of the chief reasons why we are at war with Germany." He expressed his hope that by the state fair of the following year the Allies would be celebrating the victory of democracy over autocracy. He also affirmed Japan's cooperation in the cause of the American, British, and Chinese armed forces in East Asia.[27]

Earlier in Seattle Nagai had spoken to the Japanese Club and entreated them, in light of worsening discrimination against Orientals in the United States, to demonstrate to Americans the finest aspects of the Japanese heritage and character. In that way, they, as overseas Japanese, could contribute to building a more harmonious world. Later, in his Sacramento speech, he lauded his countrymen, saying, "In this state fair, perhaps all of you have seen what the Japanese farmers have been doing to supply the country's necessities and to keep your men in the trenches well fed. Indeed Japan has been doing, both in economic and military activities, her best and bravest to conquer the common enemies of humanity and democracy and to make all mankind masters of their own!"[28]

Continuing on to New York, Nagai spoke to Japanese foreign students at Columbia University. He also met Katayama Sen, whom he had known since his student days at Waseda mainly through their mutual connection with the Heiminsha and through attendance at the Waseda Social Studies Association. In 1904 Katayama had served as Japanese representative to the Second International held in Amsterdam before returning to Japan. But after the High Treason Incident in 1910, in which four workmen patterning themselves on the radical Kōtoku Shūsui plotted to assassinate Emperor Meiji, socialism in Japan entered what is known as the "winter years." During this period left-wing activity stalled under governmental suppression, causing many socialists to defect. Katayama left the country in 1914 for America, becoming a Communist after the Russian Revolution.

During the meeting of the two men in New York, Katayama gave Nagai a copy of Trotsky's "Class Struggle," which he was editing. Nagai had shown an early interest in socialist ideas and an enthusiasm for the socialist movement, but it seems significant that his real political development was progressing along other lines during the "winter years" of socialism. Even though he retained a keen awareness of happenings within the socialist camp, he began to conform more with the mainstream of those involved in the Taishō-democracy movements in the 1910s.

Based on observations and knowledge from his first trip abroad, and supplemented by investigation into events since that time, he had written in 1912 a piece for *Shin Nippon* concerning the growth of the socialist movement. He argued that the Japanese government, by its suppression of the socialists, was dealing merely with the symptom of the social malady and not the basic cause—the suffering of the people. As a solution to the problem, he did not suggest remedies along strictly socialist lines but, rather, positive governmental action to help the poor people, and also the encouragement of colonization to develop untapped resources abroad.[29] In a book published soon after this second trip to the West, he again warned the government to heed the growth of communist and socialist movements in Europe and to initiate proper steps toward reform.[30]

Going on to England, Nagai met with James Ramsay Mac-Donald, who had resigned under pressure as parliamentary leader of the Labour party in 1914 after charging that Britain was morally wrong in declaring war on Germany. In England also Nagai met with another of his countrymen, Adachi Kenzō. Adachi had earned the title "god of elections" by his skillful handling of candidate selection for the government parties in the 1915 election and was currently in Britain for research on the electoral system.[31] Nagai's and Adachi's paths were to cross many times during their careers, as was the case with other Japanese Nagai met later at the peace conference in Paris. Among the latter was Kita Ikki, a spearhead of the later radical movement that culminated in the February 26 Incident, when young army officers rebelled and held Tokyo under a state of siege while calling for a "Shōwa Restoration."

As Nagai's personal and ideological goals had been spurred on in 1907 through first-hand observation of the handling of Japanese affairs abroad by men he considered incompetent, so it was at Paris. His indignation was clear in a January 28, 1919, letter to Gotō, wherein he complained that the Japanese delegation alone of all the major powers remained silent on major matters.[32] Others shared Nagai's feelings. As the conference wore on, the concern of many Japanese in Paris and at home turned to outrage—both at the performance of Japanese bureaucratic representatives at Versailles, and at the Anglo-American frustration of Japanese claims. Not only was Japan's proposed racial equality clause for the League Covenant defeated, it had to negotiate aggressively over what it considered rightful claims in Shantung. Moreover, instead of receiving outright the former German islands in the Pacific north of the equator as it had expected according to the 1917 secret treaties with the various European powers, Japan had to accept the Carolines, Marshalls, and Marianas as a Class C mandate under the League.

Against this background, the Kaizō dōmei organized with approximately forty-five members. Professional journalists such as Baba Tsunego, Ishibashi Tanzan, Mitsukawa Kametarō, and Nakano Seigō; journalists and professors like Uehara Etsujirō and Nagai; bureaucrats turned politicians such as Nagashima Ryūji; and figures like Suzuki Umeshirō, who was a journalist as well as a Mitsui Bank affiliate, politician, and labor movement leader—these were the types who formed the organization, in all probability with the support of Gotō Shimpei.[33] These men had a common emphasis on national unity, and they were determined to remedy what they considered inept bureaucratic handling of both Japan's external affairs (such as they saw at Paris) and her internal problems. As a solution, they demanded universal suffrage and other democratic reforms. In short, one sees in the Kaizō dōmei, the reformist coupling of democracy with a strong foreign policy line.

Others who had been at Paris—Kita Ikki, for instance—would opt for more direct action to bring about a restoration. While abroad Kita had written a tract lamenting anti-Japanese movements in the world and the cowardliness of the Japanese plenipotentiaries at Versailles. He sent this tract, later known as the Versailles letter, to Mitsukawa Kametarō, adding at the end: "I met Nagai Ryūtarō today [June 28, 1919] on his way home from the peace conference. But since there was no time to talk at leisure, please show this to him and also to Nakano Seigō, who had cautioned the people about the mis-management of Japanese delegates at the conference."[34]

Nagai himself, upon his return to Japan in July 1919, immediately gave vent to accumulated resentment over the Paris proceedings. An article written for the August 1919 issue of *Chūō kōron* entitled "Japan, Threatened by Two World Trends" is representative of his thinking at the time.[35] These two trends were Anglo-Saxonism, which he saw directed toward leading the world in line with Anglo-American culture, and the second, bolshevism, a movement aimed at rebuilding the world social structure by a global workers' revolution.

Nagai explained that the first, Anglo-Saxonism, was blatantly evident in the spirit that permeated the peace conference and also in the more concrete result of that meeting, the plan for the League of Nations. The threat, he explained, was the intense anti-Japanese feeling shared by those two countries, resulting in their cooperation to end Japanese power in the East by opposing the latter's claims at Paris. He feared that should England and the United States continue to consider Japan a danger because of its militaristic, aggressive policies, they would more than likely take steps to keep it within bounds.

Nagai warned further that Japan must be on its guard against bolshevism, for it was laboring under the same type of economic domination by aristocratic families and privileged bureaucracy as was Russia before the revolution. Either way, he argued, whether the threat be from Anglo-Saxonism or bolshevism, the situation was clear. Japan must itself take the necessary steps for reform or be coerced to do so a second time from outside, as in the late Tokugawa period.

Nagai's cynicism toward the Anglo-American bloc is even more glaring in his article for the next issue of *Chūō kōron* (September) entitled "America, Wavering Intellectually at the Crossroads—A Leader of or Threat to World Civilization?" Here he argued that America was in no position to claim world leadership because of its own low level of cultural development.[36] Many shared Nagai's pessimism. Mitsukawa Kametarō, to whom Kita Ikki had sent his Versailles letter, and also a member of the Kaizō dōmei, was writing as early as 1921 about the possible advantages and disadvantages of going to war with America over diverging interests.[37]

Still, a comparison of the attitudes and ideas of those such as Nagai and Mitsukawa on the one hand, and the pro-American, pro-Wilson stance of Minobe Tatsukichi, Nitobe Inazō, Yoshino Sakuzō, and other democrats of the period on the other, reveals a split within the Taishō movements over foreign policy. The sociopolitical phenomenon known as Taishō democracy was one aspect of Japan's reaction, as a nation and as a society, to the worldwide impact of America after World War I.[38] However, the Wilsonianism that constituted a major part of that American influence involved two aspects. One was the universal side, which consisted of Christian idealism and the theory of social evolution, and the other, the particularistic side, encompassing an ideology of special privilege according to geographical and class differences and implying the superiority of British and Americans. Accordingly the Japanese reaction to the American impact (and Wilsonianism) involved both accommodation and opposition.[39] At the same time that informed Japanese were aware that leadership in the West was shifting from Europe to America, they had diverging opinions over the pros and cons of the shift and the future meaning it would have for international affairs, especially the Japanese-American relationship within that framework.

Nagai was among those who pondered such questions. On July 2, 1919, the day he returned to Japan, he gave a talk in Osaka entitled "From Europe to America, from America, where?" In world diplomacy and economics, he explained, the focus was moving from Europe to America; and Americans themselves were aware of this. Moreover, at the Paris meeting and by way of the policies being formed there, it was clear that the United States was trying to throw a wedge between China and Japan. To make matters worse, the European nations were catering to American wishes in this and other matters. When at the meeting, Japan's position was being attacked by the Chinese and American representatives on matters like the Shantung question, England failed to come to the aid of its ally Japan, making it evident that Japan could no longer put trust in such arrangements as the Anglo-Japanese Alliance. "Whether we like it or not," Nagai said, "it has come to the point where from now on, we Japanese must struggle independently for cultural and economic superiority in the arena of the Pacific with the country that may be called the 'champion of the international struggle for survival,' the United States."[40] As this statement makes clear, his position with respect to the West—especially the Anglo-American powers—had moved considerably from his stance in Sacramento less than a year earlier.

A SECOND BID FOR ELECTION

While Nagai had been in Europe important events had taken place in Japan, both on the national and local levels. The rice riots had broken out in August 1918 in Toyama Prefecture (adjoining Ishikawa) and had spread nationwide by September. The parties had taken a rather lukewarm stand regarding the riots, but in contrast, a mass meeting of newspapermen from throughout the country had been held on September 12 to criticize the Terauchi cabinet. That cabinet ultimately resigned on September 21 to be replaced on the twenty-ninth by the first party cabinet under the premiership of Hara Takashi. The rice riots, however, had been only a symptom of deep and widespread turmoil that resulted in the acceleration of labor and social movements.

In retrospect it is evident that the emergence of party cabinets and two-party rivalry coincided with the appearance of a new set of national problems.[41] Responding to heightened social unrest and the increasingly vocal demands by the people for more political power, some elements within the parties intensified the drive begun in earnest around the turn of the century for the passage of a universal suffrage bill. They justified such a measure as a safety valve to divert the public from more radical and dangerous courses of action.[42]

The government, as formerly, opposed the plan on the grounds that it would provide an impetus to further social unrest. In the midst of heated debate on the issue, the House was dissolved on February 26, 1920, and a new election was scheduled for May 10, to be held under the revised election law of 1919 (effected by a compromise bill in the Forty-second Diet). Under this new law, the tax qualification was lowered from ten to three yen (direct tax), and the election districts were reduced in size. Passage of the bill proved to be a victory for the Seiyūkai, who, as the longtime majority party in the House, could claim credit for that body's action on suffrage. Against this background, Nagai threw his hat into the ring once more.

His electoral base followed the Taishō pattern wherein much of the reform activity originated in the cities, was led by young liberal intellectuals, journalists, and students, and was backed by an emerging working-class movement.[43] The Nagai Supporters Association, which had been formed in Kanazawa at the time of the 1917 election for the lower house, did not dissolve after Nagai's defeat. The group merely changed its name to the Kanazawa Constitutional Young

Men's Association (Kanazawa rikken seinenkai) and continued to operate with an increased membership in working for the goals advocated by Nagai during his first election campaign. The group aimed at a "new restoration"; and at the opening ceremony on August 13, 1917 (at which time Nagai spoke as advisor), they pledged themselves to the goals of extending political rights and realizing democracy, cleaning up municipal government, and attaining overall unity among the people.[44]

In July 1919 the group expanded further to include all of Ishikawa Prefecture, changing its name once more to the Ishikawa Constitutional Young Men's party (Ishikawa ken rikken seinentō). It grew eventually to encompass eleven prefectures and one urban prefecture, and in October 1925 the group was renamed the Japan Sea Young Men's League (Nihonkai seinentō remmei). From the time of its inception in the 1910s it concerned itself with issues and movements developing in the area, but duplicated in varying degrees throughout Japan.

In line with its goal of extending voting rights, for example, representatives were sent to participate in the universal suffrage movement in Tokyo. The group became involved also with growing socialist and labor activity in the area. In October 1919, the Kanazawa branch of the Japan General Labor Organization (Nihon sōdōmei yūaikai) was formed, demanding the rights of labor to organize, strike, and obtain wider political privileges. The labor movement there became even more intense when in early 1920 the region began to feel the effects of the postwar financial panic, resulting in severe personnel cuts of weavers and gilders in the factories of Ishikawa's Nomi District and in the Kanazawa silk factories.

Ishikawa was not unusual. Poor economic conditions were widespread, and there was support throughout Japan for the Seiyūkai's positive economic policy. This policy focused on national development through governmental spending, and involved, among other measures, the opening of nationwide lines of communication through the laying of railroads, building of bridges, and harbor renovation.

Such was the situation when on April 20, 1920, Nagai announced his candidacy for the Diet from Kanazawa (now the first Ishikawa district under the new election law). He based his platform on five points: correction of abuses in Diet dissolution practices; price regulation; universal suffrage; improved handling of foreign problems; and, of course, the toppling of Seiyūkai power. His backing was similar to that of 1917—the anti-Seiyūkai groups, the Kenseikai, the Kanazawa silk thread industry, the Ishikawa Constitutional Young Men's party, and the Kokumintō.

Nakahashi, who had entered the Hara cabinet in 1918 as minister of education, now had Osaka as his election base. The general interpretation is that he had purposely moved his base, fearing possible future loss to Nagai.[45] His successor as the Seiyūkai-backed candidate was the head of the Ishikawa prefectural assembly, Yonehara Otoo, who received support from leaders of many of the area's important industries, groups connected with various food concerns, and followers of Shin-shū, the largest sect of Buddhism in the region.

Nagai was suffering from pneumonia throughout part of the campaign, but he drove himself relentlessly nevertheless. Remembering his final speech at Kenrokuen when he had lost the 1917 election, many offered extra support. A representative of the silk thread industry, for instance, volunteered his office for Nagai's election activities and gave his employees three days off to campaign for him. The youth who had been so inspired by this "new man" in 1917 had formed by this time into a tight organization dedicated to Nagai's platform—especially universal suffrage—and carried the Nagai flag of a so-called Second Restoration. The end result was that in this race, Nagai could have quoted Caesar's victorious words exactly. He had received 3,305 votes to Yonehara's 1,955, and his only disappointment was that he had not been able to run against and defeat Nakahashi.

This 1920 general election for the lower house was a nationwide victory for the Seiyūkai, which won 278 seats. Following were the Kenseikai with 110 and the Kokumintō with 29.[46] Ishikawa, where the number of voters had increased from 24,809 to 45,044 under the new election law, was a Seiyūkai victory also, with four of the five seats going to their candidates. Nagai was the single non-Seiyūkai victor. On June 25 he entered the Kenseikai and joined in the opening of the Forty-third Diet on July 1.

FOUR

A Reformist in the 1920s

At the age of thirty-nine Nagai had achieved the goal toward which he had been working since he was a student in middle school. With his election to the Diet he had the opportunity to participate in the political process to effect his two long-range objectives. This duad, liberation of the socially underprivileged Japanese and Asian liberation from white domination, continued to be his main preoccupation throughout twenty-five years of public life. Entering that public life, he was representative of other contemporary politicians in his background of Ōkuma-Waseda influence and his reconstruction platform. Still, he retained a distinctiveness of political style both in his formulation of his nation's problems and his attempts to solve those problems.

It now remains to show how Nagai the reformist functioned within the milieu of the "cooperative twenties." He operated during this period within three main roles. The first was that of party man. Throughout the 1910s he had been a severe critic of the established parties. Yet very shortly after his election in 1920, he became a member of one, the Kenseikai. This choice to operate from a political party base and to try to reform the established parties from within set him apart from other young reformers of the time. Moreover, his party affiliation had important implications for his stand on foreign and domestic problems.

His second role was that of Diet member, one strongly committed to parliamentary politics and dedicated to the passage of a universal suffrage law and reform in the House of Peers. And finally was the part he played in foreign affairs. Here he was both commentator on international issues as well as actual participant in the foreign policy process through various government posts. Consideration, then, of his reformist position in these three roles during the 1920s will provide a basis for comparison with his later, more conservative position in the 1930s.

THE LATE TAISHŌ SCENE

In the early 1920s an unexpected turn of events had far-reaching effects in the political world. On November 4, 1921, Premier Hara Takashi was stabbed to death by a deranged youth at Tokyo Station. Shortly thereafter on January 10, Ōkuma Shigenobu died at eighty-five, followed on February 1 by Yamagata Aritomo, also eighty-five. It was the passing of an era, and the degree of stability that had been obtained through the tacit understanding between Yamagata and Hara (and the political forces they represented) also came to an end. The result was a period of reversion to nonparty cabinets and the stepped-up activity of antiestablishment forces.

The situation was confounded even more in that the tempo of social movements in Japan, symbolized earlier by the rice riots of 1918, accelerated under the continuing influence of the Russian Revolution and Western democratic trends. Forces within the labor movement, which had organized in 1912 as the Yūaikai (Friendship Association) under the Christian socialist Suzuki Bunji, became the General Labor Organization in 1919. In the midst of increasing tenancy disputes, the agrarian movement organized in 1920 into the Japan Farmers' Union (Nihon nōmin kumiai). Also in 1920 the women's movement which had been spurred on by the 1911 organization of authoress Hiratsuka Raichō, the Blue Stockings (Seitōsha), built up momentum with the advent of the New Women's Society (Shin fujin kyōkai). Then in 1922, the Leveling Society (Suiheisha) formed for the liberation of another disadvantaged group, Japan's social outcasts, the *burakumin*.

The socialist movement emerged from its "winter years" under the new social and ideological environment following World War I and the Russian Revolution, and the Japan Socialist League (Nihon shakaishugi dōmei) formed in 1920, the same year as Japan's first May Day. Two years later the Japan Communist party organized, followed by various proletarian parties as the decade progressed. Related to all of these movements and giving them momentum, of course, were the two great tides of thought, democracy and Marxism.

Many in Japan viewed the acceleration of these movements and the influx of foreign thought with alarm. In fact, as early as 1922 Justice Minister Ōki Enkichi and Home Minister Tokonami Takejirō introduced anti-subversive legislation into a committee of the House of Peers. After much preliminary debate, this bill for a "Law to Control Radical Social Movements" passed the House of Peers; but the

Seiyūkai cabinet did not push it through the lower house owing to the general mood of dissension both within and outside the Diet. Opposition meetings—such as that held on March 1 in Kanda, with Nagai, Ōyama Ikuo, Fukuda Tokuzō, and Ōsugi Sakae participating —were widespread, and the Seiyūkai feared that undue pressure to pass the bill then would impede other important legislation.[1]

The police used existing laws to suppress the newly formed Communist party in July 1923, but agitation continued for new and more stringent anti-subversive legislation. In the wake of the great Kanto earthquake in September 1923 that killed over 130,000 persons and destroyed close to 600,000 homes, police took advantage of an emergency ordinance to hunt out those they had tagged as radicals, and it was under such circumstances that the anarchist Ōsugi Sakae was killed by an overzealous military police officer. In December the Yamamoto cabinet, which had replaced the short-lived Katō Tomosaburō cabinet, resigned en masse after the Toranomon Incident, when an attempt was made on the life of the emperor by the anarchist Namba Daisuke. Thereafter, suppression of the labor and socialist movements intensified. At the same time, the parties' drive to reestablish party cabinets intensified after a third nonparty cabinet under the bureaucrat Kiyoura Keigo was set up in January.

Such was the domestic scene during the early 1920s, and in this stormy atmosphere Nagai firmly established his reputation as a champion of the people. His ideal had always been the formation of a people's party that would transcend the petty and corrupt politics of the established parties. This was the goal of labor and agrarian union leaders as well. Socialists, who were looking toward one nationwide proletarian party, were working for the same end. Nagai did not abandon his Kenseikai affiliation, however, to become part of that movement. As he wrote in 1920,

I can sympathize with those in the proletarian class since their interests are not represented in the Diet. I can even sympathize with their idea of not recognizing parliamentary politics, but it seems to me that these people do not understand the situation clearly. . . . Doing away with parliamentary government would not put an end to class warfare; rather, there is the danger that it would overturn the very basis of society.[2]

The Kenseikai Connection

In his early essays in *Shin Nippon* Nagai had castigated the parties for their failure to challenge the *genrō*, the bureaucracy, and the military, and for thereby endangering Japan's system of constitutional government. One of his severest criticisms concerned the lack of necessary political debate over issues, debate that would be conducive to sounder solutions of the matters involved. Instead, he insisted, the parties curried the favor of those in power, avoided taking a stand on crucial problems, and devoted themselves to building up their own factions. The reliance on such political strategies, Nagai believed, led to a lack of national unity and invited social unrest and a weak international position.[3] Still, he judged it expedient to join one of the two leading parties once his own political career had begun.

That his choice could have been only the Kenseikai was a foregone conclusion. Among the many reasons for Nagai's decision were the Kenseikai's Ōkuma-Waseda connection, its position as the opposition party, its stand in favor of universal suffrage (despite heated intraparty debate on the form of such a bill), and its bent toward reform in general. As Duus has shown, by the Kenseikai's very position as the out-party, it tended to take reform more seriously than did the Seiyūkai.[4] Moreover, by affiliating with the party in opposition to the pork-barrel politics of Hara's group, Nagai seemed to offer fresh solutions and was able to build a public image as a people's politican.

Nakano Seigō, another Waseda graduate elected to the Diet in 1920, also joined the Kenseikai. He had formerly been associated with the Kakushin (Reform) Club of Inukai Tsuyoshi, but broke away on the conviction that Inukai had failed in his attempt to build pure party government based on a popular union. Like Nagai, part of Nakano's motivation for becoming a Kenseikai member was his many Waseda friends within that party and his desire to avoid association with the corrupt political practices of the Seiyūkai. He also felt the Kenseikai had greater potential for becoming the representative of popular interests. This was especially important to him because of his belief in the need for a rational people's movement to transform politics and achieve a new restoration.[5]

Nagai also saw the potential of the Kenseikai to achieve restorationist goals, but another key factor in his decision for affiliation was personal ambition. In his determination to move ahead, he was both a Meiji man, preoccupied with *ie* (family honor), and a Taishō man, motivated by *risshin shusse* (desire for personal advancement).[6] Nagai had been of samurai stock, and though the family had been impoverished following the Meiji Restoration, the samurai pride had never been lost. Along with the desire for personal fulfillment, the restoration of family name and dignity to a standing worthy of samurai lineage was probably a significant underlying motivation spurring on his careerism.

Related to this were his inherent political aspirations. Nagai was to some extent an idealist, but he was also a realist. He was passionately involved in the present and compelled to achieve personal goals, even if this meant compromise. His chosen profession was politics, and he realistically recognized that the parties had power at the moment and could give their members support. Hence Nagai, like his doyen Ōkuma, was ready to bend in order to attain his political goals. When Ōkuma as Taishō premier found himself in a position where he could no longer stubbornly oppose the *genrō* and still remain in office, he "compromised his very principles for the advantages of *genrō* support, the very Satsuma and Chōshū cabal he had so long abhorred."[7] Similarly Nagai, though formerly an outspoken antagonist of the parties and their practices, became from 1920 an active member of the Kenseikai, a party whose origin was in the Dōshikai founded by Katsura Tarō, the model bureaucrat-politician type to which Nagai was so opposed.

His choices set him off from other Taishō reformers; likewise, his role within the Taishō movements would be different from that of a Yoshino Sakuzō. Yoshino, an intellectual with a passion for the ideal, ultimately adhered more to universalistic standards of judgment and to values transcending particular circumstances. Tetsuo Najita has suggested that Yoshino and other idealistic liberals could neither reconcile themselves to the concrete processes of government nor could they attack (by revolutionary ideology and strategy) the constitutional order that provided mediation and protection to those processes.[8] Nagai was more realistic in his acknowledgment that "ideological liberalism" is almost certain to be defeated by "concrete politics."[9]

For all that, he continued his criticism of the corrupt practices of the established parties while attempting to work from within to effect their reconstruction. In the long run his position was to cause problems for him. He said shortly before his death that although he had advanced well with his ideals while young, as the years passed, things had not worked out so satisfactorily.[10] One writer, in discussing the Young Officers who engineered the February 26 Incident in the 1930s, suggested that the affair typified "that combination of idealism and activism still prevalent in Japan, a psychology which Mishima [Yukio] characterized as the clash between 'spirit' and 'politics.' "[11] This was the dilemma Nagai faced during his career in the twenties, and even more so as the thirties progressed.

Mannequin of the Minseitō

Although the Kenseikai counted many Waseda men among its members, a great number in the party, especially those in the upper ranks, came from careers in the bureaucracy and had been educated at Tokyo Imperial University and private schools other than Waseda. Many in this group, such as Katō Takaaki, Hamaguchi Osachi, Wakatsuki Reijirō, Shidehara Kijūrō, and Egi Yoku, simply did not appeal to the common man as popular politicians.

Someone like Nagai, a people's politician, committed to commonerism and able to articulate this through his oratorical gifts, had a charm and fascination for the people. His standing as a party member, therefore, was an asset to the Kenseikai (to become the Rikken minseitō [Constitutional Democratic party] in 1927) in its appeal to a growing electorate.[12] Thus the politician Miki Bukichi, a longtime associate of Nagai since their Waseda days and popularly known as the "king of the hecklers," once referred to Nagai as the "mannequin of the Minseitō." Because of his very appeal to the common man, to women, and to youth groups, Nagai served as a camouflage for the bureaucratic hue of his party.[13] This was especially true in the later twenties when confidence in party government was on the decline owing to corruption in party politics—corruption underscored by the suffering brought on by the 1926 domestic depression and the ensuing 1927 bank crisis.

Moreover, this was an era when heated verbal attacks against the party in power were especially popular and profitable. In this connection also, Nagai, as a member of the opposition, benefited his party as well as furthered his own career through his speeches on the Diet floor and elsewhere. An incident concerning Yamagata's state funeral reveals that his reputation as a spokesman for the anti-government forces was by 1922 already well established. Matsumoto Gōkichi, confidant of Prince Saionji Kimmochi and other government leaders, recorded in his diary on January 31, 1922, a conversation he had had with General Tanaka Giichi about the condition of Yamagata. Tanaka had asked who, in the event of a state funeral, would be most likely in the House to oppose the allotment of funds. Matsumoto's reply was Nagai or Tabuchi Toyokichi (an independent), but that probably there would be no objection, even from the

Kenseikai. In a follow-up entry on February 3 after the death of Yamagata, Matsumoto noted that the appropriation for a state funeral had passed the House of Peers with no trouble; but in the lower house, opposition had been voiced by Minami Teizō and Morishita Kametarō of the Kōshin Club, fanned on by Tabuchi and Nagai. Matsumoto added that his prediction had not missed the mark by much.[14]

Nagai realized full well the importance and potential of oratory, especially under parliamentary systems, where oratorical prowess could influence greatly the direction of politics. As he wrote in 1914,

To try to be a politician under a system of constitutional government without the power of speech is like trying to go into battle without arms; and if we desire to effect constitutional government and take upon ourselves the reformation of Japanese politics, we must give very careful consideration to the practice of oratory.

He expressed also his conviction in the power of speech to bring about significant historical changes. Drawing on a saying of the novelist Thackeray to the effect that people are much like infants, Nagai explained how easily the populace could be influenced from the speaking platform.[15] His writings are filled with examples of great orators from history—the speakers of early Meiji, Chang-I (of the Warring States period in China), Caesar, Anthony and Brutus, the Buddha, Jesus, Confucius, Mohammed, Nichiren, Balfour, Churchill, Lincoln, and the list goes on.

His longtime secretary, Azuma Shun'ei, wrote that Nagai was more an orator than a politician.[16] Yet politics was his chosen vocation, and in his political style he followed in the footsteps of his mentor, Ōkuma, a "dramaturgic politician."[17] Nagai, too, fit into that category. "He never touched a drop of liquor in his life; but in front of a crowd or standing on the rostrum, he spoke as if intoxicated."[18] Unlike Ōkuma, who was prone to speak off the top of his head, Nagai labored long in preparation. He would carefully polish each speech before delivery and then revise two or three times according to the reception of different audiences.[19]

The results on the podium were electric, even before the era of sophisticated artificial amplification, when a speaker's voice might have to reach a crowd of twenty thousand practically unaided. His deliveries often betrayed bias and exaggeration. But despite his tendency to deliver tirades as a member of the opposition bent on denouncing the party in power, he is remembered for what has been considered as possibly the most famous speech of any Diet of the Taishō period, his maiden speech on July 8, 1920.[20]

In the West, Lenin—In the East, Hara Takashi

With the opening of the Forty-third Diet, Nagai delivered an attack, on behalf of the Kenseikai, at what he and they considered to be a series of evils perpetrated by the Hara cabinet.[21] Such diatribes by Kenseikai and opposition party members were not new, but Nagai's choice of words and presentation of arguments were sufficiently pointed and stinging to warrant his censure by the House and recognition as the most outstanding *shinjin* (new face) of the period.

Beginning his interrogation with the matter of dispatching troops to Siberia in 1918, he asked why adequate preparation had not been made for the expedition, thereby avoiding the great losses that had occurred. He went on to attribute much of the blame to Tanaka Giichi, who was in attendance that day as army minister in the Hara cabinet.

Nagai then questioned Hara's recent statement that foreign thought was like an infection spreading unrest among the people. More than the influence of foreign thought, insisted Nagai, social unrest was being caused by economic difficulties resulting from sudden price rises. Hara could ban Marx and Kropotkin, but he could not end the people's misery without taking measures to remedy the country's economic situation.

Neither had the Seiyūkai accepted proper responsibility in dealing with the labor problems that were growing worse by the day. This situation could turn into a class struggle unless something was done quickly. The first step should be a court for labor and law, and yet the only measure the cabinet had taken was to step up police suppression, tagging laborers as agitators disseminating dangerous thought. Even the Japanese representatives to the International Committee on Labor at the Paris Peace Conference took the attitude that such problems were really for the home government to solve. They gave a decision, therefore, on only two of the nine articles presented and deferred on the others, finally walking out of the meeting.

In short, he declaimed, Hara's policies were characterized by the tendency to repudiate constitutional government. The three-yen voting qualification was a good example. Hara's fear was that the elimination of the tax requirement would result in the breakdown of class barriers. In obstructing attempts to have a government firmly grounded in the people, however, Nagai accused Hara of going contrary to the edict of Emperor Meiji.

> In Japan and in the world today, there are those who still insist on autocratic class rule—in the West is Nicolai Lenin of the radical Russian government; and in the East, there's our own Prime Minister Hara Takashi! . . . Though the classes that raised these men up are different—for Lenin, the working class, and for Hara, the capitalists—both classes are void of the great spirit of democracy. [22]

Once House Speaker Oku Shigezōrō had regained order, Nagai went on with accusations of illegal profit making between two or three ministers and currupt businessmen. Such practices, he charged, were leading to class autocratic rule. By doing nothing about it, Hara was guilty of a moral affront against the Imperial House and the people, and Nagai closed with a direct request to Hara for an apology and an explanation.

The premier responded that no apology was in order. Furthermore, since Nagai's questions were directed to him as a political adversary, neither was an answer necessary. Hara recorded nothing concerning the confrontation in his diary. [23] Nevertheless, forces within the Seiyūkai started immediate disciplinary proceedings against Nagai, basing their charges on three points: his accusation that Hara had gone counter to the Meiji emperor's edict; the likening of Hara to Lenin; and his charge of collusion between profiteers and some government ministers.

On July 9 Nagai was given the opportunity in the Diet to retract his statements, but he declined to do so. Rather, he hoped to clarify his meaning. Speaker Oku replied that if he chose not to retract, he would have no chance to speak. Oku then called on Diet member Uzawa Sōmei for a resolution of disciplinary action, and this carried by a vote of 256 to 132. [24]

After a series of committee meetings on the case, chaired by Hatoyama Ichirō, Nagai was censured from the Diet for five days. More than the actual disciplinary measure, it was the fact that he had not been given the proper opportunity to defend himself that caused such furor in the Diet and in the press. Nagai accepted the censure, but with his reputation already established as an up-and-coming political figure. One conservative California newspaper described the situation this way:

> The liberalistic tendencies of the speeches in this year's session of the Diet has been a distinct feature of constitutional development in Japan. The

leader of the movement is a young representative named Ryutaro Nagai, whose boldness of word has attracted the attention of the empire. In the railroad train, at public meetings, wherever men gather, Nagai is on the lips of Japanese as a "coming man."

Nagai was formerly a professor at Waseda University, the most democratic of Japan's universities, which was founded by that heroic radical leader, Marquis Okuma. The young man is a great believer in the democratic development of Japanese political institutions and is an admirer of both the British Parliament and the American Congress. He is described as a man of remarkable oratorical talents, who will be heard from later in modernized Japan.[25]

Nagai's speech, delivered at the beginning of the new decade, was basically a call to bring politics closer to the people. As such, it served to further the case for universal suffrage, the cause célèbre of the Taishō-democracy movements. Indeed, it was the universal suffrage issue (building since the early years of Meiji), the activities of popular movements surrounding that issue, and the stand of the established parties with respect to both the movements and the issue that greatly determined the direction of politics during the years between 1920 and 1925.[26]

NAGAI AND UNIVERSAL SUFFRAGE

In August, a month after delivering his maiden speech, Nagai published an article in *Chūō kōron* setting forth the role he saw for parliamentary government—that is, to unite and harmonize the various class interests. He then drew a comparison between the Anglo-American legislative members and those in Japan. The former, he argued, represented all the people, not just their own classes. In Japan the reverse was true, resulting in little effort toward achieving true equality throughout society. Furthermore, the West did not consider Japan an enlightened nation because of the continuation of limited suffrage there.[27]

The Diet's future duty, he insisted, must be to establish laws that would insure the perfect representation of each class's interests in the Diet. He cautioned, however, that this move toward a new, more democratic society had to be a gradual, cooperative process, not the outcome of revolution or by dictate. Parliamentary politics had a crucial role to play in the process; and as the first step, it was necessary to enact universal suffrage to provide the basis on which the parliament could stand.[28]

Hara's decision to defeat the 1920 universal suffrage bills in the Forty-second Diet seemed to indicate that the Seiyūkai wanted only to maintain the status quo. The suffrage issue thus became enmeshed in party politics. This connection between interparty rivalry and the suffrage issue became even closer owing to the parties' natural stake in the composition of the electorate. Whereas the Seiyūkai was strong traditionally in the rural areas, urban interests and support were of greater importance for the Kenseikai. Passage of a universal suffrage bill would have increased the relative size of the urban electorate. Thus,

> . . . in the perceptions of the politicians at least, the outcome of an election did not depend solely on who controlled the government. The notable difference in the parties' reactions [to the universal suffrage issue], and especially the tenacity of the Seiyūkai's resistance, suggests that the composition of the electorate was not a matter of indifference, at least to those who had a stake in the composition of the elected house of the legislature.[29]

Helpful to consider in this connection is the thesis that two leit-motifs greatly determined the direction of Taishō democracy and reform. One was the role of the political parties, and the other, the system of national mobilization aimed at by the reform movement. Democrats, nationalists—and democrat-nationalists—were absorbed into the suffrage movement.[30] Nagai was not unusual in being involved in a multiple capacity as party man, reformer, and nationalist. He reasoned that equal voting rights were a precondition for class equality in the country, and a sine qua non for Japan's recognition as an equal among the world's democratic (and at the same time, leading) nations. This reasoning becomes more intelligible when one looks at his position on the status of women.

Women's Rights

It is clear that for Nagai the people did not signify the common man alone. Very early in Taishō he had written that he saw three major world problems at the time—racial conflict, labor, and the status of women.[31] As a supporter of women's rights, he carried on the work of some illustrious Meiji predecessors, including the natural-rights advocate and theorist Ueki Emori and Mori Arinori, education minister who supported education for women and a single standard of morality. There was also the towering intellectual and educator Fukuzawa Yukichi, who strongly encouraged changes in social mores and attitudes to effect equal opportunities for women.

Nagai, too, had criticized the traditional Japanese attitude toward women as inferiors, suggesting that it was based on an unquestioning acceptance of Confucian tenets regarding the female sex. Moreover, should women continue to accept such oppression submissively, their status could never change. To treat women as they were treated in Japan was the sign of a backward society.[32] If the country did not alter its ways so that men and women could be considered equals and work together, Nagai argued, they could never build a new Japan that would be able to "compete with and surpass the culture of the West."[33] A political speech he delivered to a women's gathering in Kanazawa was one of the first in Japan expressly for the female sex.[34] He was constantly aware of developments taking place in the women's movement and encouraged new steps and goals such as economic independence. Although not always in agreement with the ideas of some female reformers (such as opposition to marriage), he did give recognition to the work being done by Hiratsuka Raichō and the Blue Stockings,[35] and later to others in the New Women's Movement.

His trip to the West in 1918–1919 exposed him to advances in the women's movement in Europe and America, and upon his return he wrote about female liberation. On the one hand, he said, he could understand the desire of Japanese female reformers to free themselves from the traditional role of "good wife and wise mother" in that, theretofore, it had implied a status of social inequality. Still, he argued, "good wife and wise mother" was basically a sound ideal, but one that could not be brought to fruition in an unenlightened society.[36] Japan needed equal rights for women both to realize this ideal and to allow all to work together in raising the country to equal status with the enlightened nations of the world.

He also emphasized the progress that had been made in women's rights in the West, most especially in England but also in the United States, where there were hopes for equal suffrage for women by 1921.[37] He cited other examples like Finland, where already in 1906 under a revolutionary constitution women had acquired the rights of suffrage and eligibility for election at age twenty-four. It was clear to Nagai that Japan had to emulate advanced Western countries and revise its laws concerning political rights. The first step would be the passage of a universal suffrage bill.

Realization

Nagai had been involved in general suffrage activity since his student days at Waseda, and he participated in drawing up the bill that the Universal Suffrage League planned to submit in the Forty-fourth

Diet when it opened in late December 1920. The league had hoped that the Kenseikai would join with them in the bill, but the latter rejected this, preferring to act separately. Nagai's position at this point says much about the dilemma he (and other reformists) faced during the interwar years, namely, the clash between spirit and politics. The reformists were generally on the periphery of established power when they entered the public scene in 1918–1919, and a central aim of their reconstruction energies was the toppling of that power. At the same time, they were interested in using that very power and becoming a part of its base. This dichotomy led often to a dilution of goals and reform results.[38]

Nagai had acted independently of the Kenseikai in helping to draw up the bill for the Forty-fourth Diet, a step affirming, it seems, his reform zeal. In the end, however, he did not sign his name to the bill and became the object of trenchant criticism from the league and others for his apparent hypocrisy. Although he justified his position on the grounds that the plan did not provide for the right of women to participate in government, it was also well known that had he signed, he might well have been dropped from the Kenseikai ranks. Nagai was a sufficiently realistic politician to know that he could best move up in the political world through alignment with one of the established parties.[39] From that base, he continued efforts for electoral reform, one example being a 1921 book that he edited titled *Shikisha no mitaru futsū senkyo* (Intellectuals look at universal suffrage). The contributors included Ōkuma Shigenobu, Katō Takaaki, Ozaki Yukio, Minobe Tatsukichi, Yoshino Sakuzō, Tokutomi Iichirō (Sohō), and others representing the academic community, journalism, and the House of Peers.[40]

On February 23, 1922, the Kenseikai again brought up the issue in the House. Party elder Kōno Hironaka introduced a plan on the floor, and severe debate continued for four days.[41] Nagai addressed the Takahashi cabinet the day the plan was introduced, once more creating a stir as with his maiden speech two years previously. His points typified the universal suffrage arguments of the time.[42]

1. Universal suffrage was not only a problem of politics, but a "matter of logic" as well. The tide of democratic thought had awakened the people and resulted in a desire for voting rights, a desire to put sense back into politics.
2. The same change in the people's thinking had reached a critical point, as reflected in the 417 strikes that had occurred since

1918. If the Seiyūkai could not see the tendency to "turn red," then it must be "color-blind."

3. The reduced tax qualification for political rights was basically contrary to the people's wishes and had to be abolished completely. The Seiyūkai professed gradualism, but the maintenance of a tax qualification for election rights was similar to England's situation seven hundred years earlier. If the payment of taxes were equivalent to voting knowledge, then Mitsui and other economic giants would be the most qualified for the premier's office.

4. The three million or so who already had the vote should not decide on universal suffrage, but rather the people at large. A referendum should be called.

5. Although labeled "parliamentary government," the political system of Japan was rather an "autocracy under Seiyūkai rule." The Seiyūkai itself was inviting tragic events like the assassination of Hara. The Takahashi cabinet, too, in causing financial distress for so many and denying those same people the right to appeal their grievances under the law, was committing a grave injustice.

The debate was cut off on the twenty-seventh, and the Seiyūkai, by a large majority, quickly voted down the bill. Still, argument on the issue continued, causing deep dissension between parties and within party ranks as well. Shortly thereafter several Kenseikai members who felt their party was taking too mild a stand on the issue conferred with Ozaki Yukio and Shimada Saburō (both suffragist liberals who had left the party in 1921), the Kokumintō, and the Independent Club. Out of this evolved a new political group, the Kakushin Club. Inukai Tsuyoshi and his followers were the core of the group and political renovation was its goal.

Nagai had long been close to several of those who formed the Kakushin Club, but he retained his membership in the Kenseikai and spoke out later on the issue of the club's founding in *Chūō kōron*. His article, entitled "The Insignificance and Significance of Third Parties,"[43] was somewhat reminiscent of another piece he had written for *Shin Nippon* in 1914. In that case, the *Japan Advertiser* had criticized Inukai for being narrow-minded in his attitude toward the Dōshikai at a time when the constitutional order of the country was facing a crisis. The gist of the *Advertiser*'s article was that part of the country's trouble was the fighting among opposition parties. Inukai was cited as typical of that fault. Nagai agreed, closing his own article with a plea to Inukai to change his stand and "serve the emperor."[44]

In his 1922 article Nagai explained that one could not ignore the Kakushin Club nor the reasons for its formation. At the same time, he questioned the organization's justification for being on the grounds that its goals were not so different from those of the existing parties, especially the Kenseikai and the Kokumintō. To achieve necessary social reform, particularly for the laboring classes, the Kakushin Club should cooperate with the Kenseikai to achieve both universal suffrage and reform of the House of Peers. Maintaining the upper-house system in its traditional form, he said, would make it difficult for any party to represent the interests of all classes effectively.[45]

For Nagai, reform of the House of Peers and universal suffrage were linked in efforts to realize Japan's second restoration. He was not opposed to a two-house system, but he saw the upper chamber as it then existed as a holdover from the country's feudalistic structure. The separation of the nobility and the common people by family-rank was completely anachronistic, Nagai argued, and reforms should be carried out so that the peers would represent not just the upper classes and the House of Representatives not merely the lower classes. It was precisely the old dichotomy in representation that impeded social progress and encouraged class antagonism, a lesson that could be learned well from cases in foreign countries.[46]

Like universal suffrage, the peerage issue became enmeshed in partisan politics during the early 1920s. The Seiyūkai relied heavily on connections with conservative bureaucratic forces and strove to keep amendment of the old structure to a bare minimum. This approach had satisfied Yamagata as well as the Kenkyūkai, the largest faction in the House of Peers and an important support for the Seiyūkai.[47] In fact, the young noble Konoe Fumimaro joined the Kenkyūkai in 1922, and it has been suggested he did so out of the conviction that only the Kenkyūkai and its vertical alliance with the Seiyūkai could save the nobility from losing its influence.[48] On the other hand, the Kenseikai and Kokumintō took a stand as parties of the people and tried, relatively speaking, to meet more popular demands in amending the old ruling structure. Nagai reflected that position.

For example, in discussing the proliferation of proletarian parties, he conceded their significance in that they were being formed with the goal of realizing the political and economic requests of laborers and the propertyless classes, demands not being met by the existing parties.[49] A major cause for labor unrest, he insisted, was the poor living conditions in crowded cities, but a solution to the urban problem was impossible without first analyzing the reasons why it had come about so rapidly. He pointed to the agrarian plight as the major impetus for so many people to move into the cities. Policymakers had a tendency to concern themselves only with urban problems, he suggested, when the most pressing current concern was to stabilize agrarian areas and to compensate rural labor on an equal basis with urban labor. A related problem was the recent practice of the larger landowners to unite, causing more misery for the little man. To remedy the situation, the government should adopt as its standard of agrarian policy the small producers instead of the big landowners and agricultural capitalists.[50]

Yet Nagai continued to express the hope that this and other social reforms could be achieved by the existing parties, if only the non-Seiyūkai forces would join together to push through a universal suffrage bill and work for reform of the upper house. Things began to develop along these lines soon after the Toranomon Incident in December 1923 and the ensuing fall of the Yamamoto cabinet. For when a third nonparty cabinet was set up in January under the premiership of Kiyoura Keigo, the indignation of the anti-government parties became such that they joined forces to restore party government. This became known as the "second movement for constitutional government." It was not a popular movement but rather a drive by the parties to return to the practice of party cabinets begun with the Hara ministry in 1918.

As Nagai and others had urged, the Kenseikai and Kakushin Club, as well as other anti-government forces, cooperated in the movement. They were joined by a minority group from the Seiyūkai attached to Takahashi Korekiyo, a faction that found it expedient to support universal suffrage and approve of the structural reforms urged by the Kenseikai. The majority group in the Seiyūkai, which adopted the name Seiyūhontō (Main Seiyūkai), adhered to the usual party policy. Still, the opposition coalition was powerful enough to win by a good margin in the May 1924 election. The Kiyoura cabinet resigned, and Katō Takaaki, leader of the Kenseikai, became premier on June 11.

Katō had entered politics from a career as a bureaucrat and diplomat. He was known for his arrogance and to the end never captured the popular imagination. Although he was sensitive to the great changes that had taken place throughout the world as a result of World War I, especially the growing power of the masses, he often spoke of a need to inculcate in these masses the notion of duty and a spirit of cooperation. He had initial reservations about the immediate granting of universal suffrage, convinced that preparation was necessary to exercise this privilege. Nevertheless, he later indicated his willingness to go along with a suffrage bill for the 1920 Diet if his party members were in favor of it. The major goals of his own 1924 cabinet were the passage of universal suffrage, "enforcement of official discipline," administrative and financial retrenchment, and upper-house reform.

Compared with other cabinets of the Taishō period, the legislative accomplishments of the Katō government and the Fiftieth Diet were noteworthy. Still, the record was not one of unrelieved success and reflected the continued need for political compromise. The Universal Manhood Suffrage Law, promulgated in May 1925, increased the electorate from approximately 3 million to 12.5 million by granting the vote to all male citizens over the age of twenty-five who had resided in their districts for one year and who were not indigent. This law was balanced by the passage earlier in the year of a long-pending piece of legislation, the Peace Preservation Law. Aimed at repressing communism, anarchism, and forms of extreme radicalism, its passage probably eased the way for Katō to push through other legislation. The cabinet also achieved modest reform of the House of Peers, but ran into trouble with goals like retrenchment.

By the summer of 1925 internal friction in the cabinet resulted in its resignation en masse. Katō was asked to remain in office, and a new cabinet was formed under him in August. He had been in declining health since a fall in 1922 and became seriously ill in January 1926. Urged by his doctors to rest, he declined, realizing his party's weak position in the Diet. He died on January 28; but by the time of his death, it appeared that many of the goals of Taishō democracy had been realized, including the resurrection of party cabinets. Leaving that development for later examination, what about Nagai during this time?

Shortly after Katō's first cabinet had taken office, a special committee was organized to expedite the passage of universal suffrage. Nagai, who had been reelected in the May 1924 election for the lower house, served on that committee under Chairman Adachi Kenzō and Director Saitō Takao.[51] He continued to campaign actively for suffrage, and his biographers suggest that he must have felt satisfied when the bill finally passed.[52] A question that lingers, however, is why he did not speak out on the failure to extend the franchise to women. Lacking concrete documentation one can only conjecture. Most likely, his silence can be attributed to political considerations.

Heated debate over the suffrage issue had gone on within the Kenseikai while it was still an opposition party, and considerable compromise was necessary before the members could agree on the form a bill should take. Now that the Kenseikai was in power and had committed itself so strongly to the passage of universal suffrage, it had to present a united front on the issue against opposition from the Seiyūkai and conservative elements in the Privy Council and House of Peers. Here, it seems, Nagai exercised that combination of political discretion and party loyalty that would help him move up so quickly both within party ranks and in his career.

Placing this in perspective, we need only recall Nagai's position in 1920, when he had acted independently of the Kenseikai in drawing up a suffrage bill with the Universal Suffrage League for the Forty-fourth Diet. As has already been discussed, Nagai's justification for not signing the bill in the end has generally been rejected. Observers then, as now, attributed his action to his concern for his own political status, not, as he protested, to his objection to the exclusion of women from the bill. His reversal in this instance reveals that he had learned well the politics of compromise so much a part of the Taishō scene. This is nonetheless evident in his reformist position concerning Japan's international posture in the 1920s.

An integral part of the reformists' commitment to national reconstruction was their concern for Japan's international welfare, and they tended to take a strong foreign policy stand.[53] Granted, they were often split over the direction foreign policy should take, and Nagai's position was by no means universal among them. Even so, he did represent one significant current of thought and action during the interwar years. This current was found not just among politicians, but throughout a wide cross section of Japanese society, including noteworthy elements from the communications media, the intelligentsia, and the nobility.

JAPAN IN THE WORLD

Against a background of arrant social confusion following the great Kanto earthquake in September 1923, Nagai questioned Premier Yamamoto in the Diet in December on government policy regarding that disorder. He focused first on the widespread assassination of Koreans throughout Japan shortly after the quake, and provided proof that the government had circulated rumors of an impending uprising by the Korean population within the country, thereby instigating the formation of self-appointed vigilante committees. He granted that the responsibility was not that of the present cabinet, but of the former temporary Uchida cabinet and the home minister at that time, Mizuno Rentarō. Yamamoto's was a different cabinet but representative nonetheless of the same government, and therefore owed restitution and an apology to the surviving families of the Korean victims. Instead of harboring antagonism and distrust, said Nagai, Japanese and Koreans should be cooperating for the advancement of Asia.[54]

Statements about cooperation and trust between the two nationalities would be difficult to accept in isolation. Nagai, however, placed these sentiments within the context of other injustices to Koreans. His February 1923 article for *Kensei* (Constitutional government), for example, dealt with a "Fundamental Policy for the Rule of Korea." Therein he mercilessly criticized the Japanese colonial administration for many things, including the brutal 1919 suppression of nationalists in Korea—and the aftermath. Such policies, he charged, were only feeding the flames of antagonism and mistrust.

Similar mistrust, he said, was evident in the recent case of a Chinese mistakenly killed by Japanese, and the resultant demand by the Chinese government for a complete investigation into the matter. Nagai considered the Chinese demand an affront to an independent and constitutional country, treating Japan like an "area of extraterritoriality." On the other hand, he added, three months had elapsed and the Japanese government had not issued a complete report—or if it had, it had not made public the results of the investigation. In order to gain the respect of the international community, Japan must dispatch, courageously and without delay, a frank report to China in order to clear the air; but it must refuse at the same time to allow the Chinese to come and investigate further themselves.[55]

Nagai's focus in that speech on problems related to Korea and China was natural in light of current events, but his interest emanated also from his more general preoccupation with Asia and Japan's role therein, and the overall conduct of Japanese diplomacy. In the summer of 1923 he traveled with friends Matsumura Kenzō and Hirano Eiichirō to China to study the political situation. He wrote to Gotō Shimpei just as he was departing from Kobe, expressing considerable anxiety over the possibility of China's economy coming under the joint supervision of foreign countries. He concluded that "indignation at the wrongs in our China policy is becoming more unbearable each day."[56]

Certainly Nagai's experience with Japanese diplomacy and diplomats constituted a signficant factor in his decision to enter public life; it also influenced his desire to become one of the governing class and give that class a people's flavor.[57] It has been noted how during his first trip to Europe he had occasion to meet Komura Jutarō and Inoue Katsunosuke and was concerned that such men were representing Japan abroad. Experiencing even greater disquiet while attending the peace conference in 1919, he continued to write and speak out on the weakness of Japanese diplomacy after his return from Paris. In a Diet speech in 1923, for instance, he labeled the type of diplomacy he had encountered abroad as the "pinnacle of baseness," one that disregarded Japan's destiny as leader of Asia.[58]

In 1924, already one of that governing class, Nagai received his opportunity to become directly connected with diplomatic matters through his appointment as parliamentary councilor (san'yo-kan) for foreign affairs under Shidehara Kijūrō in the Katō Takaaki cabinet. Nagai went to pay his respects to the new premier and came away quite impressed. For one thing, he found Katō a much warmer person than appearances would have led one to expect. Then too, there existed some common bonds linking the two men despite their different backgrounds. Both, for example, had had close ties to Ōkuma (Katō, in fact, had become private secretary for Ōkuma in 1887 when the latter was foreign minister); and the two shared a deep admiration for the English parliamentary system. Nagai later said that one of the most striking things about the meeting was Katō's warning that Japan's servile attitude toward Western countries was making it impossible to have foreign relations with them on an equal basis. The premier added that anyone engaged in foreign affairs should give this serious consideration. Indeed, said Nagai, the warning came back to him time and again, serving as an inspiration.[59]

He served off and on in the Foreign Ministry until 1931, next as parliamentary councilor under the first Wakatsuki cabinet and then as parliamentary vice-minister (seimu-jikan) under the Hamaguchi cabinet.[60] Both the seimu-jikan and san'yo-kan were parliamentary officials whose function was to assist a particular minister with special tasks; but whereas the former participated more in policy and planning, the latter's special duty was to serve the minister in negotiating matters with the Diet. Some have suggested that Nagai's retention of both positions makes him in part responsible for the direction of Shidehara diplomacy.[61] It may be that he had a hand in the formation and implementation of that diplomacy, which was committed to joint action with the powers and noninterference in China (while continuing to protect Japan's economic interests there). Still, the generalization needs qualification.

Shidehara Diplomacy

As Nagai perceived foreign affairs in the early 1920s, there were two major policy objectives. One was to check white imperialism, and the other to prevent interference in China. Shidehara was of a similar mind, but Nagai's attitude toward white imperialism was much more antagonistic than his superior's. His cynicism concerning the United States in the post–World War I period has been described; and if one uses his writings and speeches as an indicator of his true feelings, it seems his antipathy toward American "power diplomacy," "moralism," "Monrōshugi" (Monroe doctrinism), and the like deepened with each passing year—despite the governmental position of cooperation and friendship maintained during his service in the Foreign Ministry. As the situation in China grew more critical during the 1930s, this point of opposition to white imperialism, which had been controlled (relatively speaking) for several years, resurfaced with even greater vehemence than before.[62]

When Nagai's appointment as parliamentary councilor in the Katō cabinet became known, Matsumura Kenzō called on him to express congratulations and was taken aback at Nagai's show of disappointment over his new position. Nagai then explained, "To achieve the restoration in Japan that I've been secretly planning for so long, it is necessary to use the active military and reservists. For that, I'd have to first become parliamentary councilor for military affairs and establish a definite tie with the military." He then handed Matsumura a mimeographed copy of Kita Ikki's radical "Outline Plan for the Reorganization of Japan" (Nihon kaizō hōan gaikō) and said, "Here, take a look at this."[63] Still, he accepted the assignment and cooperated with Shidehara in pursuing diplomatic policy in line with the "new international order" and Japan's attempts at economic and peaceful expansionism (as advocated earlier by the journalist Kayahara Kazan and Waseda professor Ukita Kazutami).

Nagai's position during that period, and in this particular instance, resembles closely that of one of the "reformist nobility,"[64]

Konoe Fumimaro, at the time of the Versailles Peace Conference. Even before leaving for Paris as a member of the Japanese delegation, Konoe had written a piece vigorously criticizing the Anglo-American powers, charging that their advocacy of certain international moral principles was born out of their sense of self-interest and desire to maintain the status quo. He also interpreted their proposed international peacekeeping organization in the same light. He returned to Japan both frustrated at the failure of the Japanese delegation to achieve certain aims and fearful that the British-American plans for a new international order would prove inimical in the long run to Japanese interests and security. Yet, wise and realistic enough to size up the uselessness of opposition to the major powers at that point, he agreed to serve on the Japanese Commission of the League of Nations. Moreover, he subdued his open criticism of the new order until events in the early thirties brought it forth again with new fervor.[65]

Konoe, like Nagai, continued throughout the 1920s to press for national strength and unity so as to insure the success of future foreign undertakings; but the efforts of these men to adjust to the post–World War I international milieu in the meantime were representative of a large body of Japanese. As one writer has interpreted the national climate at that time,

Although the new economic foreign policy [implicit in Shidehara diplomacy] never completely replaced the idea of forceful expansionism, the years between the Versailles Peace Conference and the Manchurian Incident witnessed the fruition of economistic thinking. This was the time when the Japanese were willing to try to integrate themselves into the liberal international order and to avow that they belonged to the world, that they were world citizens as well as Japanese subjects.[66]

The use of the phrase "liberal international order" in the above context is open to some question, but the noteworthy point of the passage is its emphasis on Japanese internationalist thinking and efforts. Accordingly, Japan cooperated with the 1924 International Federation, and signed a basic treaty with the Soviet Union on January 20, 1925, resuming diplomatic relations. Shidehara also worked for noninterference in major incidents of warlord fighting in China during 1924 and 1925 but was less successful here in light of maneuvering by the Japanese Army.[67]

As a member of the government Nagai went along with this new international diplomacy. Even when Tanaka Giichi replaced Shidehara as foreign minister later in the decade in Tanaka's own cabinet, Nagai continued to serve as Shidehara's spokesman on the Diet floor in attacks on Tanaka diplomacy.[68] Still, his statements from earlier years indicate that his endorsement of Shidehara's policies must have been given with some personal reservation (as was the case with other Minseitō members). Nagai's contacts with Ukita Kazutami at Waseda and in political activities had given him sufficient exposure to the type of peaceful expansionism espoused by the latter,[69] and he had even addressed himself at times sympathetically to the ideas of the journalist Kayahara Kazan.

Kayahara had traveled in Europe and America between 1905 and 1910 and became the leading popularizer of the idea of expansion when he returned home. He stressed, however, that the age of militaristic imperialism was over. In the future, imperialism must take the more peaceful form of economic expansionism, such as through emigration and capital investment. Moreover, Japan should not limit this expansionism to Manchuria and Korea; it should also direct its activities to North America, Brazil, the South Seas, Australia, and New Zealand. For this endeavor to be successful, however, the Japanese had to study the wider world and learn to live in that world. They must constantly question their own past, shed their parochialism, absorb Western ideas, and work toward a total renovation of Japanese life. This more cosmopolitan approach, he insisted, would equip them to meet the various demands of future expansionistic endeavors.[70] Nagai liked many of these ideas, though he was not so pessimistic as Kazan about the shortcomings of the Japanese.[71] In many ways, he would prove to be more defensive of their actions.

Japan in Asia

"An independent China policy," a speech Nagai delivered in the Diet on March 15, 1923, the year before his affiliation with the Foreign Ministry, reveals clearly his position on Japan's Asian policy.[72] In that speech he attacked Foreign Minister Uchida Yasuya and others for having sold out Japan both at Versailles and the Washington Conference of 1921–1922. The Manchurian-Mongolian Railway rights as well as most of the Twenty-one Demands had been eroded one by one until only four of the original demands remained, and there was no telling how long Japan could retain even those four under the leadership of such diplomats. The most opprobrious aspect of the matter, he lamented, was that these concessions had been made to

China not through Japanese goodwill, but rather through the fear of Anglo-American disdain on the part of Uchida and company.

In the first place, the demands should not have been discussed at the Paris and Washington meetings since they were a private agreement between China and Japan. "If we follow blindly the China policy of Great Britain, the United States, and others now, we'll be pulled eventually into a relationship where we'll have to follow."[73] To make matters worse, China had requested that the pact with Japan be abrogated by 1925. But, insisted Nagai, from the very standpoint of Japan's independence, it was imperative that the two nations work together for coexistence and co-prosperity. Japan's policy must be to show its basic disagreement with Western imperialism—that, as leader in Asia, it would safeguard the freedom and independence of the weaker countries.

Included in Nagai's conception of coexistence and co-prosperity was the necessity for Japanese colonization abroad. Yet, as is seen from his writings, his notion of imperialism differed from that of a Tokutomi Sohō.[74] Tokutomi came to espouse his brand of imperialism because he saw it as the most viable way of dealing with the realities of world politics at the time. He initially had supported peaceful expansion through emigration, trade, and colonization. The events of the Sino-Japanese War and later the Triple Intervention, however, led him to believe that only by a powerful military force could Japan's interests abroad be protected and extended. Likewise, only by that means could the people's welfare as well as the Japanese nation be secured.[75]

Whereas Tokutomi tended to evaluate the good resulting from expansionism more in terms of the benefits to the colonizing country, Nagai's emphasis was on the possibility for positive results for both the colonizer and the colonized. His 1912 and 1913 articles criticizing Tōtaku, or Tōyō takushoku kaisha (Oriental Development Company, established in 1908), are representative of his faultfinding with ventures that reaped one-sided advantages and profit.[76] The two initial aims of Tōtaku were the large-scale agricultural settlement of Korea and the improvement of Korean agriculture. Instead, the company soon became Korea's largest tenant landlord, having decided already by 1911 to have the greater portion of its lands cultivated by Korean tenants rather than by Japanese settlers.[77]

While Nagai was in Korea on an observation tour in 1915, he wrote to Governor-General Terauchi Masatake in Seoul of his fear of

Korean opposition should Japanese residents not change their de-
meaning attitude toward the native population.[78] The letter is significant for at least three reasons. First, it shows that Nagai had exten-
sively studied colonial policy in general and Japanese policy in
particular. This is evident in his suggestions about taxation practices
(drawing on examples from the English and German colonial experience) and also in his recommendation that the seat of supervision be
moved from Seoul to Pyongyang in order to effect more complete
economic and political control over the entire area.

This suggests a second reason for the letter's import, namely, the
extent to which it illustrates the pattern mentioned earlier that to
scratch a reformer in this context is to find a nationalist. In the same
breath that Nagai was urging a change in attitude by Japanese in
Korea, he explained that the change was necessary to bring the
Koreans fully under imperial authority and make them loyal subjects
of Japan. But one must qualify this with a third significant matter in
his Terauchi letter—his conviction that Japan's colonial policy had to
be based on different premises than those of capitalistic imperialism.
The focus of such policy must shift from the colonizing nation to the
colonies.

In a 1923 article for *Chūō kōron*, he built on this same theme in
theorizing about colonization. Evidently overlooking the high level of
sophistication attained by the Korean and other Asian cultures, he
concluded his article as follows:

No matter how low the level of culture, how backward and inefficient—if a
people can be given the proper environment [for advancement] and the
appropriate education according to their special characteristics as a people,
enlightenment is possible. That has got to be the basis of colonization
policy.[79]

When Nagai became minister of colonization in 1932, he tried to
carry out policy and personnel reforms to implement this philosophy
of colonization, but confronted once more the spirit-politics conflict.
As the journalist Baba Tsunego observed, Nagai's capacity to realize
his goals would be defined by the specific situations and general environment in which he found himself.[80]

Nagai had experienced this right at the beginning of the decade
when he had attempted as parliamentary vice-minister to gain support for the governmental position on the London Naval Conference
proceedings. At this follow-up to the earlier disarmament conference
at Washington, Premier Hamaguchi agreed to limitations on naval

construction that were extended to include a ratio for heavy cruisers of 10:10:7 among Britain, the United States, and Japan. This evoked a strong reaction at home. There were few, either within the government or the incumbent Minseitō, who attempted to negotiate with those groups and individuals taking a hard foreign policy stand in protest to the treaty signed on April 22. Among those who did try to ameliorate the situation were Nagai and Colonization Minister Matsuda Genji. Nagai approached Katō Kanji (chief of the naval staff) and Kita Ikki, cautioning the latter against instigating the military and interfering in the controversy over the right of supreme command.[81] Although his efforts went for naught, it is significant that he did make an attempt here and in another area in the face of military opposition to the London Naval Treaty.

The Dai-issen dōmei (Front-line League) had been formed in May 1930 to investigate urgent national and international problems and, as the occasion demanded, to assume a vanguard position in movements connected with those issues. This league supported the Hamaguchi government's decision to reduce armaments on the grounds that a cutback in military expenditures would free funds for social welfare purposes. Asserting also that the military had overstepped its bounds, the league sponsored study groups and lecture meetings to bring its case to the people. Here too Nagai gave time as a lecturer, joining others (many of whom had a Waseda and a Christian background) in trying to win support for the government's position.[82]

At first glance it appears incongruous that Nagai, who was stressing cooperation with the Western powers and a program of arms limitation in 1930, could within two years be supporting Japan's actions in Manchuria, and before the decade was out, the invasion of China. Yet, he found it possible—and exigent—to adopt this stance on the conviction that "in a new era, new policies are necessary."[83] He may have referred to a new era, but taking into account the significant lines of continuity that cut across the divisions of the interwar period, the changes in his position seem more natural than incongruous—especially when those continuities are coupled with new domestic and foreign developments.

From the mid-1920s many Japanese began to lose faith in the peaceful expansionism and international cooperation to which they had made a commitment as world citizens in the early interwar period. That disenchantment emanated mainly from two causes. One was the national economic and social ills that were attributed in part to the basic orientation of Japanese foreign policy during those years; a second was the conviction that other nations were willing to forego international cooperation in order to pursue their own interests in China.[84] Accordingly, undercurrents of thought evident particularly from the time of World War I resurfaced with new intensity and implications. Along with the widespread distrust of Anglo-American motives, many Japanese perceived the international order mapped out by those powers at Versailles and Washington as basically out of accord with Japanese interests and security. Many, too, had a deep conviction of their country's special position in China and Manchuria.

These ideas received further impetus from the London Naval Treaty controversy. Prominent political leaders as well as a large sector of the general public stated openly that the Hamaguchi government had overstepped its constitutional bounds in violating the right of supreme command and in so doing had compromised national security. Those security issues became entwined with domestic politics, and the Seiyūkai platform increasingly emphasized two major planks. It advocated, first, a foreign policy that minimized the necessity of cooperation with the Anglo-American powers in matters regarding naval armament agreements and at the same time committed itself to the defense of Japan's continental interests. The second plank sought the preservation of Japan's privileged position in Manchuria.[85]

The treaty controversy resulted in extensive political unrest, which in turn substantially reinforced the long-held belief of Nagai, Konoe, and others of a reformist bent that national unity and strength were the sine qua non for the success of future foreign ventures. Concurrently, the overall complexion of Japanese democracy began to change and continued to do so as the 1930s progressed.

Toward Totalistic Reform

ON October 1, 1930, Japan's Privy Council approved ratification of the London Naval Treaty, and the emperor affixed his seal shortly thereafter. The same month, Nagai went on an inspection tour of China, his second visit to that country. His plan was to stay for two months, and while there he met with several Chinese leaders, including Chiang Kai-shek. He continued on to Mukden and then Korea, where he received a telegram from Shidehara informing him of the November 14 assassination attempt on Prime Minister Hamaguchi. Cutting short his trip, he returned immediately to Japan, paid his respects to the wounded premier, and resumed his work in Tokyo.

When Nagai visited Hamaguchi the premier cautioned him about possible attempts on his own life.[1] Indeed, the attack on Hamaguchi was a portent of things to come during the 1930s, a critical decade when Japan would undergo numerous changes as it attempted to cope with the internal and external situations. Along with the London Naval Treaty controversy, the growing instability caused by the world depression and the Manchurian Incident set the tone for the thirties. It was a time when many of those involved in policymaking would adjust their thinking and behavior, modifying the stance they had taken in the rather different climate of the twenties.

This was the case with Nagai. When he and other reformists had become active in the public arena in the late 1910s, much of the world was caught up in revolutionary change. They were convinced that, in contrast, Japan had been stagnating. National reconstruction was deemed necessary; and throughout the twenties, Nagai felt that the best way to effect this was to work within the parties. His position by the mid-thirties was that since the parties were not maintaining their grip on the situation, a new type of political action was essential. From that point on, he became increasingly receptive to extraparty political alternatives.

Amid all the changes, he continued to voice as his two goals "a political order to most benefit the Japanese people" and "Asian liberation from white domination." His articulation of these goals was consistent throughout the interwar period, and even into the 1940s. The inconsistencies came in his incremental redefinitions of "Asian liberation," "the people," and the things that would "benefit the people." Although this is evident to us now in historical perspective, one wonders how clear it was to Nagai as he made his way through that tumultuous time. And yet, he must have felt some sense of optimism in 1931, for he was being given new opportunities to work toward achieving his objectives.

MINSEITŌ LEADERSHIP

Shidehara Kijūrō served as proxy prime minister while Hamaguchi was recovering, but the Seiyūkai continued to push for the cabinet's resignation. By April 1931 they were successful. Wakatsuki Reijirō, newly elected president of the Minseitō and head of the majority party in the House, was asked to form a new cabinet, which was set up on April 13. Shidehara remained in his post as foreign minister, but it is said that Nagai resigned as parliamentary vice-minister to make way for someone else from the Minseitō to hold the post. All along he continued his reformist push for new directions in Japan's internal and external policies. For one, he advocated that Japan, like other countries, send a representative to the Soviet Union to study communism. Japan, he insisted, could not ignore what was happening there.[2] Then in early September 1931, he was appointed, along with Nakano Seigō, to a special Minseitō committee on China, particularly significant in light of Japanese aggressions in Manchuria that followed so soon after.[3]

On the night of September 18, middle-grade Japanese officers blew up a small section of the Japan-owned South Manchuria Railway. Claiming it had been Chinese sabotage, they used the occasion to begin taking control of Manchuria. The civilian government in Tokyo tried to keep the "incident" under control; as early as September 19, in fact, the cabinet made a decision to localize the matter, but to no avail. The Kwantung Army succeeded in gaining greater army support for its actions and finally separated Manchuria from China. Japan recognized this puppet state of Manchukuo in September 1932. In the meantime the army became firmly committed to an expansionist policy on the continent, all with significant effects on the country's foreign policy. In the words of James Crowley:

The hallmarks of Japanese diplomacy during the 1920s—armaments control and cooperation with the Anglo-American nations—were soon obliterated in the wake of the Manchurian Incident. In part, this was the consequence of Japan's move into Manchuria; in part, it was caused by the reactions of the powers, typified by the Stimson Doctrine. Whichever one chooses to stress, the creation of Manchukuo radically altered Japan's relations with China and with the Western powers.[4]

This reversal in Japan's foreign policy was followed by a shift in the balance of power within the civilian government. The Manchurian Incident and the rapid conquest of Manchuria had created at home both a nationalistic euphoria and support for the Kwantung Army. This changed public mood contributed to the civilian power shift, leading also to developments such as the increased influence of the military in foreign policy and the terrorist activities of some of the younger officers. Within this milieu, Nagai became increasingly active in the Minseitō, the party that had been the standard-bearer of Shidehara diplomacy and that was now under such heavy attack. A growing number within and outside the party were questioning the Minseitō's ability to handle not only the Manchurian crisis, but also the economy and other national policy matters.

After the abortive October Incident of 1931, when a group of young officers planned to exterminate the cabinet and replace it with extreme nationalists, Nagai presented to Prime Minister Wakatsuki and Home Minister Adachi Kenzō a plan to reorganize the national ministries. The goal was to unify certain aspects of the military and civilian sectors and thereby to make the ministries more economical and efficient. He had two main recommendations: to combine the army and navy into a national defense ministry headed by a civil official, and to set up a social or labor ministry. Two of his other recommendations deserve mention in view of posts he later held. Concerning the Colonization Ministry, he suggested that a nonparty governor-general reside in each colony and be in communication with the home minister of the country. He also proposed that the Communications Ministry be abolished and its functions distributed among new boards and a new transport ministry.[5]

The plan was not accepted, of course, though a labor ministry was established eventually. Nagai was equally unsuccessful in another serious undertaking shortly thereafter—the case involving his senior in politics and old friend Adachi Kenzō. By this time the Minseitō was undergoing critical internal dissension and factional struggles, all exacerbated by differing stands over Manchuria. Despite Adachi's post as Minseitō vice-president and home minister in the cabinet, he had been for some time dissatisfied with party policies and leadership. He disagreed with Shidehara's foreign policies, and he opposed the gold embargo and retrenchment program of Finance Minister Inoue Junnosuke. Moreover, he had aspirations himself for the party presidency and eventually the premiership.

In late October 1931, Wakatsuki had approached Adachi with the possibility of a Minseitō-Seiyūkai coalition cabinet to help win Seiyūkai support for the party's policies.[6] Adachi was strongly in favor and began to work toward realizing the premier's plan. Backing his efforts were such notable party members as party advisor Tomita Kōjirō, Nakano Seigō, and Nagai. In November, however, Wakatsuki discarded the plan owing to opposition from Shidehara and Foreign Minister Inoue, two extremely influential men in maintaining the party's ties with business and the bureaucracy. Adachi nevertheless continued to work publicly for a coalition government. The matter came to a showdown in December.

By then Nagai's opinion was that a coalition cabinet would be acceptable if it were merely that and did not result in the transfer of political power to the opposition party. On the evening of December 10, he went to Adachi's home to present his case, arguing that Wakatsuki was making every effort to draw closer to the will of the people and the Diet and therefore deserved support from party members. For Adachi to try to topple the cabinet from within would be to betray the people's trust in him, and Nagai appealed to him to throw his support behind the present cabinet. This dialogue took place in the presence of about ten important Minseitō members gathered there, including Nakano Seigō, Matsuda Genji, and Tomita Kōjirō. Nagai and Nakano had been friends for many years, but they came close to blows that night over the question of support for the Wakatsuki cabinet. Nagai returned home in the early hours of the next morning, having failed to persuade Adachi and other insurgent members to change their plans.[7]

Adachi brought the cabinet matter to a climax on December 11, when he would neither attend an emergency cabinet session nor resign from his post as home minister. Unable to achieve cabinet unity, Wakatsuki submitted his government's resignation. On December 13 a new government was set up under the Seiyūkai leader Inukai Tsuyoshi, who excluded the Minseitō from his cabinet. The coalition plans of Adachi and sympathetic elements from the Seiyūkai had come to nothing for the time being, and Adachi left the party soon after. Wakatsuki planned to step down as Minseitō president, taking responsibility for the turn of events, but Nagai called on him also, arguing that many in the party wanted him to stay on. Moreover, his retirement would only precipitate additional turmoil in the organization. Wakatsuki acceded to the request and remained on in the post until 1934.[8]

In the meantime Nagai had accepted office on December 14 as chief secretary of the Minseitō. While he was still a parliamentary vice-minister Wakatsuki had spoken of him as one who had much to learn about the political game.[9] He was soon to learn, for by moving up in the Minseitō he gained even greater exposure to the maneuvering for political power that took place within the parties. Nagai Michio wrote that on his father's return from party headquarters, he would often say that he had just left "a den of robbers and swindlers."[10] Later when Michio was a student at Kyoto University, his father advised: "If you're going to enter politics, it might be better to go the route of entering the House of Peers from the academy." But he added that a rather innocent scholar would do well not to get mixed up in the misery and ugliness of party politics.[11]

Like Nakano Seigō, Nagai regarded Ōshio Heihachirō (1793–1837) as a model and, in fact, left behind when he died an unfinished manuscript for a drama on the life of that samurai Confucian scholar. Ōshio had led the people in the Tempō Uprising of 1837 in opposition to shogunate misgovernment. Nagai saw his own times as a reflection of Ōshio's, but now it was government and party malpractices that were creating social injustices.[12] Despite this disillusionment with party machinations, Nagai as yet remained firm to the principle of constitutionalism. He maintained also his long-held conviction that "without parties, it is almost impossible to carry out constitutional government."[13] Still, he continued to chastise the parties for their failure to reform and focus on the people.

The Saitō "National Unity" Cabinet

If 1931 had ended on a sour note for Nagai as a party man, 1932 brought more troubles. In the February 1932 general election the Minseitō was defeated soundly, winning only 146 seats in the House as compared with the 301 garnered by the Seiyūkai. The latter, however, was so riddled by factions that it was unable to present a strong united front in dealing with the country's problems—and this at the very time the country needed forceful civilian leadership to counter escalating military intrusion into domestic politics and foreign policy.

Economic hard times both in the cities and rural areas, partly the result of the world depression, convinced many that the ruling elites, including the parties and the *zaibatsu* (financial combines), were going their self-serving ways at the expense of the people. The Manchurian crisis compounded these current uncertainties and aggravated the already widespread sense of crisis. In this atmosphere right-wing ideas proliferated, as did patriotic societies, all fed by younger military men calling for a "Shōwa Restoration." By direct action, they insisted, power must be wrested from the civilian elites and restored to its rightful locus, the emperor. This would save the country from its present plight of internal and external threats, just as the Meiji Restoration had rescued the country in the nineteenth century.

On February 9, 1932, Inoue Junnosuke, formerly minister of finance, governor of the Bank of Japan, and a member of the Minseitō, was assassinated by radicals; and on March 5, Baron Dan Takuma of Mitsui interests met the same fate. A turning point came on May 15, when a group of junior navy officers and members of a rural patriotic society attacked the Seiyūkai headquarters, the Bank of Japan, the Tokyo Police headquarters, and official residences, murdering Prime Minister Inukai and other political figures. At this juncture the man chosen to form a new cabinet was head of neither major party, but a compromise candidate, Admiral Saitō Makoto.

Prince Saionji, who as the last of the *genrō* was greatly responsible for choosing new premiers, hoped that a "national unity" cabinet under Saitō would restore confidence in the government and give the parties the opportunity to consolidate their forces and play once more a major role in leading the country by providing premiers.[14] The parties, too, pictured a Saitō cabinet as an interim solution to the governmental leadership problem and gave their support.[15] Moreover, the parties were represented in the Saitō government by supplying cabinet personnel, among whom was Nagai as colonization minister and Hatoyama Ichirō (who had chaired the censure committee meetings on Nagai in 1920) as education minister.[16]

Shortly before, in April of 1932, Nagai had summarized what he felt to be the most important problems facing the country and what he saw as solutions. One was his appeal for a "nationalist masses party," in which all worked together for the common good.[17] This idea of a masses party had been a recurrent theme throughout

Nagai's career and would become more pronounced as the 1930s progressed. While it hardly sounds like the talk of a man aligned with one of the major parties in a two-party system, neither does his entering a coalition cabinet seem like the behavior of one committed to *kensei no jōdō*, or "constitutional government as the normal way of running the state." If, as the journalist Baba Tsunego observed at the time, Nagai's venture was so risky, why did he undertake it? Baba himself suggested that Nagai's rationalization was that the government should be not merely a *kōbu gattai* setup—that is, simply an amalgamation of civil and military power—but rather should emulate the "new government of the Meiji Restoration with representatives of each powerful clan." Most likely, he also looked on it as an opportunity to effect reform.[18] At the same time, personal ambition cannot altogether be discounted.

Was he qualified to fill the position? From the perspective of his academic background in colonial policy and his definite views on the importance of colonization for Japan, he was not without some degree of preparation for the post. Still, he was basically an idealist and one of the progressive-reformists described at the outset of this book. As such, could he survive in such a high public office and remain true to his ideals and goals—especially at a time when the progressive-reformists were coming under increasing governmental pressure? Nagai's experience in the Saitō cabinet suggests the pitfalls inherent in such an attempt.

Just as his dual ideals of expanding abroad and easing the burden of Japanese at home caused a dilemma for him, so his dual role as a people's politician and representative of the governing class resulted in additional contradictions and problems. His expressed faith in the people necessitated his evaluating issues from their perspective, but he could not stray too far from the governmental and party line if he wished to maintain his position. Already in 1932, as he was beginning his rapid climb to success, the dilemma inherent in his objective of reconciling the ideal with reality was apparent. After observing him as colonization minister for a few months, Baba commented on Nagai's major shortcomings as a politician, namely, his ineptitude in the machinations and Machiavellian tactics of the political world.[19] Nagai's longtime secretary, Azuma Shun'ei, also commented that Nagai lacked the qualities necessary to be either a successful politician or administrator.[20]

In examining his first performance as cabinet minister, certain factors concerning his post deserve mention. First, Nagai would be responsible in part for supervision of the South Manchuria Railway in Manchukuo. Administration of the Oriental Development Company was included in his duties as well. And despite a low budget, the territory for which he was responsible in formulating policy was extensive, including Korea, Taiwan, Karafuto (South Sakhalin), and Kwantung.

The general theme of his tenure seemed to be the need for cooperation among Asian peoples to preserve the common concerns that bound them together as a group vis-à-vis other peoples. He explained his goals on various occasions as follows:

1. Establishment of an economic policy that would prevail in the homeland and colonies to secure Japan's welfare in a time of growing economic blocs
2. Expansion of foreign colonization by breaking down barriers in Japan, the colonies, and other countries
3. Encouragement of and proper leadership for colonists going abroad
4. Establishment of policies to prevent the monopolization of Manchurian resources by any one class or group[21]

Before attempting to implement this program, he had to resolve the more basic problem of keeping his post, for he was in office barely three months when the Seiyūkai placed a motion of nonconfidence against him in the Diet. This action was the result of a fundamental administrative weakness—his handling of personnel matters.[22] Upon coming to office, he had decided on a shake-up in personnel, mainly in Taiwan and Karafuto. He met with trouble in this undertaking, but it was his appointment of a president for the South Manchuria Railway that caused a storm of protest.

Nagai foresaw public finances as a potential stumbling block in the future prospects for Manchukuo. He believed that a sound economic base would be imperative for the country's development, and reasoned further that the South Manchuria Railway would be crucial as a catalytic agent in building that base, as would be its president, who must have certain qualifications. His choice for that post was Kajiwara Nakaji, who had been president of Kangyō ginkō (Kangyō Bank). Kajiwara was a man of good character, adept in public finance, and not affiliated with the parties. Evidently, Nagai had consulted with hardly anyone about the appointment. He brushed aside recommendations from the Minseitō and other sources, moving ahead on his own convictions.

The rumor circulating at the time was that the choice was made for reasons unrelated to Kajiwara's qualifications. Nagai had appointed as his parliamentary vice-minister Tsutsumi Yasujirō, with whom he had been familiar since his Waseda days. Tsutsumi, through the connection of a Hakone real estate firm, had borrowed about ¥3 million from the Kangyō ginkō when Kajiwara was president; and the perception that this had influenced the appointment led to unfortunate results. Nagai apologized later, explaining that he had not talked with Tsutsumi at all about the appointment and had not realized the connection. Nevertheless, Seiyūkai and army opposition made Nagai retract his choice. The task of filling the post then went to Premier Saitō. His selection was Hayashi Hirotarō from the House of Peers, who, as it turned out, clashed with the military and railway personnel once in office.[23]

Nagai was able ultimately to retain his post, but not without a struggle. In January and February 1933, he appeared before the House of Peers to defend his policies, including distribution of profits from Manchurian development. On February 2 he also was questioned by Viscount Mimurodo Yukimitsu for attending the funeral of the socialist Sakai Toshihiko. Mimurodo argued that a person in Nagai's position had erred in paying his respects to one whose basic goals were oriented against the state, and he urged Nagai to resign. Nagai held his ground with the retort that it was in deference to old ties with Sakai, his senior at Waseda, that he had attended the memorial service; his action was unrelated to Sakai's political and economic views. The prime minister came to Nagai's defense, and he kept his position.[24]

He was in the post for over two years, long enough to effect some reform in the colonies and establish a degree of continuity in policy. A significant influence on the efficacy and limits of his progressive and ambitious program, however, was Japan's international position. The country withdrew officially from the League of Nations in March 1933 over the previous month's condemnation of Japan's actions in Manchuria. Accordingly, emphasis on a consolidated Asian bloc increased, and controls in the colonies tightened. Within this context, the following are examples of Nagai's achievements—and frustrations.[25]

1. The Marriage Law for Taiwanese and Japanese: Although marriage between a Korean and a Japanese was recognized as being legitimate as of June 1921, marriage between a Japa-

nese female and a Taiwanese male was not recognized from the legal standpoint. A child born to such a couple was recorded in the woman's locale as illegitimate offspring. The new marriage law of October 1932 ended this practice.

2. Karafuto: Nagai pushed for a long-term colonization plan for the area that would continue despite cabinet changes, and he was able to accomplish some reform in the administration of the forested areas. He was also working toward the granting of citizenship for Ainu and other tribes, but the final results of his efforts were limited by time and also by subsequent international developments in the colony.

3. Korea: He achieved some change in agrarian laws, more assistance to tenant farmers, and the introduction of advanced agricultural techniques. He was not so successful with attempts to put elementary education standards for Koreans on a par with those of the Japanese.

4. Manchuria: Just as Nagai ran into opposition here regarding personnel, so he encountered obstacles to other projected reforms, such as plans to prevent monopolization of profits from the area by specific groups.

Nagai's public statements during this period were considerably more limited than before, but we do have indications of what he was thinking about domestic and foreign developments. Like so many others, he saw the early thirties as a time of crisis. Speaking out in *Chūō kōron* in January 1933, he pointed out that Japan was not alone in experiencing political, economic, and social turmoil. Similar conditions existed abroad, especially in Europe where, in addition to the depression, the aftershocks of the Great War were still being felt. He added that those countries experiencing such distress shared a common feature—namely, the political awakening of the masses and the formation of new popular movements. The latter resulted from economic and other hardships attendant on class divisions; concurrently, the existence of people's movements signified the demand for national unity. It was a period when strong leadership was imperative, but too many leaders and politicians (including those in Japan) were looking out only for themselves. For all that, he voiced his confidence in the country's existent political system, if only it could renovate itself from within.[26]

In September 1933 Saitō called a special cabinet meeting to discuss such problems, explaining that any real confidence in Japan's parliamentary system was dissipating quickly and that something had to be done. Nagai's input centered on the need for reform in four areas. He advocated, first, an increase in the length of the Diet session. In a time of worldwide economic upheaval, the government could not keep up with a whole year's economic changes in three short Diet months; it should therefore consider a session duration like that of the English Parliament. Second, since consistent confrontation between the government and the Diet had hindered the expedition of state business, the government should look into the American president's authority with respect to the Congress and consider the expansion of its own executive power. Third, to insure that the Diet truly reflected the will of all the people, the government should refer to German practices such as the electoral district federations and the vocational representative system. Finally, revisions to the present bicameral system were necessary to insure closer cooperation between the two houses.[27]

He did not use this or other occasions, it seems, to speak out in an official capacity on another of his longtime concerns, women's rights, though he did continue his general support for that cause. In the first Diet session Nagai attended after entering the cabinet, Abe Isoo proposed revisions to the Law for the Election of Members of the House of Representatives that would give women voting rights. Nagai said that since his official position prohibited him from proposing such revisions himself, he was greatly pleased that his senior, Abe, had done so.[28] Abe's plan was rejected however; the Manchurian Incident and the increased role of the military in government had greatly altered the women's movement and almost ended the suffrage issue.

This turn of events in the women's rights issue brings us to one more important development in Nagai's years in the Saitō cabinet, namely, his increasing closeness to the military. He became friendly with General Ugaki Kazushige, who was governor-general in Korea at the time.[29] He also had good rapport with General Araki Sadao, war minister in the Saitō cabinet.[30] There were contacts with the young but influential Colonel Suzuki Tei-ichi, who served in significant bureaucratic policymaking positions,[31] and ties with Generals Hayashi Senjūrō and Abe Nobuyuki from Ishikawa. (On occasion he even reported information from Abe to the prime minister.[32]) Nagai also became quite intimate with Yatsugi Kazuo, a civilian advisor of the army and head of the Kokusaku kenkyūkai (National Policy

Research Association) formed in 1933. Nagai himself was one of the
original members of the group, eventually becoming one of the Man-
aging Committee.[33]

The Saitō cabinet continued for two years, but could not withstand
forces working for its downfall, the various factions within the parties
as well as right-wing nationalist groups for example. The cabinet
resigned in July 1934 and was followed by another national unity
cabinet under the moderate Admiral Okada Keisuke (July 1934–
March 1936). The parties, severely splintered into factions, gave
repeated evidence of their overriding self-interest at the expense of
greater national interests. Discontented elements within both major
parties put forth a plan in late November 1934 for the merger of the
Minseitō and the Seiyūkai, proclaiming the need for change if the
parties were to maintain a strong voice in governmental affairs.
Already in October of that year the army had published its pamphlet
The Essence of National Defense and Proposals to Strengthen It. Though
many party members took the Diet floor in sustained and vigorous
criticism of the growing power of the military, the years of the Saitō
and Okada cabinets nevertheless saw a steady drift away from the
policies and general tone of the 1920s. This same tendency can be
seen in Nagai.

A Reformist at Midstream

In my introduction I outlined a pattern of reformist development. It
might be useful to reiterate some of the points made there before discussing Nagai's career at mid-course. I suggested that Nagai was
representative of a composite political type active in the Taishō–early
Shōwa period—the reformist. As a group the reformists represented
a range of opinions extending to both ends of the political spectrum,
but the fact that there were substantial differences among individuals
should not obscure the existence of large areas of agreement. Consensus was symbolically registered by such concepts as "Japan,"
"nation," "emperor," and "the West." Reformists were generally
people in their twenties and thirties who emerged on the political
scene after World War I with aspirations for relieving their fellow
Japanese of the burden of injustice imposed on them by the political
status quo. Through renovation and reconstruction of the existing
system they hoped to create a new era for Japan both nationally and
internationally.

Just as there were undeniable differences in ideological positions and political affiliations among the reformists, the means they envisioned and adopted to achieve their renovationist goals varied. But again, there were striking commonalities amid the disparities. For example, one principal objective held in common at the beginning was the destruction of the established political power bases in Japan. At the very same time, however, this group deployed a strategy of using these bases of power to secure authority for themselves. Reformists were alike also in their disposition toward a strong foreign policy. Many doubted the reliability of the international order set up at the Versailles and Washington conferences, but were nevertheless willing to cooperate with that order in the 1920s. Toward the end of the decade, however, it began to seem that the international order might fail to safeguard Japan's interests, and it was then that they began to withdraw their support.

Although the reformists participated in various Taishō-democracy movements during the twenties, they began to move in divergent directions, many far to the right in the wake of internal and external crises during early Shōwa. The device I have presented for analyzing these shifts is that of Itō Takashi, who has viewed the original reformist group as split into two camps, the progressive-reformists and the restoration-reformists. By 1935 the progressive-reformists, who included socialists, communists, and liberals most sympathetic to these two, had largely succumbed to governmental pressure. Though there were those who remained steadfast in their former beliefs or who continued to be active without their former organizational affiliations, many realigned with the restoration-reformists, who comprised, generally speaking, the right wing. The resultant amalgamation came to represent the reformists, and it was this group that went on to gain ascendancy within the power structure.

Nagai Ryūtarō fits this pattern very closely. One of the leading Taishō democrats and progressives during the period of florescence of the more liberal reform movements in prewar Japan, he was searching by the mid-thirties for new solutions to Japan's problems. For him, as for many Japanese by that time, two factors were present in his thinking and subsequent courses of action. He had a growing doubt about the viability of Japan's two-party system based on the English model; he was also growing increasingly close to the military. For Nagai, the latter was coupled with his belief that international conflict was bound to come to Asia.[34] The end result of these changes was his own move from the progressive-reformists to the restoration-reformist camp. This is evident beginning about 1935.

In fact, in the 1935 New Year's edition of the *Hokkoku shimbun* he expounded on a merger of the parties.[35] Centering on abuses within party politics, he stressed that if the parties wanted to maintain public support, they must establish a new image as public parties. Only if they worked for the people instead of themselves could they have the public's support. Pointing out that without such party reform there could be no change on a national level, he summarized his arguments with his familiar theme of the relationship between the domestic and international situations. Only with a national party comprising all the people could Japan attain the international power necessary to perform her special world mission.

He picked up the theme of party renovation and carried it one step further in a July 1935 article dealing with regulation of the Diet.[36] As he saw it, two related internal problems required immediate solution —the people's livelihood and the growing pessimism about parliamentary government. Nagai reasoned that the pessimism was the outgrowth of a system wherein the dominant party also controlled government. As was the case in England, he said, the system invited abuses and led to voting interference. He explained that however much the basic principle of constitutional politics was respected in Japan, it was essentially unrealizable as long as a dominant first party existed. An alternative would be a coalition cabinet, for by the very fact that it would consist of many different factions, such a cabinet would be in consonance with the principle of majority rule, which is at the heart of constitutional government.[37]

In short, by 1935 Nagai was trying seriously to reconcile the *kensei no jōdō* principle with the contemporary problems facing Japan. But even though he had advocated consistently the ideal of a party of the masses, his position in the mid-thirties was considerably different from that of the mid-twenties. He was moving from a more pro-parliamentarian position to one relatively less so. At the same time, he was giving serious consideration to the military as the group by which a national renovation could be achieved. This is not surprising in light of factors in Nagai's background, such as early aspirations for a military career and his remark in 1924 to Matsumura Kenzō: "To achieve the restoration in Japan that I've been secretly planning for so long, it is necessary to use the active military and reservists. For that I'd have to first become parliamentary councilor for military affairs and establish a definite tie with the military." His growing deference to the military was not unusual either, given the nature of the times and the emphasis placed on that group in Japanese tradition.

By 1936, then, Nagai was at once vigorously pressing for his old idea of a popular party, advocating coalition cabinets, and moving closer to both the military and the bureaucracy. Concurrently, another element appears more frequently in his writings, speeches, and comments—his growing consideration of German and Italian leadership as a partial model for political reform in Japan.

Shortly after the February 26 Incident of 1936, Nagai wrote for the *Asahi* on the relationship between the rebellion and the general state of society.[38] As noted earlier, he had been a rather close acquaintance of Kita Ikki, whose influence was at work in the incident, and, like Nakano Seigō, had given him some financial support over the years.[39] Still, he called the February Incident (and its predecessor, the May 15 Incident of 1932) deplorable. But he added, as did other commentators, that the root of the problem was to be found not in internal military problems but rather in the social and economic problems of the day.[40] Concluding, he pointed to developments in Germany and Italy, emphasizing how Hitler and Mussolini had once shared their people's suffering and were thus able to give strong leadership in rebuilding their countries. They were party politicians *and* politicians of the masses; that was precisely why their cabinets were strong.[41]

From late 1936 Nagai participated in conferences held at the Ogikubo residence of Count Arima Yoriyasu. Discussion there centered on various matters concerning the parties, including the military's attitude and the possibility of a new party led by Prince Konoe Fumimaro.[42] Then, at a Minseitō general meeting on January 20, 1937, Nagai, as chief secretary, criticized the Hirota cabinet for isolating itself from the people's wishes and trying to impose political reform from above according to the ideas and plans of a very few.[43] When the Hirota cabinet fell shortly thereafter and a new cabinet was being formed under General Hayashi Senjūrō (who also had attended the Ogikubo conferences), Nagai from the Minseitō and Nakajima Chikuhei from the Seiyūkai were asked to enter on the condition that they leave their respective parties. Both refused,[44] but Nagai's reasons were more complicated than they appeared on the surface. Correspondence to his close friend and election aide Ichikawa Kiyoshi shows that his basic motivation for the decision was that he feared his leaving the Minseitō to enter the government would cause friction between the party and the new cabinet, thereby hindering the chances of a successful premiership for Hayashi. Such friction also would impede "the progress of national renovation wherein the military and civilians work together."[45]

Nagai's caution notwithstanding, the Hayashi cabinet lasted only four months owing to Diet opposition. Hayashi believed that cabinets should be above the factional strife that the parties represented, and shortly after getting the budget passed he dissolved the Diet on March 31 and announced that new elections would be held in April. At the same time, he gave governmental support to the pro-militarist Shōwakai party. In this 1937 election, however, the Minseitō and Seiyūkai campaigned on platforms of opposition to militarism and fascism in government, and won three-quarters of the Diet seats. Despite a last show of resistance, Hayashi resigned on May 31.

With this resurgence of the parties in opposition to an army-dominated government, Prince Saionji turned to Prince Konoe to form the next cabinet. It was felt that Konoe could resolve the conflict between the parties and the government because he had ties with the army, the parties, the bureaucracy, and the financial world—in a word, the elites. Therefore, although by mid-1937 Japan was less parliamentarian than in 1931, it was not totalitarian. The turning point came, it seems, in 1937 with the China Incident, which led to wartime controls. In November of that year the political power of the military services was institutionalized with the formation of the Liaison Council, and war became an increasingly irresistible national cause. For Nagai too 1937 was a watershed. Since the early 1930s, he had been moving away from his more liberal position of the 1920s, but the events of 1937 proved to be a catalyst for significant changes in his thought and action.

Turning Point

As with the Hayashi cabinet, Nagai and Nakajima Chikuhei were invited to accept posts in the Konoe government. This time they accepted. But as there had been no prior negotiations with their respective parties, they entered the cabinet as individuals and not as representatives of those parties.[46] The Minseitō reluctantly approved Nagai's action (after considerable discussion and criticism),[47] and it was from this time especially that a growing breach became evident between Nagai and others in the Minseitō leadership—most notably, Minseitō president Machida Chūji.

Nagai had been considered originally for the post of foreign minister, but Privy Seal Yuasa Kurahei's response to the suggestion was unmistakably negative, and he received the portfolio of communications instead.[48] It was apparent that some consideration had been given to this appointment, for Nagai was of a faction in the Minseitō that had been advocating nationalization of the electric power industry.[49] Control of electric power would be an important component of the "Five-Year Plan for the Production of War Material" drawn up by the Japanese Army in the summer of 1937 to help Japan match Soviet power in East Asia. It was anticipated that Nagai would be an effective supporter of the new government's policies.[50]

In fact, the Electric Industries Control Bill, which eventually placed over six hundred private electric companies under a system of unified national control, has been called a major accomplishment of Nagai's career.[51] The problem had been long pending in Japan, with concrete research into the matter of water power resources conducted under Gotō Shimpei as communications minister in 1910. Later, plans to introduce legislation nationalizing control of the electric power industry were shelved in 1937 by the Hayashi cabinet, but the outbreak of hostilities between China and Japan after the Marco Polo Bridge Incident of July 7, 1937, added urgency to the matter.

On various occasions, Nagai summarized the basic issue as the balance between capitalism (free enterprise) and the public good. His argument was that it was contradictory to grant individuals the water rights that were necessary for the good of the greater populace. In the course of debate over the proposed legislation, however, it became clear that, apart from the factor of natural vested interests, a confrontation was taking place between two main groups. One group (composed of people like Nagai and others in the reformist camp) had become convinced that greater state control of the economy was necessary to mobilize the full potential of the country in times of crisis. Those in the opposing group found nationalization of utilities contrary both to their concept of the role of government and to their belief that the potential of the existent capitalist system could be marshaled to build up Japan's strength.

On July 15, 1937, Nagai presented to Ōwada Teiji, chief of the electricity board, a "Policy for the Regulation of Electricity." Essentially a plan to put electricity under national administration in the form of company consignment, it called for large-scale development of electrical resources and rationing in accordance with a national plan.[52] In addition, a basic electric plan was decided on August 31, 1937, in the Kokusaku kenkyūkai and presented to Nagai by Yatsugi Kazuo.[53] Thereafter, the proposed legislation went to a series of governmental and nongovernmental commissions and groups for review, and Nagai's office finally presented the package to the Diet on January 20, 1938.

In the ensuing heated debate, which lasted for over two months, Nagai frequently countered arguments by stressing that a reform policy nationalizing electric power would be the first step toward a new Japan. Nationalization of the industry would be beneficial in both peace and wartime, but especially during the latter; it was impossible to think of separating weapons production and general military preparation from the electric power industry. In facing a war situation, time was crucial and nationalization of all-important industries imperative.[54] He remained staunchly opposed to any of the proposed revisions aimed at weakening the degree of state control written into the original plan, and this stance evoked severe challenges from many quarters, including both Seiyūkai and Minseitō members.[55]

Illness compounded Nagai's problems. Acute attacks of rheumatism necessitated constant doses of strong medicine, fogging his thinking and causing permanent stomach damage. He presented a sorry spectacle as he commuted from the hospital in his determination to see the bill through. The debate continued, and Saionji voiced fear that Nagai's failure to get the bill through might result in his resignation as communications minister, thereby bringing down the cabinet.[56] Indeed, Nagai did write up a resignation as well as a withdrawal notice from the Minseitō, but withheld final action on these at the urging of Matsumura Kenzō. About the same time, Colonization Minister Ōtani Son'yū suggested to the influential peer Inoue Tadashirō that blocking cabinet efforts could have serious repercussions for the China situation; and Konoe himself let rumors circulate that he might resign and form a new party.[57] In the end Nagai remained at his post and the cabinet continued, as a significantly revised plan passed both houses on March 26, 1938. This whole controversy over electric power, however, has implications for both Nagai the reformist and the situation in Japan during the late 1930s.

As to why Nagai gave such staunch backing to this plan, two possibilities stand out immediately—his ties with the military and bureaucracy, and his reformist position. Actually, it was probably a combination of these, along with the fact that he had put his political career on the line in working for the successful passage of the bill. The army generally gave strong support to the plan, as did General Sugiyama Hajime (Gen), war minister in the Konoe cabinet, in discussions concerning it.[58] In addition, Nagai's tenacious backing of the bill as well as his arguments in defense of it reveal a lingering socialist influence, for the original plan bore the qualities of national socialism. Related to this, the plan also reflected his ongoing goal of making "Japan a Japan of all the Japanese" through the reconciliation of class antagonisms. Finally, his commitment to the legislation reveals the reformist pattern of linking national strength and unity to national mission—the coupling of national reform (increasingly totalistic in nature) to a strong foreign policy stand.

In perspective, what is important is that Nagai's efforts constitute an important step forward in the building of a national defense state and a significant step back from his earlier, more liberal democratic ideals. By 1938, his position can be described as statist in the sense that Tokutomi Sohō's earlier, more liberal position had become statist by the period following the Sino-Japanese War of 1894–1895— statist, that is, in the "primacy [Tokutomi] gave to building national power, and in demanding total dedication and sacrifice on the part of the people for the advancement of national goals."[59] The counterpart to this is the shift in Nagai's perceptions of the people and what would best benefit them. The populace as he now defined them was not so much that body of autonomous individuals whom the state serves, but more the group working as a concerted whole to contribute to the national good. Likewise, what would benefit them was not so much Western-style liberal reforms as adherence to indigenous ways and values.

By this time, too, one sees in Nagai's perception of democracy less stress on diversity and pluralism and more on conformity throughout the nation to insure that all of the nation's subjects, having developed their individual potential through the opportunities afforded under democratic institutions, could work more effectively with each other to serve the emperor and nation. A unified, harmonious state had become an urgent need calling for immediate and direct action. There was no time, so he thought, to work through the process of trial and error, nor could the situation indulge the lack of coercion inherent in a more liberal democratic approach. In a word, he found it difficult to remain loyal to principles transcending the Japanese state and to sustain the spirit of challenge to the prevailing particularistic, emperor-centered ethic of his society.

At another level of the Electric Industries Control Bill question, it is noteworthy that the government found it necessary to make concessions to corporate interests in the spheres of directorship, financial recompense, and the degree of state control over the electric power industry in order to get the bill through. As of the late thirties, bureaucratic proposals dovetailing with reformist ideology still had to contend with the status quo forces—in this case, particularly those forces connected with Japan's capitalistic system. It may be as Duus and Okimoto have suggested:

The hard political battles of the late 1930s were fought not over the budget or foreign policy, but over the extent to which the bureaucracy could define the limits of corporate decision-making. The National Electrical Industries Law, and the so-called Hoshino Plan for economic control all prompted intense debate in the Diet, and led to confrontation between the bureaucracy and big business leadership.[60]

Indeed, one of the charges leveled against Nagai during the controversy was that he espoused bureaucratic ideology. What is important, though, is that the restrictions placed on both Nagai and the bureaucracy for passage of the bill indicate conditions with which the government would have to deal in setting up and administering a wartime economy. A similar situation can be seen in concessions the government had to make to get its National Mobilization Law through the Diet about the same time.

Views on the Foreign Situation

A main reason for Nagai's urgency concerning the electricity bill, of course, was the stream of events in China. He believed wholeheartedly in supporting the China expedition in 1937, just as he had supported the Manchurian venture earlier in the decade. Writing in April 1932, he had reasoned that Japan's actions in Manchuria were necessary to maintain peace and equilibrium in the area. He feared that should the turmoil from China proper spread to Manchuria, it would create an opportunity for the Soviet Union to move south, threatening the stability of all Asia.[61] Nagai's views were not unusual for a party man. One writer has pointed out that "with the exception of certain proletarian groups, all political parties officially approved the course of national foreign policy from 1931 to the summer of 1937."[62]

In a speech Nagai delivered in July 1938 on the first anniversary of the Marco Polo Bridge Incident, he further justified Japan's position in China by distinguishing between the Chinese people and the Chinese government. The latter, he insisted, had become the lap dog of the white imperialists, and it was incumbent on Japan, as a leader in

Asia, to help liberate the Chinese people from such a regime.[63] But although Nagai is advocating here his longtime goal of Asian liberation from white domination, his meaning of liberation has changed considerably. As he is using the term by this time, it is nothing more than a euphemism for Japanese imperialism.

On November 3, 1938, Konoe announced the New Order in East Asia which would, in effect, replace the existing treaty system with Japan's overlordship in the area. On November 26, the Cabinet Information Commission submitted a plan supporting a spiritual mobilization movement to realize this East Asian Order. The cabinet members decided to examine the plan; Nagai, Nakajima, and the Overseas Development Minister Hatta Yoshiaki were invited to join in the discussions, which became known as the Eight Minister Conferences.[64] Through his subsequent writings, speeches, and actions, Nagai became one of the most avid supporters of Japan's New Order and must, therefore, bear partial responsibility for it.

An essay he wrote in 1939 summarizes his arguments concerning China as the decade was drawing to an end.[65] He agreed with Konoe's remarks before the cabinet that Japan had not dispatched troops to China for land or indemnities, but rather to cooperate with Manchukuo and China for the mutual well-being and prosperity of the area and to help free China from control by imperialist powers. Moreover, if Japan did not work quickly to build up Manchuria, the Communists would move into that area just as they had into other parts of China. Communism, wrote Nagai, was at odds with Japanese democracy, and if Chiang Kai-shek had not submitted to the early communist demands in China, Japan probably would have supported him. But Chiang's actions had engaged all of China in civil war, thereby endangering East Asia—a situation exacerbated because of his anti-Japanese stance.

Going more deeply into economic factors, Nagai insisted that Japan had invested great sums in Manchuria with good results, one example being the doubling of Manchuria's trade. He took issue with the Open Door and Equal Opportunity doctrines the West espoused concerning Asia. Should it not also work in reverse, he asked, with the opening of Europe and America to Asians? If that were unacceptable to the West, the Asian peoples should be free to monopolize their own resources and establish self-supporting economies. In short, he argued that it was only natural that Japan, Manchuria, and China should cooperate in East Asia in the same spirit that the Western blocs were working toward their own goals.[66]

In early January 1939 Baron Hiranuma Kiichirō, president of the Privy Council, replaced Konoe as premier. With the end of the first Konoe cabinet, Nagai's official voice in national policy ended temporarily, but he continued to speak out concerning foreign policy. At the April 1 session of the Kokusaku kenkyūkai dealing with the possibility of Japan's entering a military alliance with Germany and Italy, Nagai stated his position clearly. Chastising England for its global economic policies, he insisted that it must be prevented from reestablishing English imperialism. This was imperative to narrow the gap between the haves and have-nots, and it could be effected best through Japan's predominance in Asia and that of Germany and Italy in Central Europe and on the Mediterranean coast. As Nagai saw it, the answer to Japan's whole foreign problem was to support the anti-communist Axis powers. That was one side of the coin, the other being to separate completely from England and the United States. He explained also that Japan's efforts to remove powers like England, France, and the Soviet Union from the Far East did not mean war; it implied only that they should be prevented from imperialistic activities in the area.[67]

Some, like former Vice Admiral Wada Senzō, agreed with Nagai, while others took issue, but it would be only a short time before Nagai's voice would become official once more. The Hiranuma cabinet fell in August 1939, partially the result of the signing of the Soviet-German nonaggression pact about which Japan had not received prior notice from Germany (its ally under the 1936 Japanese-German Mutual Defense Pact). General Abe Nobuyuki from Kanazawa succeeded Hiranuma as prime minister. Nagai had been a major force in the establishment of the cabinet and became, subsequently, a member of the Abe government on August 30, 1939, with joint ministerial posts in communications and railways.[68]

The Reformist Wave Crests

FORMER ambassador to the United States Shigemitsu Mamoru evaluated the Abe cabinet as "so weak that its like had never been seen before."[1] Whether or not one would agree with Shigemitsu's 1958 assessment, the fact remains that the latter part of 1939 was a period of worldwide crisis, a time when any country would require strong leadership. The Abe cabinet was by all standards inadequate for the tasks before it.[2] Nagai's entrance into that cabinet was to be among the last three major undertakings of his career, a career that had only five years remaining. His other two ventures were active participation in Japan's New Political Order at home and in its New Asian Order. As at the beginning of the decade, he must have had a certain sense of optimism in 1939—despite the traumas of the times—for the opportunities before him appeared conducive to the fulfillment of his renovationist goals.

In fact, the few remaining years of Nagai's life were to be the crest of the reformist wave. To recapitulate the final segment of the pattern outlined at the beginning of this book, it was stated that during the late thirties, many progressives realigned with the restoration-reformists, with the combination going on to gain preeminence within the power structure. Having become part of that structure, however, they were drawn into the confrontation which was taking shape within the rightist ranks, that between the reform right and the spiritual right. The first cliques to form from the core of the reformists tended to align with the reform right, groups generally aiming at a New Political Order and a New Order in East Asia, and looking in the process toward a state-controlled economy and a monolithic political party. They also favored the Tripartite Pact, the push south, and, if necessary, war with the United States. This reform right gained predominance in the power struggle, but had to contend with constant resistance from the spiritual right. Like the former, the spiritual right opposed the status quo; but rather than committing themselves to a new order, they looked back to Japan's pre-Western age and what they perceived as the country's ideal emperor system.

Nagai too, initially a progressive-reformist, moved into the restoration-reformist camp from the mid-thirties. Then, as one of the power elite during the late thirties and Pacific War years (and as an important member of the Imperial Rule Assistance Association), he worked with many of the reform right. He had become committed to Japan's new orders at home and in East Asia, and can be counted among those reformists who initially wanted to change Japan along the lines of the West, but who later helped lead his nation into war with Western nations. As with his involvement in the Abe cabinet, his commitment to Japan's new orders also led to dead ends. Mass mobilization of the Japanese people initiated and administered from above did not mean a greater degree of democracy for the people— unless by democracy one means the freedom to suffer. Furthermore, Japanese subjugation of Asia, while displacing the white man, did not constitute liberation.

It is relatively easy to draw these conclusions now. What is important is to try to understand how Nagai and others perceived the situation during the late 1930s and early 1940s.

THE ABE CABINET

Nagai's appointment to the Abe cabinet further aggravated the tensions generated between him and others in the Minseitō at the time the first Konoe government was formed. Party president Machida Chūji and those in party headquarters were loath to allow Nagai's participation since they did not like Nagai's associations with the army nor the fact that he might try to use the post to effect radical reform. The Abe forces applied pressure, however, and permission finally came after personal visits to Machida from Nagai and Endō Ryūsaku (cabinet secretary).[3] Nagai's participation seemed necessary to those behind Abe, notably Colonel Arisue Seizō. It appears Arisue hoped to use Abe's tenure as prime minister to push through major domestic and political reforms in support of the army's program to establish a national defense state. Expecting opposition to the reform program, it was planned to have the premier dissolve the Diet and hold new elections, at which time a new nationalist masses party would demonstrate strong support for the government's proposals. It was common knowledge that Nagai's ideal for many years had been such a masses party, and he was to be the major force behind the marshaling of the party.[4]

Nagai was agreeable to such plans of the army; the Minseitō was not. Moreover, Abe had made the basic decision that it was more important in the long run to appease the parties, and he quickly shelved the above-mentioned reform plans. Nagai's ideas, therefore, had little impact on national policy at this time, but as Gordon Berger has suggested, the opposition that he and like-minded members of the army encountered pointed to two important developments.

First, pressures were again emanating from the Army for the creation of a new party to mobilize political support for its program of reform. Second, Nagai and other lesser party figures were prepared to create a new mass political organization on behalf of the Army, in the belief that the military's reform proposals were vital from the viewpoint of national defense and essential to the welfare of the citizenry.[5]

Nagai had relatively greater success with more concrete undertakings in the areas of traffic and transportation (expansion of domestic railway services, inter-Asian airways, and the like), but the cabinet's tenure was too short for any of the ministers to effect major achievements. Moreover, soon after the cabinet was set up, the emperor expressed to Abe two doubts about Nagai. One concerned his holding the joint ministerial positions of communications and railways, and Nagai was relieved of the latter on November 29, being replaced by Nagata Hidejirō.

The emperor's second misgiving was Nagai's reputation as a leader in the anti-British movement.[6] This movement had been escalating in Japan from about the fall of 1937, spearheaded by right-wing groups and influential sympathizers. The agitation grew to such an extent that by July of 1939, there were 387 anti-British rallies attended by some 850,000, with over 400,000 participating in street demonstrations.[7] Indeed, Nagai used his highly charged article of that month, "Some questions for President Roosevelt," not only to criticize United States policies and leadership but to lambaste the British as well. As he wrote, "Roosevelt often says, 'It's America's special work to help put down world oppressors and to cooperate with England and China.'" But didn't Roosevelt realize, asked Nagai, that his very ally England had been the world's greatest oppressor for the past three centuries, creating the empire on which the sun never sets? His conclusion was that conflict with England would be natural.[8]

The other dimension of Nagai's opposition to the Anglo-American powers was his "friendly to Germany" arguments, which he was pushing strongly by the late 1930s. He was convinced that factors like competing in the arena of bloc economics, strengthening the Anti-Comintern Pact, and harnessing Roosevelt's "wild desire" to dominate the world necessitated this. At a cabinet meeting held immediately after Great Britain and France declared war against Germany in September 1939, Nagai expounded at length on the need to draw close to Germany. The prime minister disagreed;[9] in fact, on September 4 the cabinet spoke out unequivocally that it would stay out of the conflict. As would be the case with his successor to the premiership Admiral Yonai Mitsumasa, Abe repelled new German diplomatic advances, and during the period of the Abe and Yonai cabinets (August 1939–July 1940), many leaders attempted to improve Japanese relations with the United States and England. Still, Nagai continued his "friendly to Germany" stance in cabinet meetings.[10]

The cabinet had a short life, however, for in addition to its inherent weakness, external factors worked against it from the beginning. Japan had sought for some time an alliance which would protect it against its traditional enemy Russia. This became increasingly crucial in 1938 when, along with the problem of increased Russian aid to China, Japanese and Russian troops fought a "Small War" along the Russian-Korean border near Changkufeng.[11] Then, from May to September 1939, Japanese troops battled with Russian divisions near Nomonhan on the Mongolian-Manchurian border, and though an armistice was signed in September, victory went to the more advanced Soviet forces. In addition, the Russian-German nonaggression pact had been signed in August 1939, all resulting in the considerable strengthening of the Soviet Union's position in East Asia.

At the same time, Japan was sinking deeper into the China quagmire. This put a drain on national resources such as coal, which when coupled with a severe drought, resulted in an insufficient electrical power supply. The Abe cabinet's inability to deal with such shortages incited severe criticism of the government—especially since one of the cabinet ministers was Nagai Ryūtarō, the one greatly responsible for the previously enacted Electric Power Industries Law.[12] A parallel development was the growing agitation among that group of Diet members whose goal was the formation of a reformist party in alliance with the army as a last possible means to restore party power in the government.[13]

Despite Abe's attempts to stay in office, the premier succumbed to intense pressure to step down. The cabinet resigned in mid-January 1940 to be succeeded by a new government led by Admiral Yonai Mitsumasa. Admiral Yonai was known for his pro-British/American stance, but certain factors worked against that particular position. China remained the stumbling block in efforts to improve relations with those nations. Moreover, with the German victories in Europe and what seemed to be the imminent fall of England, German sympathizers in Japan gained a stronger voice, as did the growing number from the rank and file who supported a strong foreign policy. The greater public input gained by the common man during the Taishō era seemed to be benefiting the advocates of militant action as Shōwa progressed.

It became increasingly difficult, too, to criticize the military. In February 1940, Minseitō member Saitō Takao spoke out on the New Order in East Asia and censured the government's position on the Sino-Japanese conflict. Two years earlier he had found fault with the General National Mobilization Law when it was being debated in the Seventy-third Diet. Now, though, the military looked on his remarks as "blasphemy against the Holy War"; and the Diet, by majority resolution at its plenary session, voted his expulsion from the House of Representatives.

Nagai and Saitō had served together as Minseitō committee members in 1924 in efforts to achieve general suffrage,[14] but by 1940 they diverged considerably on the solutions they envisioned for Japan's problems. For Nagai, one solution centered on major changes in the existent political system.

THE NEW POLITICAL ORDER

The Yonai cabinet and the army had not been in close cooperation, and ultimately War Minister Hata Shunroku brought down the cabinet by resigning on July 16, 1940. A second Konoe cabinet was set up on July 22, aimed at strengthening Japan's position with respect to the Anglo-American powers, tightening controls over the economy, and working toward a new political order. The cabinet appointments reflected this. The pro-German Matsuoka Yōsuke, for example, became foreign minister and General Tōjō Hideki, war minister. Former economic planner in Manchuria, Hoshino Naoki, held the posts of minister without portfolio and head of the Planning Board, and Kazami Akira, a Diet leader of the new party movement, became justice minister.

It is argued that Konoe had been frustrated in attempts to control the Army during the tenure of his first cabinet. It was not so much that he disagreed with the overall thrust of army policy as that he was dissatisfied with the existing political system that allowed the military services independence from the premier in determining their operations. His conclusion was that the military could be checked only by a mass organization rooted in the people—different from the parties but with the political strength necessary to keep a handle on the military.[15] By the spring of 1940, Konoe's supporters Arima Yoriyasu and Kazami Akira were putting plans into motion for a New Political Order.[16]

As devised by the various participants who had been working toward the New Order since the Ogikubo talks of 1936–1937, the new party was to consist of those members supporting Nagai and Sakurauchi Yukio in the Minseitō, the mainstream group in the Seiyūkai, and other smaller splinter groups in the parliament. The mainstream faction of the Minseitō and the Hatoyama faction of the Seiyūkai were to be excluded.[17] During the summer of 1940 the parties dissolved themselves one by one; and their replacement, the New Political Order, appeared in its initial stages to be an all-embracing sociopolitical system along the lines of a one-party state. That Nagai gave his support to this New Order is natural considering factors already emphasized here, but two more background elements help to explain the apparent ease with which he made the transition from support of two-party constitutional government to endorsement of a one-party system. One was the evolution in his thinking about liberalism, and the other, his continued and deepening ties with the military and bureaucracy.

By the beginning of the new decade, Nagai no longer saw liberalism as a viable basic philosophy for modern societies and state systems.[18] More precisely, he pointed to several shortcomings in a liberal system that rendered it deficient for the times. These included the inherent contradictions in such a system between individual and state actions; class antagonisms that prevented mobilization of all the people for national needs; the connection between money interests and politics, which heightened the potential for class warfare; and the plethora of political parties that resulted in short-lived cabinets and difficulty in executing state policy. Moreover, insisted Nagai, world trends showed that the age of liberalism was over. Proof of this was not just in the one-party states of Germany, Italy, and the Soviet Union, but also in the widespread power of the English cabinet and in the tremendous growth in authority of the American executive, especially since the days of the New Deal.

Coupled with Nagai's declining faith in liberalism was a deepening conviction that only the military could rescue Japan from its present critical situation. His consistent inclination toward the military establishment has been traced earlier. Still, he had tried to place the parties above the military throughout the 1920s and even into the 1930s. As has been shown, however, events like the February 26 Incident persuaded him that the parties' capacity for handling Japan's problems was severely impaired by their extreme preoccupation with power to the detriment of the people. He did not reason, it seems, that part of the parties' inability to cope with the country's problems was army activity abroad and terrorist tactics by activists at home. Failing to take the ratiocination process that far, he came to see the established parties as more of a danger to Japan than the military. This perception conveniently coincided with a view of some in the military and bureaucracy that Nagai could be of use to them.[19] One might almost say that he had made the transition from "mannequin of the Minseitō" to "mannequin of the military" and bureaucracy.

As Baba Tsunego analyzed the development, the idea had been gaining momentum in many circles since 1933–1934 that the parties and the military did not have to be in opposition, but could cooperate instead for the country's progress. On the other hand, the military continued to stress the degeneration of the parties, an assertion with which Nagai could empathize, as he could with some of their other revolutionary ideas. In Nagai's consciousness, too, were his long-held self-image as a people's politician and his ideal of a people's party, both of which made him more than receptive during the later thirties to the increasing talk of a new political organization.[20] Often drawing a comparison between his own times and Bakamatsu Japan, Nagai, it seems, came to look on himself as a latter-day Kido Kōin spreading the message that the people must give up the old order for a new if the country were to survive.[21]

He was particularly active in this connection in June of 1940.[22] Finally on the twenty-fourth of that month, Konoe Fumimaro resigned from his position as president of the Privy Council and announced his aspirations for establishing a New Political Order. On the twenty-fifth, members of the Minseitō met to decide what action to take in the face of Konoe's plans, but party president Machida continued to voice doubts concerning Konoe. Other parties and political factions were not so cautious, and beginning with the Shakai taishūtō (Social Mass party) on July 6, they disbanded one after another during that summer.

Nagai, meanwhile, was putting forth every effort to convince Machida that the Minseitō must join in the movement.[23] At this point the breach that had been growing within the ranks of the party, especially since 1939, developed into a complete split. Machida challenged Nagai to the effect that if he really considered himself a follower of Ōkuma, was he not obliged to stay with the party until the end. Nagai countered that it was precisely because he was a follower of Ōkuma that he was convinced the party should disband in the greater interests of the country.[24] The outcome of this confrontation was that Nagai became more determined to separate from the organization and consulted with close associates like Sakurauchi Yukio. Ultimately on July 25, he led thirty-nine members out of the party, pledging support to Konoe's Shintaisei (New Political Order);[25] and on August 15 the Minseitō itself dissolved (much against the wishes of Machida), the last of the prewar parties to do so.

Reflecting on the significance of Nagai's action and the clash between him and Machida, one cannot discount the play of personal and party power. But the import of the matter transcends that level of meaning. At the personal, party, and national levels, Machida was representative of the status quo position in that he, like Hatoyama Ichirō, was more the traditional parliamentarian. Nagai stood for the reformist protest to that position. Machida and other more mainstream figures continued to hope that Japan's internal and external problems could be handled by working through established channels and without further disruption of the political, economic, and social systems. Conversely, reformists like Nagai had despaired of that course already by 1940 and were convinced that only extraordinary measures could save Japan. Their envisioned action involved cooperation with the military and various reform groups, as well as the establishment of a new political order that would include more totalistic economic, social, and political controls on a par with the magnitude of Japan's problems. So while Machida had tried to hold fast to the *kensei no jōdō* principle, he ultimately lost out to the reformists.

Still, Nagai's action was not effected without considerable uneasiness, as is evident from his July 29 letter to Arima Yoriyasu, his compatriot in the new party plans since the days of the Ogikubo talks of late 1936. In that correspondence Nagai explained how, at Arima's urging, he had tried to convince Machida and other Minseitō members of the necessity to fall in with the New Political Order; but unable to get the desired compliance, he had had to resort to leading a contingent out of the party. He realized that this was not what Arima had been hoping, but at least he and his group would be able to participate in the New Order. He closed with a request for Arima's thoughts on how the ex-Minseitō group could cooperate.[26]

By the end of August a preparatory commission was formed, with Nagai a member. They began their work on the twenty-eighth and continued through to September 17 with meetings at which heated debate took place over the nature of the proposed organization. Konoe had indicated back in May that he preferred the designation "New Order" rather than "party," since such nomenclature would be less likely to convey the impression that he was seeking political power.[27]

The main focus of debate at the meetings was what the nature of the core body of the organization should be—a political or public organ. Nagai spoke out very strongly that it should be a political party.[28] His reasoning was, as it had been from years earlier, that only with an all-encompassing political party structure could selfish partisan struggles be lessened and greater benefits be made possible for all society. He had no illusions however. He had stated often that no matter how absolute a government, there was sure to be opposition power.[29] He did not, in other words, visualize Japan's New Order to be an imitation of the one country, one party set-up of Germany and Italy.

What resulted from the meetings of the preparatory commission was a compromise between those who wanted a new party and those who visualized the New Order as an all-embracing popular movement.[30] At the sixth and final meeting on September 17, the acting commission chairman announced that the nuclear body of the order would be named the Taisei yokusankai, or Imperial Rule Assistance Association (IRAA), and that this nuclear body would lead a popular movement to be named the Taisei yokusan undō (Imperial Rule Assistance Movement).[31] In reality this was an uneasy compromise, and already by early October Nagai was complaining that members of the former party groups were engaged in frantic activity to hold onto their old political power bases in preparation for the next election. He protested that this did not bode well for the IRAA and the hopes the people had for its shaping up into a truly new order.[32]

The IRAA was inaugurated officially on October 12. Arima Yoriyasu was made chief of office, and Nagai was one of the eleven selected as permanent directors to supervise the work of the organi-

zation (as was his longtime comrade in arms Nakano Seigō).[33] As for
the actual work and nature of the IRAA, there was perhaps even
more ambiguity concerning these points after Konoe's inaugural
speech than before. *New York Times* correspondent Otto Tolischus
made the following observations:

As stated by its founder, the I.R.A.A. was to transmit the *will* of those above
to those below, and the *wishes* of those below to those above. But it was not to
be an imitation of the Nazi or the Fascist party aiming at total power. Such a
party, said Konoye, would be contrary to the constitution, guaranteeing free
speech and association. He, like the Emperor and Hiranuma, had seen in
Germany and Italy how a totalitarian party usurped control of the Government and forced the head of state to make its chief the Premier; and they did
not want this to happen in Japan. Therefore, the Premier himself was to be
head, and he was to appoint the directors of the movement, whom a new
Premier might change. But this made the I.R.A.A. an organ of the Government, which had no standing under the constitution. The I.R.A.A. was thus
neither fish nor fowl, and the many divergent elements amalgamated in it
promptly started to fight within the movement, as they had done heretofore
in separate parties.[34]

The disagreement centered, as before, on whether the IRAA was
to become a new political body, an administrative organ within the
aegis of the Home Ministry in other words, or a nonpartisan public
body with the goal of popular mobilization in support of the government.[35] Although Konoe was vague in his speech on October 12, it
gradually became clear that his sympathies were with the public body
idea.

One factor responsible for his swing in that direction was the
IRAA position concerning the late 1940 controversy over the new
economic order devised by the Planning Board as part of a greater
design to set up a national defense state.[36] The army, IRAA, and
Planning Board were staunch supporters of the new economic order,
while the business community, major party leaders, and some right-
wingers were opposed. Konoe had to effect a compromise to get cabinet consensus, which was achieved finally on December 7, 1940.
However, the IRAA staff continued in their campaign for more radical economic measures, and Konoe realized all too clearly the organization's potential for opposition to governmental policies.

Effecting a shake-up in his cabinet in December 1940, Konoe
brought Hiranuma Kiichirō in as minister without portfolio, eventually to become home minister. Hiranuma's position concerning the

IRAA was clear. He had opposed the political nature of the organization from the beginning and indicated in remarks made in January 1941 that it was to be regarded as a public organization to serve as an agency of spiritual and economic mobilization.[37]

The IRAA was beleaguered not only by dissension from within and attacks from the Home Ministry, it was under fire from other sources as well. The Diet, fearful that the organization would cut into its own prerogatives, held up the IRAA budget, even after it had been greatly reduced to ¥8 million. The press also joined the attack, the conservative as well as the jingoistic papers. The army and navy then openly entered the foray, and their support for the IRAA facilitated the passing of the ¥8 million budget. Still, widespread demands for IRAA reorganization continued, and in the midst of all this Nagai retorted that the association *was* a political grouping and that efforts to enfeeble it would be met with strong opposition. About the same time, he was promoting with Kamei Kan'ichirō and Akamatsu Katsumaro a popular political and ideological movement in connection with the East Asia Section of the IRAA (of which Kamei was chief).[38]

Nevertheless, the organization was forced to bow ultimately to the onslaught of attacks. In March both Nakano Seigō and Hashimoto Kingorō resigned from their positions as permanent directors. Major structural and personnel changes were carried out by early April, and at that point it was obvious that the IRAA was not to be the political organization Nagai and others had envisioned. It would not, in other words, play a major role in the national decision-making process. Instead, the reorganized structure was tied closely to the government, much like a business organization. It assisted the government in policy research, in the carrying out of orders, and in mobilizing public support for official policy. Actual power lay in the governmental structure, not in the association, with real direction in the latter coming from governmental leaders.[39] It has been likened to a "facade plastered over great heterogeneity,"[40] with the political parties continuing their factional struggles within its boundaries. In essence, then, the IRAA can hardly be likened to the one-party systems operating at the same time in Germany and Italy.

In the reorganized structure Nagai Ryūtarō was placed in charge of the newly created East Asia Bureau on April 12, 1941. This was later changed to the Development of Asia Bureau, over which Nagai presided as well. He also headed the Board of Directors for the Spiritual League for the Development of Asia. None of these constituted the political type of organization for which he had hoped, but were, in reality, part of an ideological movement to promote Japan's aims in Asia. Nakano and others left the IRAA when it failed to take shape as they had planned. On the other hand, Nagai, perhaps the highest-ranking politician in the IRAA and a chief advocate of its core body's becoming the nucleus of a new mass-based political party, stayed with that organization until his death in late 1944.

Several possible reasons account for his behavior. Personal factors figured in—Nagai's determination, his ambition and drive to move up in the world, continued to be an influence. Another factor at this time, however, was his deteriorating health, which necessitated heavy medication. In addition was his partiality for the military, his sympathy for their point of view, and the fact that he had been working closely with them for several years now. They generally had come out in support of the IRAA, and Nagai himself had articulated that one objective of the organization should be to realize a unity between the military and the government.[41]

Perhaps another reason for his remaining with the IRAA was that throughout much of his political career he had belonged formally to the faction in power, and he evidently saw his affiliation with the IRAA in this light. Most probably, too, he pictured his positions within the organization as a last opportunity to achieve the goals toward which he had been working throughout his career, *kyokoku-itchi* (national unity within Japan) and the end of white domination in Asia. Accordingly, just as he threw himself wholeheartedly into Japan's New Order at home, so he was one of the most ardent supporters of the New Order abroad.

JAPAN'S NEW ASIAN ORDER

Nagai was never able to break away completely from the Anglo-Saxon frame of reference of his early years. His studies of the civilization, his admiration for figures like Gladstone, and his years as a student and observer abroad all left an indelible mark—in some ways favorable toward the Anglo-Saxons but frequently antagonistic, particularly regarding Western imperialism. The British and Americans especially, he said, mouthed one thing concerning the equality of all races, but their colonial activities and subjugation of the colored peoples betrayed their real intentions. He was unable, too, to forget his treatment at the hands of British authorities during one trip when he had been prevented from going ashore at Singapore on the basis that his sympathy with the Indian independence movement made him a subversive threat.[42]

From the latter part of the thirties down to Pearl Harbor, Nagai was clear and firm in his position regarding the Axis and Allied powers—favoring close ties with the former in an anti-Comintern alliance and separation from the English and Americans. At a meeting of the Shintaisei Preparatory Commission called by Konoe in September of 1940 to consider the Tripartite Pact with Germany and Italy that Foreign Minister Matsuoka was promoting, Nagai, along with Matsuoka and others present, became emotional to the point of tears.[43]

In the different investigatory groups active in Yatsugi Kazuo's Kokusaku kenkyūkai during the latter part of 1940, Nagai, along with Tsurumi Yūsuke, was a member of the group dealing with British-American matters. His views during this period were consistently anti-British/American, but since he was unable to rid himself of the Anglo-Saxon perspective, he found it necessary to justify his international position within that frame of reference. His March 1941 speech entitled "The unity and popular nature of the New Political Order" is representative. Along with other problems, he tackled the concept of dictatorship, which he analyzed to include the following elements: constant intervention by leaders in the people's lives; governmental selection of talent from the populace, and the setting up of such talent in responsible positions; unparalleled unity between leaders and the governed; and goals geared toward general mobilization. When judged by such standards, he reasoned, Roosevelt could be considered a dictator, and he extended his analysis to the Emergency Wartime Cabinet of Churchill and to past governments in Britain.[44]

Outside observers like *New York Times* correspondent Tolischus read Nagai well. Writing in September 1941, Tolischus noted that even though some recent developments had given him reason for optimism concerning Japan,

At the same time, Commander Itaro Tashiro, of the Navy press section, called on the Japanese people in a nation-wide broadcast to be prepared for total war; Ryutaro Nagai, director of the East Asia Bureau of the I.R.A.A., called on America and Great Britain to withdraw from the Far East; and the press hewed along the same line. My new-found optimism began to fade.[45]

Tolischus' forebodings were borne out. On October 16 the third Konoe cabinet resigned with the explanation that it had been difficult to reach agreement on the manner of executing national policy.[46] The discord had been over whether Japan should pursue a settlement with the United States or continue close ties with Germany. On October 18 a new government took over headed by General Tōjō Hideki as premier, war minister, and home minister, and within two months World War II in the Pacific had begun. Nagai himself did not live long enough to travel the whole way from Pearl Harbor to Potsdam, but he helped to chart the course—just as he had helped move the country from Paris to Pearl. At home and abroad, he was one of the most ardent supporters of Japan's "Holy War."

In September 1942, for example, he traveled as ambassador extraordinary to Nanking with Hiranuma Kiichirō and former foreign minister Arita Hachirō. There he met Wang Ching-wei, whom he had met before in 1930 at Tientsin and in 1941 in Tokyo. Wang had set up a government in Nanking in March 1940 under Japanese aegis and in opposition to Chiang Kai-shek's government, now removed to Chungking. Nagai spoke in Nanking on September 25, expounding on one of his favorite themes, the "coexistence and coprosperity of China and Japan"—ironic considering Japan's atrocities in that city close to five years earlier. His talk that day was one of those flights of wartime rhetoric that became more frequent and vociferous for him as Japan's situation deteriorated. Assassination threats had been made against him before he spoke, but he went through with his speech, firing away on topics such as European oppression and the war as a contest for leadership of various world cultures more than a struggle for resources; Chiang's betrayal of the Chinese by collaborating with the Anglo-Americans to perpetuate his own power; and the necessity of Sino-Japanese cooperation for the advancement of East Asia.[47]

His rhetoric at home was similar as he pursued his hectic pace of activities and involvement with the IRAA. In September 1941 the Yokusan giin dōmei, or Yokudō (Yokusan Dietman's League), had formed to fill the political void in the Diet. Nagai became a leader of that group. The government also had pegged him as one of the "reliable 85" supporters in the Diet and employed his services accordingly to prepare for the upcoming election of April 1942.[48] In anticipation of this so-called Yokusan Election, Abe Nobuyuki became head of a temporary political organization to nominate and help elect candidates. Nagai was one of the seven selected to participate. He

also became a member of the Political Council (Yokusan seiji taisei kyōgikai—Imperial Rule Assistance Political Organization) assembled in February 1942 to work toward establishing a Diet that
would pursue successfully the Greater East Asian War objectives. He
was one of the four Yokudō Special Executive Committee members
who acted as liaison agents between the Yokudō and the Political
Council. He campaigned for other candidates in their election districts and made recordings for the places he could not appear. He
himself won reelection by a large majority.

Shortly after the election the government announced that no
longer would it merely appeal for national unity; instead, every effort
would be made to realize it. Accordingly, on May 7 Tōjō assembled
powerful representatives of the Diet, press, economic world, and the
like, explaining to them the government's position and the need to
work together toward the goal of national unity. The government
went one step further and stressed that for the successful completion
of the Greater East Asian War, it desired the formation of a Yokusan
political organization that would take the proper steps to regiment
nationwide political power. Nagai became a member of the Preparatory Committee, set up on May 8 under the chairmanship of Gotō
Fumio, as well as a member of the Administrative Committee
(Sōmukai) of the Yokusan Political Association (Yokusan seijikai)
formed later in the month.[49]

Secure in his positions as head of the Development of Asia Bureau
and as an official of the Yokusan Political Association, Nagai kept up
his drive for his last two years. As president of the Greater Japan
Education Association, his stated goals were to equalize national
educational opportunities and to establish a Greater East Asia system
of education (a plan for the latter being presented in the House as
early as February 1942).[50] He threw himself into other projects like
the Greater East Asia Conference and the Greater East Asia Collected People's Meeting (held in Tokyo in November 1943); and to
the end, he remained an enthusiastic supporter of the Indian independence movement.[51]

He also continued his efforts for the Spiritual Mobilization movement, with increasingly nationalistic speeches and writings, such as
his 1942 *Sekai o senku suru Nihon* (Japan taking the lead in the world).
But despite all of this optative rhetoric, he realized the war was not
going well. He placed much of the responsibility on Prime Minister
Tōjō and did not hesitate to voice his opinion on the matter.[52] His
feelings show through very clearly in correspondence of July 16,

1944, to Privy Seal Kido Kōichi.[53] There he contended that a new cabinet was necessary to gain Diet support for the government and to give Japan better direction in the war. The letter is revealing also of the lingering importance for Nagai of both the Bakumatsu patriots and the English model as frames of reference. Both the patriots and England's Lloyd George, he pointed out, had had to overthrow existing governments to save the situation in the face of enemy threats.

Tōjō's cabinet finally fell on July 22. The senior statesmen had hoped to replace him with the former premier Admiral Yonai Mitsumasa, but the army considered Yonai too moderate. Instead, General Koiso Kuniaki became prime minister, with Yonai his deputy prime minister and navy minister. The Yokusan Political Association continued to function, and Nagai retained his Administrative Committee position despite various committee shake-ups. He also kept up his own factional activities, but only for a short time, for by this point he was very ill.[54]

Troublesome symptoms had been reoccurring since his trip to Nanking in 1942, but examinations then had revealed nothing. During the summer of 1944, his condition deteriorated so that on September 10 he entered the Greater East Asia Hospital in Tsukiji (now St. Luke's) for more tests. The diagnosis this time was contractile cancer of the stomach. Those who visited him during his hospitalization said that these last months were extremely painful for Nagai both physically and psychologically. He expressed frequently to callers such as Arima Yoriyasu, Godō Takuo, and Tsutsumi Yasujirō the realization that his career had taken a wrong turn.

Worse, it seems, was the remorse he felt for Japan's present plight. Tsutsumi relates that when B-29s hit Tokyo in an air raid on November 30 Nagai stood transfixed at his hospital window watching Kanda go up in flames and blaming himself for his role in bringing this to pass. Though Nagai's son Michio had often disagreed with his father over Japan's direction, he was there with his mother throughout this time, reading and keeping Nagai company. In this final stage of his illness Nagai entreated his son to avoid repeating his mistakes; at the same time, he urged him to do all he could to advance education in the country. After Nagai died quietly on December 5, among the things placed in his coffin were his bible, his cane, and his worn copy of the life of Gladstone.[55]

On the day of his death the Rising Sun merit of the first degree was conferred on him, and he was raised to the court rank of junior second class by special imperial command. Shidehara, Kido, Premier

Koiso, and other ministers attended the funeral on December 6, though Tōjō did not.[56] On the twenty-seventh, Sakurai Hyōgorō, speaking for the Diet, delivered an address on the Diet floor in Nagai's honor. It was laudatory; Sakurai and Nagai had been close. He summarized Nagai's work, his talents, his transition from the Minseitō to the Shintaisei, and the honors accorded Nagai at his death. One of the most salient passages of the memorial address was his depiction of Nagai as a pioneer in the political arena, "a parliamentary politician of individual stamp, who, in spanning the Taishō and Shōwa eras, left numerous contributions behind. With his fiery enthusiasm for politics and revolutionary spirit, he has long been considered a 'new man' in the political world and one who cut a conspicuous figure therein."[57]

Nagai's life did span an era—the very years when Japan was making every effort to catch up with the West by becoming a modernized, powerful nation. This process involved necessary internal reforms and the ability to meet external challenges and threats. Japan's leaders were prepared to do both. Nagai was born in 1881, the year of the imperial rescript declaring that a national assembly would be formed. He also belonged to the "generation of 1905" that came to maturity during the years between Japan's victories in the Sino-Japanese and Russo-Japanese wars.[58] He made his name in the political world in the period immediately following the Paris Peace Conference, a time when many Japanese were determined to become world citizens by effecting democracy at home and cooperating in the international community with peaceful economic expansion abroad. As world trends became more conservative and nationalistic in the 1930s, however, so did the Japanese—and Nagai. As his career was drawing to a close in late 1944, so too was an era in Japan's history. The reformist wave had crested, and the Allies' Potsdam surrender ultimatum was not far off.

SEVEN

Conclusion

KATAYAMA TETSU, Japan's only socialist prime minister (1947–1948) and longtime acquaintance of Nagai Ryūtarō, was banned from various political positions in the period directly preceding the war because of his adverse stand on governmental and party policies. When asked how he viewed Nagai's career in perspective, he replied that in the years leading up to the war concerned Japanese were grasping at any straw they thought would save the situation. "I grasped at one, and Nagai at another."[1]

Nagai was not alone. It can be said that he walked the usual path of the reformists. For like many others who appeared on the public scene in 1918–1919 pledged to the goal of social and political reform along progressive lines, he was absorbed ultimately into the one-party system, the Taisei yokusankai—a commitment that appeared to negate the very ideals he had embraced earlier when he and other concerned Japanese had entertained more liberal ideas and had endeavored to become international citizens. In conclusion, therefore, it would be salutary to add some final comments on the reformist pattern, Nagai Ryūtarō as the case study for that pattern, and the implications of both reformism and the Nagai experience for democracy in prewar Japan.

THE REFORMIST PATTERN

This study has used the reformist concept only in a hypothetical way, but research centering on the various groups and individuals who followed this pattern (as suggested by Itō Takashi in his various writings cited earlier) could contribute to a clearer understanding of sociopolitical developments in twentieth-century Japan. This is true for not only the period preceding World War II, but also the relationship between the pre- and postwar periods. One reason is that many of those affiliated with the 1918–1919 reformist organizations (the New Men's Society, Dawn Society, People's League, Founders' League, League for the Realization of Universal Suffrage, Reconstruction

League, Old and Young Society, Constitutional Young Men's party, North Wind Society, Yūzonsha, and the like) became active politically again after the war. Moreover, just as leading reformists were absorbed into the New Political Order while failing to become the real locus of power in that order, neither did they succeed in taking the lead in postwar Japanese politics. In the years following 1945 it looked as if this group—particularly the left wing—had a major opportunity to grasp power, but it did not work out that way. For example, reformists who constituted the center of the postwar Socialist party did not become the power center in the political world.[2] To understand why would be helpful.

The reformist pattern is relevant also to an understanding of prewar Japanese nationalism and internationalism. As shown, reformists had a general lack of faith in the new international order set up at the Versailles and Washington conferences. Although people like Nagai and Prince Konoe, one of the reformist nobility, cooperated with this new order in the 1920s and tried to protect Japan's interests within its framework, they gradually began to withdraw their endorsement of that order in the late 1920s, when the order no longer appeared to protect and enhance Japan's interests. Accordingly, at the international level, as well as at the national, the concept of *tenkō,* or "ideological conversion," is not wholly adequate to explain the reformists' behavior pattern, since consistencies ran throughout the two main periods of the interwar years.

The ongoing influence of Spencerian thought and the concept of Darwinian struggle whereby the strong triumph over the weak was one strand of continuity. In addition, and as suggested earlier, it appeared that the philosophy of the Edo scholar Sakuma Shōzan, "Japanese spirit and Western knowledge," persisted into the Taishō and early Shōwa periods. This is seen in the parallel lines of thought and action adopted by Nagai and others in trying to cope with Japanese problems during those years—the pragmatic, changing line represented by the democratic reforms and practices that have contributed to the Taishō-democracy image, as well as the traditional, more consistent line of Japanese nationalism and the emperor system about which that nationalism revolved. These parallel threads would account for the contrasts apparent in the two periods of the interwar years. More than an actual contradiction, however, it is most likely that in the late teens and early twenties, the pragmatic, changing line was predominant, with the traditional line regaining supremacy by the thirties.

THE NAGAI EXPERIENCE

As it was with the country, so it was with Nagai, who represented those trends in his attempts at reform. Subtleties and tensions in the reform ethos, as some have observed, cannot be viewed in absolute terms; and "although we may prefer our reformers and conservatives pure, men may harbor reactionary and progressive impulses not only at the same time, but for the same reasons."[3] As a young new liberal, Nagai had received strong Western influence through his study and observation tours abroad. He was struck especially by the English constitutional monarchical system, which remained his model for life. Because of this very inability to break away from an English-American framework, Nagai has been portrayed as a pseudo-reformist as opposed to a pure reformist like Nakano Seigō.[4] What is significant, though, is that Nagai's perception of Western developments and systems was colored by and mixed with the more particularist Japanese emperor-centered orientation.

He adhered to the tradition that government should be run jointly by the emperor and the people *(kummin kyōji)* in accord with the inseparable bond that had existed between them from ages past *(ikkun bammin),* an ideal that had special meaning for political party men. For them, "this bond between Emperor and people symbolized the change from the feudal, class-oriented Tokugawa society to the modern, egalitarian order of Meiji; it guaranteed equality and unlimited mobility to all; it was the bedrock on which 'Japanese democracy' and the claim for party government rested."[5] It is likely that it was Nagai's dedication to the working out of this bond between the emperor and people that led him to espouse some tenets of Woodrow Wilson's "New Liberalism" (even though he became an increasingly staunch opponent of the man Wilson as the Taishō and Shōwa periods progressed). For example, he liked the idea of working "with the people" instead of "for them"; and even though he realized that such an ideal was not completely applicable to Japan, he found it in many ways compatible with the concept of *kummin kyōji.*[6]

Nagai also came to represent that strain within the reformist group who elected to work toward their goals through the established parties. Furthermore, as a "Taishō democrat," he stuck with the parties far into the thirties—considerably longer than many of his compatriots of the Taishō period—even though he continued to chastise those parties for their failure to reform and focus on the people. His motives for making the effort were complex, it is sure, based partly on his early conviction that a strong two-party system was necessary to effect true constitutional government and partly on his personal ambitions. Nagai's concern about advancing his career as a politician was strong enough to insure that his political behavior did not become too out of step with the mood of the period.

This ability to adjust to the times enabled him to remain more mainstream throughout his career than others who came into the public arena during Taishō with renovationist goals. For instance, Nagai did not become associated intimately with the proletarian party movement embraced by Ōyama Ikuo. Ōyama, like Nagai, had been considered a defender of Taishō democracy, but in 1926 became chairman of the pro-communist Labor-Farmer party. For him and many other liberal intellectuals of the early 1920s, the proletarian party movement represented a possibility for cleaning up political corruption, which they blamed on the established parties.[7] Ironically, when Ōyama and Nagai graduated from Waseda in 1905, Nagai was portrayed as a radical and Ōyama as one whose ideal was "to walk the middle path."[8] In the course of their careers, the roles would be reversed.

To say that Nagai was more conservative or mainstream does not imply that he did not stand out. A true example of the Ōkuma-Waseda type of politician, he broke into politics armed with oratorical and journalistic talents; and with those same abilities plus a sensitivity to the concerns of the general public, he became a celebrated politician of the people. Nagai's very popularity and his dramaturgic style, part of his Ōkuma heritage, distinguished him from the style of the professional Hara.[9] Moreover, the fact that Nagai could win such political popularity by his eloquence reveals something about the special character of Taishō as an era in Japanese politics.

Through his role and campaigning in the universal suffrage movement, he made his name as a champion of the people, and it was within this context and because of this image as a defender of popular causes that Yatsugi Kazuo suggested that Nagai was exploited throughout his career by various professional politicians, however much they may have looked down on him. It was along these lines also that Miki Bukichi referred to him as a "mannequin of the Minseitō." As a member of that party (and despite the fact that he became eventually chief secretary of the organization), Nagai was always to some extent apart from many Minseitō leaders in the way he linked his populist cause of social democracy to Japan's mission. As it turned out, his alternative associations were, first, the people—

the "common man," women, and youth.[10] It was primarily to them that he appealed, and with them that he won acceptance. Next came those connected with journalism, reformist-type bureaucratic elite groups, and, ultimately, the military.

REFORMIST PERCEPTIONS OF DEMOCRACY

Going back to the setting with which this book began, it will be remembered how upon returning from Paris in 1919, many Japanese (including members of the Kaizō dōmei) such as Mitsukawa Kametarō, Baba Tsunego, Nakano Seigō, and Nagai, had insisted on the need for universal suffrage as one step toward consolidating and strengthening the country. In this sense universal suffrage was a necessary precondition not only to achieve true constitutional government, but for national mobilization as well. Nagai, a democrat and an ardent nationalist, was in the vanguard of that and other Taishō movements aimed at broadening the base of power to include the people. He was also in the forefront of support for Konoe and the New Political Order, which had as one goal mobilization of the people for national and international objectives.

In short, by the early 1940s Nagai's position, including his espousal of democracy, had moved along that spectrum from a more liberal orientation in the 1910s and 1920s to one more totalitarian. One cannot deny the countercurrents in his position over the course of his career. We do not find as we might expect, for instance, his staunch support of universal suffrage corroborated by opposition to the Peace Preservation Law—legislation some see to be part of the swan song of Taishō democracy. But the reformist Nagai was not a product of the Taishō era alone. Born only thirteen years after the fall of the Tokugawa Bakufu, he was one of the Russo-Japanese War generation, a Meiji man with an intense loyalty to his country. With his cultivated, keen awareness of the problems Japan had faced since late Tokugawa, he took upon himself a type of mission and made an early commitment to the realization of reforms that would help guarantee the stability, security, and advancement of his country.

Nagai's conception of democracy reflects this, for he placed more emphasis on a certain degree of conformity throughout the country and less on diversity and pluralism. As he saw it, the primary goal was to have individuals develop their potential through the opportunities afforded under democratic institutions so that all could work together more effectively to serve the emperor and nation and at the same time ward off foreign threats.[11] In short, democracy for Nagai was a tool to be used in solving Japan's problems. As such, his approach to it was not primarily from the standpoint of individual-ism but rather from that of nationalism—as was likely the case with many Taishō democrats, including Yoshino Sakuzō.[12]

Nagai's perception of democracy as a means to state power, how-ever, was ineluctably vulnerable to the fact that there are shorter means to that end. As he and other concerned Japanese perceived the national and international environment in the 1930s, the need for a unified, harmonious Japanese state became increasingly a matter of immediate urgency. They had no time, so they thought, to work through that process essential to achieve the "higher synthesis" of a more liberal democratic approach.

Maruyama Masao has answered his own query concerning this move away from Western liberal ideals by referring to the "interfu-sion of ethics and power" that took place in Japan.

National sovereignty was the ultimate source of both ethics and power, and constituted their intrinsic unity; this being the situation, Japanese morality never underwent the process of interiorization that we have seen in the case of the West, and accordingly it always had the impulse to transform itself into power. . . . The "total mobilization of the people's spirit" during the war was a typical manifestation of Japanese morality emerging as outward action.[13]

Related to this is Robert Bellah's thesis on the tradition of submerged transcendence in Japanese history, which may be summarized as the difficulty of retaining loyalty to "some principle transcending soci-ety" and challenging the prevailing particularistic ethic in that so-ciety.[14]

This movement away from Western liberal ideals has been charac-terized as an ideological conversion, even reversion. Given the greater context of modern Japanese history and Japan's prewar emperor system, however, the Nagai experience and the reformist pattern may be interpreted in another way. The ideological adjust-ments made by reformists such as Nagai may be viewed as an ongo-ing response to the major threats and problems the country had faced since the nineteenth century, when, after a long period of introver-sion, the conscious decision was being made to move back into the international community. In this sense the reformist course ulti-mately did not end in retreat, but rather continued, by adapting itself to contemporary realities, in its attempt to carry Japan forward.

Notes

Introduction

1. Mitsukawa, *Sangoku kanshō igo,* pp. 228–32, including a list of the forty-five original members (p. 229); Nakano S., "Kaizō dōmei ron"; Uehara, *Demokurashii to Nihon no kaizō,* esp. preface, pp. 1–5; and Tokyo Nichinichi shimbunsha and Osaka Mainichi shimbunsha, *Meiji, Taishō, Shōwa gikai seiji rimen shi,* pp. 79–80.

2. Nagai R., *Kaizō no risō,* pp. 31–32.

3. Ibid., pp. 32–33.

4. Suzuki, *Nihon kaizō no dōgi oyobi,* pp. 134–35.

5. Ibid., pp. 136–37.

6. Ibid., p. 137.

7. Mitani, *Taishō demokurashii ron,* p. 33. A discussion of the origins and popularizing of the term "Taishō democracy" appears in Eguchi, *Taishō demokurashii,* p. 9ff. Eguchi suggests that the term became common vocabulary among scholars following Shinobu Seizaburō's use of it in his *Taishō seiji shi* and his *Taishō demokurashii shi.*

8. Nagai R., *Kaizō no risō,* p. 20.

9. Kisaki, *Kisaki nikki,* p. 227. "Nagai Ryūtarō" hensankai, *Nagai Ryūtarō,* p. 156 passim. This is the standard biography of Nagai. There is little on him in English other than two articles by Peter Duus: "Nagai Ryūtarō and the 'White Peril' " and "Nagai Ryūtarō: Tactical Dilemmas."

10. Mitani, *Taishō demokurashii ron,* p. 32. See Chang, *Historians and Taisho Statesmen,* pp. 1–3, for a discussion of recent ranking of Taishō leadership by Japanese scholars of the period.

11. Itō works with this concept, including organizations and individual names, in "Nihon 'kakushin' ha no seiritsu," "Shōwa seiji shi kenkyū e no ichi shikaku," *Taishō ki 'kakushin' ha no seiritsu,* and in other writings. Some in this reformist group would overlap with the "new liberals" described by Duus in *Party Rivalry,* pp. 113–17.

12. "Yūzonsha" is difficult to translate as an isolated term, though "yet remaining" would come close. The phrase *"yūzon"* appeared in a poem by a scholar-official of ancient China, T'ao Yüan-ming: "Though all paths lie overgrown, the pines and chrysanthemums still survive." And Ōkawa Shūmei, a right-wing reformist member of the Yūzonsha, explaining the origin of its obscure name, said, "Those were the days when countless organiza-

tions, large and small, were established, some being radical organizations with democratic or anarchical principles, while others had socialistic or communistic principles. At that time . . . we considered ourselves the pine trees and chrysanthemums of Japan, and decided on the name 'Yusonsha' [*sic*]" (Wilson, *Radical Nationalist in Japan,* pp. 97, 188); Storry, *Double Patriots,* p. 39.

13. Mitsukawa, "Rōsōkai no ki."

14. Itō T., "Shōwa seiji shi kenkyū e no ichi shikaku," pp. 223–26.

15. Ibid. For his analysis, Itō has drawn partly on the May 1941 statements of the active professor and public figure Yabe Teiji, as they appear in Imai and Itō, *Gendai shi shiryō* 44, pp. 484–88.

16. See Craig, *Japan: A Comparative View,* pp. 6–7, for his hypothesis on the rapidly occurring "waves" of westernization in modern Japan—the first after 1868, the second during and after World War I, and the third after World War II. Also, Shūichi Katō, "Japanese Writers and Modernizaton," in Jansen, *Changing Japanese Attitudes,* pp. 443–44.

17. Several writers have used the juxtaposition of diverse sets of themes or groupings to explain modern Japan. See, for example, Tetsuo Najita's discussion of "bureaucratism" and "restorationism" in *Japan,* pp. 2–7; David Titus' treatment of "constitutionalists" and "renovationists" in *Palace and Politics,* pp. 325–26; and Itō Takashi's thesis concerning "Progressives" (westernization) vs. "Reactionaries" (restoration) in "The Role of Right-Wing Organizations in Japan," trans. Shumpei Okamoto, in Borg and Okamoto, *Pearl Harbor as History,* pp. 488–91.

18. Ben-Ami Shillony treats the "restoration" concept succinctly in his *Revolt in Japan,* pp. 57–58.

19. Morley, *Dilemmas of Growth,* p. 3.

20. A discussion of the problem appears in Mitani, *Taishō demokurashii ron,* p. 291.

CHAPTER ONE *Taishō Democracy*

1. Gay, "Weimar Culture," p. 64.

2. Tsuda, *Shisō, bungei, Nihongo,* pp. 226–33.

3. Ibid., pp. 219–22.

4. Mitani, *Taishō demokurashii ron,* p. 8ff.

5. Ishida Takeshi, in his *Kindai Nihon seiji kōzō,* takes the position that the growth of political party consciousness did not turn into a general denunciation of bureaucratism. Rather, changes which took place occurred gradually as integrated methods within the administrative system (p. 151). A similar position is taken by Tetsuo Najita in his study of Hara Kei (*Hara Kei,* see esp. pp. viii, xii).

6. Kimbara, *Taishō ki no seitō to kokumin,* p. 8.

7. On periodization, see Eguchi, *Taishō demokurashii,* pp. 14–16; also Matsuo, "Development of Democracy in Japan," pp. 614–15.

8. Duus, review of *The Japanese Oligarchy and the Russo-Japanese War.*

9. Matsumoto Sannosuke, *Kindai Nihon no chiteki jōkyō* (The intellectual climate of modern Japan) (Tokyo, 1974), p. 117ff.

10. For another perspective on the Shinjinkai, see Smith, *Japan's First Student Radicals,* pp. x–xi. Smith suggests that the generation of Japanese youth that appeared in the decade between the Russo-Japanese War and World War I usually could be seen as engaged in negative retreat from the heroic, outgoing nationalism of the earlier generation. Whereas formerly, the focus had been on nation, there emerged a new stress on self, whether in the "selfish acquisition of wealth" or in "existentialist despair."

11. Nagai R., *Zampan,* pp. 197–200.

12. Throughout, the term "commoners" means the greater body of people outside the ranks of the nobility, other ruling groups, and the intelligentsia. In Nagai's time, many still referred to this greater body as the *"heimin,"* a term employed by the Meiji government in 1869 to signify those people who had belonged formerly to the peasant, artisan, and merchant classes. In its first issue (Nov. 15, 1903), *Heimin shimbun* (Commoners' news) referred to this larger group as the "laboring classes," as opposed to the "ruling classes."

13. Matsuo, "Natsume Sōseki to," p. 41; and his *Taishō demokurashii,* p. 5. Also Yoshino, "Minshūteki jii undō o ronzu," p. 87.

14. Okamoto, *The Japanese Oligarchy,* pp. 227–29. Matsuo, *Taishō demokurashii,* pp. 13–27.

15. For this summary I have drawn on Kazushi Ohkawa and Henry Rosovsky, "A Century of Japanese Economic Growth," in Lockwood, *The State and Economic Enterprise,* esp. pp. 77–81; Kozo Yamamura, "The Japanese Economy, 1911–1930: Concentration, Conflicts, Crises," in Silberman and Harootunian, *Japan in Crisis,* pp. 299–328; and Jansen, *Japan and China,* pp. 95–97.

16. Yamamura, "Japanese Economy, 1911–1930," pp. 300, 310, 327.

17. Duus, *Party Rivalry,* pp. 124–25.

18. Ibid., p. 121.

19. See esp. Yoshino, "Kensei no hongi o toite."

20. Matsuo, "Profile of Asian Minded Man," pp. 389–92; Tetsuo Najita, "Some Reflections on Idealism in the Political Thought of Yoshino Sakuzō," in Silberman and Harootunian, *Japan in Crisis,* pp. 39–40.

21. Takeda, "Pioneers of Modern Japan," pp. 516–17; Silberman, "Political Theory of Yoshino Sakuzō," pp. 316–17.

22. Najita, "Idealism in the Thought of Yoshino Sakuzō," pp. 39–40.

23. Nagai R., *Zampan,* pp. 200–208.

24. Itō T., "Nihon 'kakushin' ha no seiritsu," p. 53. This trend is evident in the following case. The Kōwa mondai dōshi rengōkai (Federation of Like-minded Men Concerning the Peace Problem) was active at the time of the Russo-Japanese War. The rengōkai was a federation composed of diverse elements such as the Tai-Ro dōshikai (Association of Like-minded Men vis-

à-vis Russia), the Kokuryūkai (Black Dragon Society), the Dōshi kisha kurabu (Like-minded Journalists Club), and others that had been opposed to Russia and in favor of war before hostilities finally broke out. In 1905 the rengōkai became the Kokumin kurabu (People's Club) with the goals of "constitutionalism within" the country and "imperialism without." When the power of the extreme rightist group, the Kokuryūkai, weakened within the association, leadership moved to the anti-*hambatsu* group made up of lawyers, journalists, and anti-Seiyūkai politicians, the same group active in the Universal Suffrage League (Fusen dōmeikai) established in 1901 (Matsuo, *Taishō demokurashii,* pp. 19–20, 36–37).

25. Nagai M., "Bikko to seiji," p. 61.

26. Ibid.

27. Katayama Tetsu, interview with author, June 27, 1972.

28. Saitō, *Kikuchi Shigeru chosakushū,* pp. 464, 606. Kikuchi and Nagai attended Waseda together and were later fellow party members.

29. See, for instance, *Shūgiin giji sokkiroku* 45, no. 16 (Feb. 24, 1922): 329–33.

30. Nagai R., "Jōin tai minshū no mondai," p. 167.

31. *Shūgiin giji sokkiroku* 43, no. 6 (July 9, 1920): 82.

32. Nagai R., "Nihon sansen no riyū oyobi kōka" (Japan's participation in the war: The reasons and results), in *Nagai Ryūtarō shi daienzetsushū* 1:2–3. Italics mine.

33. Nagai R., "Gikai shukusei yori mitaru."

34. Shisō no kagaku kenkyūkai, *Tenkō* 2:95. Similar ideas appear in Hokkoku shimbunsha henshūkyoku, *Fūsetsu no hi,* p. 308; and Kawasaki, *Waseda no seijika-tachi,* p. 199.

CHAPTER TWO   *Liberal Beginnings*

1. Ruggiero, *History of European Liberalism,* p. vii.

2. Ibid., pp. vii–viii.

3. Ibid., p. 379.

4. General facts concerning Nagai's life are from his biography edited by Matsumura Kenzō.

5. Nagai R., *Zampan,* p. 281ff. Tsutsumi Kōjirō gives a character sketch of Tsuru in his memoirs, *Taiheiyō no kakehashi,* pp. 322–28.

6. Lebra, *Ōkuma Shigenobu: Statesman,* p. 9.

7. Enomoto hōreikan henshūbu, *Kare wa ika ni shite,* p. 156. One of Nagai's heroes, in fact, was Napoleon.

8. Albert M. Craig, "Introduction: Perspectives on Personality," in Craig and Shively, *Personality in Japanese History,* pp. 26–27.

9. "Nagai Ryūtarō" hensankai, *Nagai Ryūtarō,* p. 12.

10. Nagai M., "Bikko to seiji," p. 61.

11. Ōta, "Ōyama Ikuo no mimponshugi ron," p. 31. Ōta points out that little is known about the Kokumin sakushinkai because of insufficient

resources, but he adds that more information concerning it would be valuable toward understanding the thought-formation process of many later involved in the Taishō-democracy movements (p. 34).

12. Nagai R., *Zampan*, pp. 94–96.

13. See "Nagai Ryūtarō" hensankai, *Nagai Ryūtarō*, p. 41. According to this source Nagai did collaborate on answers; but in talking about it in later years, he passed it off to youth and having been "audacious and wily."

14. Nagai M., "Bikko to seiji," p. 60. In his writings, Ryūtarō paid tribute to these two men. Representative are the essays on Ōkuma and Abe included in his *Watakushi no shinnen to taiken*, pp. 172–78, 192–221; also his drama of Ōkuma's life published on the tenth anniversary of the latter's death, *Ōkuma Shigenobu: Gikyoku*, evaluated positively by Ōkuma's eldest daughter for its insights into her father's behavior (Horibe, *Ōkuma Kumako fujin genkoroku*, pp. 105–107).

15. Saitō, *Kikuchi Shigeru chosakushū*, pp. 357–58; 436. Gail Lee Bernstein, "Kawakami Hajime: A Japanese Marxist in Search of the Way," in Silberman and Harootunian, *Japan in Crisis*, p. 95.

16. Notehelfer, "Japan's First Pollution Incident," pp. 351–83; and his *Kōtoku Shūsui*, pp. 65–66.

17. "Nagai Ryūtarō" hensankai, *Nagai Ryūtarō*, pp. 48–49.

18. Hirano, *Nakamura Tahachirō den*, p. 53.

19. Nagai's connection is mentioned in Tanaka, *Kōtoku Shūsui*, pp. 212–13; Komaki, *Tanemaku hitobito*, pp. 130–31.

20. A biography of Ono in English is now availabe by Sandra T. W. Davis. See her *Intellectual Change and Political Development*.

21. Lebra, *Ōkuma Shigenobu: Statesman*, pp. 56–60.

22. Nagai R., *Guraddosuton*.

23. Nagai R., *Watakushi no shinnen to taiken*, pp. 245–46.

24. Nagai R., "Shakaiteki jiyū o ronzu."

25. Nagai R., *Zampan*, pp. 51–52.

26. "Nagai Ryūtarō" hensankai, *Nagai Ryūtarō*, pp. 80–81.

27. Nagai R., *Zampan*, p. 117.

28. Shisō no kagaku kenkyūkai, *Tenkō* 2:93.

29. Ishikawa, *Jijoden* 1:71.

30. Nagai R., *Watakushi no shinnen to taiken*, pp. 178–82; and "Nagai Ryūtarō" hensankai, *Nagai Ryūtarō*, pp. 71–83.

31. Nagai Ryūtarō, "Beikoku gakusha no."

32. Ibid., no. 148, pp. 21–22.

33. Iriye, *Pacific Estrangement*, pp. 78–80.

34. Nagai R., *Eijin kishitsu omoide no ki*, p. 411.

35. Matsumura, *Sandai kaikoroku*, p. 134.

36. Nagai R., *Zampan*, pp. 3–4. A similar appeal appears in the preface to his 1939 drama about the Tokugawa merchant Zeniya Gohee (*Zeniya Gohee: Gikyoku*, p. 4).

37. Nagai R., *Zampan*, pp. 173–74.

38. "Shakoku" (Announcement), *Shin Nippon* 1, no. 1 (Apr. 3, 1911).

39. Ōkuma, "Shin Nippon ron."

40. Waseda daigaku shuppanbu, *Meiji bummei shi ni okeru Ōkuma Shigenobu,* p. 395.

41. A summary of the so-called Ōkuma Doctrine is found in Ichijima, *Ōkuma kō hachijūgo-nen shi* 2:435–39.

42. Ōkuma, *Ōkuma haku shakai gan,* pp. 27–30.

43. Nagai R., "Tai-Shi gaikō no shippai," p. 76.

44. Nagai R., "Sekai no hammon," esp. p. 13.

45. Duus, "Nagai Ryūtarō: Tactical Dilemmas," p. 411.

CHAPTER THREE   *Toward Democratic Reform*

1. Matsumura, *Sandai kaikoroku,* p. 132.

2. Lebra, *Ōkuma Shigenobu: Statesman,* p. 148.

3. Ishikawa kenchō, *Ishikawa ken shi* 1:97; also author's interviews with widows of Nagai's former campaign aides Ichikawa Kiyoshi and Sawano Tomoji, Kanazawa, June 25 and 26, 1973.

4. "Nagai Ryūtarō" hensankai, *Nagai Ryūtarō,* p. 334.

5. Discussing the oratorical tradition in his memoirs, Matsumura Kenzō suggests that the majority of orators were traditionally connected with the Kaishintō and the Kenseikai, with almost none appearing with a Jiyūtō (Liberal party) or Seiyūkai affiliation (*Sandai kaikoroku,* p. 130).

6. Duus, *Party Rivalry,* pp. 91–92.

7. Ueda Sotoo gives a contemporary view of the election in his *Sōsenkyo ki.*

8. Ishikawa kenchō, *Ishikawa ken shi* 1:97.

9. Nagai R., "Yo wa naze daigishi nara'n to hossuru ka" (Why do I wish to become a Diet member?) (Speech delivered in Kanazawa on April 1, 1917), in *Nagai Ryūtarō shi daienzetsushū* 1:1–15; Tokyo Nichinichi shimbunsha and Osaka Mainichi shimbunsha, *Meiji, Taishō, Shōwa gikai seiji rimen shi,* pp. 29–30.

10. Ueda, *Sōsenkyo ki,* p. 201ff.

11. Itō K., *Washi ga kuni sa,* pp. 361–62.

12. Ishikawa kenchō, *Ishikawa ken shi* 1:85.

13. Nagai eventually did marry this same woman, Miura Tsuguyo (the daughter of a Christian minister), who exerted a positive influence on his life and career. Shisō no kagaku kenkyūkai, *Tenkō* 2:93–94; Tsutsumi, *Taiheiyō no kakehashi,* p. 321.

14. Shisō no kagaku kenkyūkai, *Tenkō* 2:93.

15. Masumi, "Japanese Political Studies" 2, no. 2:157–58.

16. Hokkoku shimbunsha henshūkyoku, *Fūsetsu no hi,* p. 299.

17. Ishikawa kenchō, *Ishikawa ken shi* 1:92–95.

18. As Nagai's career progressed he became proficient in collecting money. It was not that he really solicited it—rather it was given to him from

fans, as it would be given to actresses or to sumo wrestlers. Matsumura, *Sandai kaikoroku,* p. 356.

19. "Nagai Ryūtarō" hensankai, *Nagai Ryūtarō,* p. 8.

20. Ishikawa kenchō, *Ishikawa ken shi* 1:97–98. Asano, "Kanazawa seisen no tsuioku," pp. 73–75.

21. *Nagai Ryūtarō shi daienzetsushū* 1:15–25.

22. The juxtaposition of those within and outside the Diet was a favorite Nagai theme and one he was to use repeatedly in the battles preceding final passage of the universal suffrage bill in 1926. Representative is his 1914 essay, "Innai no gikai to," esp. p. 123.

23. Ishikawa kenchō, *Ishikawa ken shi* 1:99.

24. "Nagai Ryūtarō" hensankai, *Nagai Ryūtarō,* pp. 148–60.

25. Ibid. Ozaki Shirō portrays Nagai's difficulties during the Waseda turmoil in his historical novel *Waseda daigaku,* pp. 94, 126–35.

26. Nagai R., "Sekai o shite zenjinrui no sekai tarashime yo," in *Nagai Ryūtarō shi daienzetsushū* 1:68–85.

27. Nagai R., "Nihon sansen no riyū oyobi kōka," in *Nagai Ryūtarō shi daienzetsushū* 1:2–4.

28. Ibid., p. 5, "military activities" referring here mainly to Japan's intervention in Siberia.

29. Nagai R., "Shakaishugi no Beikoku ni furawazaru yuen o," pp. 88–89. Nagai's analysis of the reasons for socialism's failure to take root in the United States as it had in Europe (pp. 86–87) resembles closely the "expectant capitalists" theory put forth later by the American historian Richard Hofstadter. See Hofstadter, *American Political Tradition,* pp. viii–xi; and his *Age of Reform,* p. 10.

30. Nagai R., *Kaizō no risō,* p. 53.

31. Adachi, *Adachi Kenzō jijoden,* pp. 354–56.

32. "Gotō Shimpei monjo," Nagai Ryūtarō shokan (Nagai Ryūtarō correspondence), R83. See discussion of greater problem in Thomas Wesley Burkman's "Japan and the New World Order," pp. 176–77.

33. Itō T., *Taishō ki 'kakushin' ha no seiritsu,* pp. 184–86.

34. Hayashi et al., *Ni/ni-roku jiken hiroku,* special vol., p. 132.

35. Nagai R., "Sekai no ni-daiseiryoku yori." See also his "Ei-Bei no sekaiteki shidō to Nihon" and "Han-Amerikashugi no bō o haisu."

36. Nagai R., "Shisō-jō no jūjiro ni samayoeru Beikoku, esp. p. 91.

37. Mitsukawa, *Ubawaretaru Ajia,* pp. 350–56.

38. Mitani, *Taishō demokurashii ron,* pp. 34, 124.

39. Ibid., pp. 133–35.

40. Nagai R., "Ōshū yori Beikoku e, Beikoku yori doko e," in *Nagai Ryūtarō shi daienzetsushū* 2:264–300, quotation, p. 299.

41. Duus, *Party Rivalry,* p. 5.

42. Griffin, "Universal Suffrage Issue," p. 280.

43. Matsuo, *Taishō demokurashii,* p. vi; Duus, *Party Rivalry,* pp. 108–109.

44. Ishikawa kenchō, *Ishikawa ken shi* 1:99–100. Kobayashi Akio covers the group's history in "Taishō ki ni okeru shimin seisha no dōkō." According to this source, Nagai gave the group financial support, as did Nakano Seigō (notes section, p. 95).

45. "Nagai Ryūtarō" hensankai, *Nagai Ryūtarō,* pp. 178–79; Ishikawa kenchō, *Ishikawa ken shi* 1:104. Hokkoku shimbunsha henshūkyoku, *Fūsetsu no hi,* p. 305. Even though Nagai and Nakahashi were on opposite sides of the political fence throughout their careers, they had a mutual respect, and Nagai represented the House in delivering the memorial address in the Diet when Nakahashi died in 1934.

46. Election statistics throughout are from Tōyama and Adachi, *Kindai Nihon seiji hikkei.*

CHAPTER FOUR   *A Reformist in the 1920s*

1. Shinobu, *Taishō seiji shi,* pp. 922–35, 939.

2. Nagai R., "Gikai seiji no shimei," pp. 56–57.

3. Nagai R., "Reigo netsugo" 3, no. 2:29–30.

4. Duus, *Party Rivalry,* pp. 142–43.

5. Tetsuo Najita, "Nakano Seigō and the Spirit of the Meiji Restoration in Twentieth-Century Japan," in Morley, *Dilemmas of Growth,* pp. 396, 403. Mikuriya Takashi compares the political positions of Nagai and Nakano during the Taishō and early Shōwa eras in his essay "Taishō demokurashii kara Shintaisei e."

6. Enomoto hōreikan henshūbu, *Kare wa ika ni shite,* pp. 154–55. For the historical significance of the concept *"ie"* within the Japanese political system, see Ishida, *Kindai Nihon seiji kōzō,* p. 44ff.

7. Lebra, *Ōkuma Shigenobu: Statesman,* p. 130.

8. Tetsuo Najita, "Some Reflections on Idealism in the Political Thought of Yoshino Sakuzō," in Silberman and Harootunian, *Japan in Crisis,* p. 65.

9. Hegel, quoted in ibid., pp. 62–63.

10. Nagai M., "Bikko to seiji," p. 61.

11. Falconeri, review of *Revolt in Japan,* p. 712.

12. Nagai (along with Nakano Seigō) was a chief advocate for the name change to Minseitō. Shidehara heiwa zaidan, *Shidehara Kijūrō,* p. 348; "Nagai Ryūtarō" hensankai, *Nagai Ryūtarō,* p. 254.

13. "Nagai Ryūtarō" hensankai, *Nagai Ryūtarō,* pp. 273–74.

14. Matsumoto Gōkichi, *Taishō demokurashii ki no seiji—Matsumoto Gōkichi seiji nisshi* (Politics during the era of Taishō democracy—the political diary of Matsumoto Gōkichi), ed. Oka Yoshitake and Hayashi Shigeru, (Tokyo, 1959), pp. 137–38.

15. Nagai R., *Zampan,* pp. 101–103.

16. Azuma, *Omitsusa,* p. 128.

17. Lebra, *Ōkuma Shigenobu: Statesman,* p. 147.

18. Tsurumi Shunsuke, quoted in Shisō no kagaku kenkyūkai, *Tenkō* 2:98.

19. Matsumura, *Sandai kaikoroku*, p. 133. Matsumura also comments that listening to Nagai speak impromptu was almost unbearable. On one occasion, when the latter delivered a toast at the wedding reception of the daughter of a hot springs innkeeper for whom he and his wife had acted as go-betweens, he went on for over an hour about the origins and utility of hot springs, unable to bring his talk to a conclusion. Wakatsuki Reijirō, who was sitting next to Matsumura, leaned over and whispered that Nagai's giving the toast as a go-between at a wedding reception was like "brandishing a halberd in a four-and-a-half mat room."

20. Duus, *Party Rivalry*, p. 157.

21. The text of this speech is included in the Diet proceedings, *Shūgiin giji sokkiroku* 43, no. 6 (July 9, 1920): 81–84; see also Nagai R., "Nishi ni Reenin, higashi ni Hara Takashi," in *Nagai Ryūtarō shi daienzetsushū* 1:25–44.

22. *Shūgiin giji sokkiroku* 43, no. 6:84.

23. Hara, *Hara Kei nikki* 8:585–87. He did make note on the tenth regarding the joint bill of nonconfidence in the cabinet submitted by the Kenseikai and the Kokumintō, but the entry does not suggest that the premier was greatly concerned about the bill or the resultant agitation among some elements of the population.

24. *Shūgiin giji sokkiroku* 43, no. 7 (July 10, 1920): 87–90. Uzawa Sōmei (1872–1955), a graduate of the Law Department of Tokyo Imperial University and a practicing lawyer, was first elected to the House of Representatives in 1906 and figured as a leading member of the Seiyūkai. In Nagai's 1914 book *Zampan*, he had criticized Uzawa for claiming to represent the people in the Diet when in reality he was representing merely the large landowners and great capitalists (p. 206). It is not surprising, therefore, that Uzawa introduced the censure resolution against Nagai.

25. *Fresno Republican* (Calif.), Sept. 11, 1920. See also coverage for July 9, 1920, and succeeding days in *Yomiuri shimbun* (Tokyo), *Kokumin shimbun*, *Hōchi shimbun*, *Tokyo Asahi shimbun*, and the *Tokyo Nichinichi shimbun*.

26. Kenseikai member Koizumi Matajirō has detailed the events leading to the passage of the suffrage bill in his *Fusen undō hishi* (Koizumi had become deputy speaker of the House by the time of publication). See also Nagai's recollections in Tokyo Nichinichi shimbunsha and Osaka Mainichi shimbunsha, *Meiji, Taishō, Shōwa gikai seiji rimen shi*, pp. 79–81.

27. Nagai's praise of the West in this case in no way contradicts the criticism he expressed upon his return to Japan in 1919, for his writings and speeches throughout his career indicate that he drew a dichotomy between the political system of a country and its foreign policy.

28. Nagai R., "Gikai seiji no shimei," pp. 53–57.

29. Griffin, "Universal Suffrage Issue," p. 290.

30. Mitani, *Taishō demokurashii ron*, p. 41.

31. Nagai R., *Zampan,* pp. 177–78. The ideas expressed in this book appear later in a 1920 speech Nagai prepared for a gathering sponsored by the *Kokumin shimbun* on the "woman problem" (see Nagai R., "Yo no fujin kan" 1:1–37).

32. Nagai R., *Zampan,* pp. 51, 239–40, 247.

33. Nagai R., "Ningyo ka, ningen ka" (Are they dolls or are they human?), in *Nagai Ryūtarō shi daienzetsushū* 1:219.

34. Azuma, *Omitsusa,* p. 141.

35. Nagai R., *Zampan,* pp. 257–70.

36. Nagai R., "Danshi sensei yori danjo dōchi e" (From male despotism to male-female equality), in *Kaizō no risō,* p. 122.

37. Ibid., pp. 113–16.

38. See discussion in Itō T., *Taishō ki 'kakushin' ha no seiritsu,* pp. 10, 299–300.

39. *Tokyo Asahi shimbun,* Dec. 27 and 28, 1920; *Kokumin shimbun,* Dec. 28, 1920.

40. Nagai R., *Shikisha no mitaru futsū senkyo.*

41. A summary of the debate appears in the *Rikken minseitō shi* 1:519–21.

42. *Shūgiin giji sokkiroku* 45, no. 16 (Feb. 24, 1922): 329–33. Nagai R., "Futsū senkyo no kompongi" (The basic meaning of universal suffrage), in *Nagai Ryūtarō shi daienzetsushū* 1:44–67.

43. Nagai R., "Daisan tō."

44. Nagai R., "Inukai Tsuyoshi kun ni atau" (To Inukai Tsuyoshi), *Shin Nippon* 4, no.7 (July 1914): 44–45.

45. Nagai R., "Daisan tō," pp. 123–26.

46. Nagai R., "Jōin tai minshū no mondai," pp. 169–71.

47. Matsuo, "Development of Democracy in Japan," p. 631.

48. Berger, "Japan's Young Prince," p. 462.

49. Nagai R., "Daisan tō," p. 123.

50. Nagai R., "Nōsei no hon'i o," pp. 88–90.

51. Adachi, *Adachi Kenzō jijoden,* pp. 198–99.

52. "Nagai Ryūtarō" hensankai, *Nagai Ryūtarō,* p. 233.

53. Nagai's coupling of these two elements is especially evident in a 1923 speech to the Sekishunkai of Ibaraki entitled "Iki'n to hosseba, tatakae" (If you want to live, fight!) (*Sekishun,* Ibaraki Prefecture, November 20, 1923).

54. *Shūgiin giji sokkiroku* 47, no. 5 (Dec. 16, 1923): 104–107. Nagai R., "Seigi jindō ikubaku ni ka aru" (How much justice and humanity?), in *Nagai Ryūtarō shi daienzetsushū* 1:159–63.

55. *Shūgiin giji sokkiroku* 47, no. 5 (Dec. 16, 1923): 107–108; *Nagai Ryūtarō shi daienzetsushū* 1:164–68.

56. Gotō Shimpei monjo, June 8, 1923.

57. Tsurumi Shunsuke, in Shisō no kagaku kenkyūkai, *Tenkō* 2:93.

58. *Shūgiin giji sokkiroku* 46, no. 32 (Mar. 16, 1923): 725.

59. "Nagai Ryūtarō" hensankai, *Nagai Ryūtarō,* pp. 223–25.

60. Itō Takashi, in *Shōwa shoki seiji shi kenkyū,* shows how Nagai's appoint-

ment in the Hamaguchi administration was tied in with his connection with Adachi Kenzō as one of the Adachi *shitennō* (big four), who, in addition to Nagai, were Nakano Seigō, Suzuki Fujiya, and Yamamichi Jōichi (pp. 29, 69–70).

61. "Nagai Ryūtarō" hensankai, *Nagai Ryūtarō*, pp. 230–32.

62. Similar views are expressed by Mikuriya Takashi in "Nagai Ryūtarō," pp. 17–18.

63. "Nagai Ryūtarō" hensankai, *Nagai Ryūtarō*, p. 226. Kita's book was written in 1919 and called for sweeping changes in Japanese society. Its 1920 distribution was forbidden by the police; the 1923 revised edition was published but banned again soon after; and the 1926 edition was also later banned.

64. Itō T., *Taishō ki 'kakushin' ha no seiritsu*, p. 299.

65. Berger, "Japan's Young Prince," pp. 457–59.

66. Akira Iriye, "The Failure of Economic Expansionism: 1918–1931," in Silberman and Harootunian, *Japan in Crisis*, p. 239. See also Bamba, *Japanese Diplomacy in a Dilemma*, p. 19.

67. See discussion in Takemoto, *Failure of Liberalism*, pp. 62–65.

68. An example would be the Tsinan Incident (see *Shūgiin giji sokkiroku* 55, no. 7 [May 5, 1928]: 74–77). Nagai's general ideas at this time appear in his "Shidehara gaikō no honryō," and correspondence of September 11, 1928, to Kikuchi Shigeru reveals that he was planning further publication to clarify Shidehara's policies (Saitō, *Kikuchi Shigeru chosakushū*, p. 630).

69. Ueda, *Sōsenkyo ki*, p. 245. Nagai and Ukita had campaigned together in Kanazawa for the 1915 general election.

70. Iriye, *Pacific Estrangement*, pp. 213–14; also Iriye's essay "Kayahara Kazan and Japanese Cosmopolitanism" in Craig and Shively, *Personality in Japanese History*, pp. 373–98.

71. Nagai R., *Zampan*, pp. 56–58, 294–307.

72. *Shūgiin giji sokkiroku* 46, no. 32 (Mar. 16, 1923): 724–26; see also Nagai R., "Jishu dokuritsu no tai-Shi gaikō," in *Nagai Ryūtarō shi daienzetsushū* 1:86–100.

73. *Shūgiin giji sokkiroku* 46, no. 32 (Mar. 16, 1923): 725; Nagai R., "Jishu dokuritsu no tai-Shi gaikō," p. 91.

74. Miyamoto, "Mimponshugisha to shite no Nagai Ryūtarō," pp. 5–9, 14. For points of similarity and dissimilarity between the two men, see also Nagai's articles on Tokutomi Sohō in *Shin Nippon*: "Tokutomi Sohō shi no," pt. 1; "Sohō sensei no," pts. 2, 3. See also Nagai's piece on "Tokutomi Sohō sensei," in his *Watakushi no shinnen to taiken*, pp. 162–72.

75. Pierson, "Liberal Thought of Tokutomi Sohō," p. 224; and his *Tokutomi Sohō*, pp. 234–47.

76. Nagai R., "Tōtaku kaisha no kaiaku"; Nagai R., "Tōyō takushoku kaisha bokumetsu ron" (serialized in *Shin Nippon*).

77. Very early on Itō Hirobumi had voiced opposition to the proposed Tōtaku because he did not visualize its proving beneficial to Korea. More-

over, since the resident-general would have no direct controls over the company, it was possible that its operations could increase anti-Japanese feeling, thereby rendering the resident-general's position even more difficult. Moskowitz, "Oriental Development Company," pp. 74, 102, 91.

78. "Terauchi Masatake kankei monjo," vol. 13, no. 183, Nagai Ryūtarō shokan (Nagai Ryūtarō correspondence), August 15, 1915.

79. Nagai R., "Shokumin shisō no kakumei ki," pp. 118–19.

80. Baba, "Nagai Ryūtarō ron," pp. 156–57.

81. Itō T., *Shōwa shoki seiji shi kenkyū*, p. 111. Nagai's concern is indicated also in Nihon kokusai seiji gakkai—Taiheiyō sensō gen'in kenkyū-bu, *Taiheiyō sensō e no michi* 1:98.

82. Itō T., *Shōwa shoki seiji shi kenkyū*, p. 118.

83. Nagai Ryūtarō, "Rūzuberuto daitōryō ni tou" (Some questions for President Roosevelt) and "Futatabi Rūzuberuto daitōryō ni tou" (Once more, some questions for President Roosevelt), both in his *Sekai o senku suru Nihon* p. 58. This piece also appeared as "Some Questions for President Roosevelt" in the July 1939 issue of *Contemporary Japan*.

84. Iriye, "Failure of Economic Expansionism," pp. 262–69.

85. A summary of this controversy is included in James B. Crowley's *Japan's Quest for Autonomy*, pp. 80–81.

CHAPTER FIVE   *Toward Totalistic Reform*

1. "Nagai Ryūtarō" hensankai, *Nagai Ryūtarō*, pp. 274–78.

2. Nagai Ryūtarō, "Roshia haken'in o okuru." Since the early 1920s Nagai had maintained a rather open attitude to developments in Russia, as is indicated in his correspondence of June 8, 1923, to Gotō Shimpei ("Gotō Shimpei monjo"); and also in his essay, "Ro-Doku o shite," esp. p. 84. As a party the Kenseikai had supported Japanese recognition of the Soviet Union.

3. *Rikken Minseitō shi* 2:872.

4. Crowley, "Japan's Military Foreign Policies," p. 54.

5. "Nagai Ryūtarō" hensankai, *Nagai Ryūtarō*, pp. 293–94.

6. For the coalition cabinet problem, see *Rikken Minseitō shi* 2:893–907; Adachi, *Adachi Kenzō jijoden*, pp. 262–64; "Nagai Ryūtarō" hensankai, *Nagai Ryūtarō*, pp. 293–300; and Berger, *Parties Out of Power*, pp. 39–43. Berger's research has been of immeasurable help in working through this chapter.

7. Baba, "Nagai Ryūtarō ron," pp. 157–59.

8. Wakatsuki, *Kofūan kaikoroku*, pp. 388–89.

9. Yatsugi, *Shōwa dōran shishi* 1:80.

10. Nagai M., "Bikko to seiji," p. 60.

11. "Nagai Ryūtarō" hensankai, *Nagai Ryūtarō*, p. 229.

12. For Nakano's thoughts regarding Ōshio, see Tetsuo Najita, "Nakano Seigō and the Spirit of the Meiji Restoration in Twentieth-Century Japan," in Morley, *Dilemmas of Growth*, p. 390; for Nagai, see "Nagai Ryūtarō" hen-

sankai, *Nagai Ryūtarō*, p. 228. More recently, the novelist Mishima Yukio referred to Ōshio in a plea to postwar Japanese to revive the spirit of revolutionary commitment.

13. Nagai R., "Daisan tō," p. 115.

14. Berger, *Parties Out of Power*, p. 52.

15. Sasaki Takashi deals with the Seiyūkai's rationale for support in his "Kyokoku-itchi naikaku ki no seitō."

16. Consultations on the new cabinet makeup appear in Kido, *Kido Kōichi nikki* 1:165–66; Harada, *Saionji-kō to seikyoku* 2:295; and "Nagai Ryūtarō" hensankai, *Nagai Ryūtarō*, pp. 311–14.

17. Nagai R., "Kokkashugi taishutō no geki" (Appeal for a nationalist masses party), in his *Watakushi no shinnen to taiken*, pp. 281–91.

18. Baba, "Nagai Ryūtarō ron," p. 155.

19. Ibid., pp. 160–61.

20. Azuma, *Omitsusa*, pp. 101–102, 128.

21. "Nagai Ryūtarō" hensankai, *Nagai Ryūtarō*, pp. 319–23.

22. Azuma, *Omitsusa*, pp. 101–102. In addition to Nagai's troubles while colonization minister, Azuma tells of his unsuccessful experience as head of *Hokkoku Mainichi shimbun* in the mid-thirties.

23. Harada, *Saionji-kō to seikyoku* 2:318–19, 335; Baba, "Nagai Ryūtarō ron," pp. 156–57.

24. "Nagai Ryūtarō" hensankai, *Nagai Ryūtarō*, pp. 322–27. It was this same Viscount Mimurodo who, along with Barons Kikuchi Takeo and Inoue Kiyosumi, attacked the theory of Minobe Tatsukichi in the House of Peers a year later. Itō Takashi, "The Role of Right-Wing Organizations in Japan," trans. Shumpei Okamoto, in Borg and Okamoto, *Pearl Harbor as History*, p. 499.

25. "Nagai Ryūtarō" hensankai, *Nagai Ryūtarō*, pp. 327–30.

26. Nagai R., "Kokka hijōji ni chokumen shite."

27. "Nagai Ryūtarō" hensankai, *Nagai Ryūtarō*, pp. 333–34.

28. Ibid., p. 322.

29. Ibid., p. 352.

30. Harada, *Saionji-kō to seikyoku* 2:354, and 3:280.

31. Itō and Sasaki, "Suzuki Tei-ichi nikki—Shōwa 8 nen," p. 69; Itō and Sasaki, "Suzuki Tei-ichi nikki—Shōwa 9 nen," p. 72.

32. Harada, *Saionji-kō to seikyoku* 3:280.

33. Yatsugi, *Shōwa dōran shishi* 1:102, 261–62; Yatsugi Kazuo, interview with author, Tokyo, April 16, 1979.

34. Nagai's reasoning on the certainty of Asian conflict comes through clearly in a speech he delivered for the fiftieth anniversary of *Chūō kōron*, "Gaishū no hitori to shite" (As one of the masses), *Chūō kōron* 50, special anniversary issue (Nov. 1935): 356.

35. Nagai R., "Seitō saiken no aki."

36. Nagai R., "Gikai shukusei yori mitaru."

37. David Titus suggests that the prewar Japanese government existed

"not in order to legislate but in order to govern." The power to govern was lodged in the executive, and the competition over that office was fierce. One result was that between 1885 and 1945 there were forty-three cabinets (or one every 1.4 years) (*Palace and Politics,* p. 315).

38. Nagai R., "Ni/ni-roku jiken igo" (After the 2/26 Incident), reprinted in his *Watakushi no shinnen to taiken,* pp. 266–75.

39. Hayashi et al., *Ni/ni-roku jiken hiroku* 1:282, 361, and 2:3; Yatsugi, interview with author.

40. Nagai R., "Ni/ni-roku jiken igo," p. 266; see also, for example, Matsumoto S., "Seian jiken no chūkan hōkoku," p. 91.

41. Nagai R., "Ni/ni-roku jiken igo," pp. 274–75; Tokyo Nichinichi shimbunsha and Osaka Mainichi shimbunsha, *Meiji, Taishō, Shōwa gikai seiji rimen shi,* p. 98.

42. Harada, *Saionji-kō to seikyoku* 5:210; Arima Y., *Seikai dōchūki,* pp. 117–19. Itō Takashi, "Shōwa jūsan-nen Konoe shintō mondai kenkyū oboegaki" (Research notes on the Konoe new party issue of 1938), Nihon seiji gakkai, *Nempō seijigaku, 1972: "Konoe shintaisei,"* pp. 138–39.

43. Yatsugi, *Shōwa dōran shishi* 1:193; "Nagai Ryūtarō" hensankai, *Nagai Ryūtarō,* pp. 350–51.

44. Matsumura, *Machida Chūji-ō den,* p. 333; Harada, *Saionji-kō to seikyoku* 5:251; "Nagai Ryūtarō" hensankai, *Nagai Ryūtarō,* pp. 354–55.

45. Letter and newspaper draft from Nagai Ryūtarō to Ichikawa Kiyoshi, Feb. 4, 1937, in author's possession.

46. "Nagai Ryūtarō" hensankai, *Nagai Ryūtarō,* p. 357. A comparison of the two men (including a negative evaluation of Nagai) appears in Kanechika, *Konoe naikaku no shimei,* pp. 96–99.

47. Matsumura, *Machida Chūji-ō den,* pp. 342–43.

48. Harada, *Saionji-kō to seikyoku* 6:3; Kido, *Kido Kōichi nikki* 1:567–68.

49. Yatsugi Kazuo expressed the view that Nagai originally was not enthused about such nationalization, being basically opposed to a controlled economy, but that his ideas began to change around 1936–1937 because of Western "bloc economics" (Interview with author).

50. Berger, *Parties Out of Power,* p. 123.

51. "Nagai Ryūtarō" hensankai, *Nagai Ryūtarō,* p. 362, also 362–425 for an overview of the entire problem.

52. Ibid., pp. 370, 374–75; Yabe Teiji, *Konoe Fumimaro* 1:480–82.

53. Yatsugi, *Shōwa dōran shishi* 1:300. Nagai wrote that while in office, he had received assistance on several matters from the Kokusaku kenkyūkai ("Taikan ni atatte").

54. "Nagai Ryūtarō" hensankai, *Nagai Ryūtarō,* pp. 409–410, 380.

55. An example of the opposition's stand is found in Kojima Naoki's "Makaritōru," a serial concerning Matsunaga Yasuzaemon.

56. Harada, *Saionji-kō to seikyoku* 6:263–64.

57. "Nagai Ryūtarō" hensankai, *Nagai Ryūtarō,* pp. 416–17; Berger, *Parties Out of Power,* p. 338.

58. "Nagai Ryūtarō" hensankai, *Nagai Ryūtarō*, p. 385; Yatsugi, interview with author.

59. Pierson, *Tokutomi Sohō*, p. 243.

60. Duus and Okimoto, "Fascism and Pre-War Japan," p. 72.

61. Nagai R., *Watakushi no shinnen to taiken*, pp. 288–91.

62. Ward, "Party Government in Japan," p. iv.

63. Nagai R., "Sensō o kataru" (Talking of war), in his *Watakushi no shinnen to taiken*, pp. 337–38.

64. Berger, *Parties Out of Power*, p. 196. As Berger also points out, "The invitations to Nagai and Nakajima to attend . . . indicated that mobilization and reform could not be carried out by excluding the political parties and their supporters from the formulation and execution of domestic policies" (p. 225).

65. Nagai R., "Rūzuberuto daitōryō ni tou" (see chap. 4, n. 83).

66. Despite this escalating emphasis on blocs, I agree with Mikuriya Takashi that Nagai did not equate blocs with war. Rather, it was that the world was moving in the direction of bloc patterns, and it was necessary that Japan join with Manchuria and China to keep up with this trend (see Mikuriya, "Nagai Ryūtarō," pp. 20–21).

67. Yatsugi, *Shōwa dōran shishi* 2:4–13.

68. Ibid., 86. Nakano Yasuo notes that the cabinet combination of three from the same locality—Abe, Godō Takuo, who held the joint posts of Commerce-Industry and Agriculture-Forestry, and Nagai with his two posts—was seen as reflecting clan government with a military mentality (*Seijika Nakano Seigō* 2:420).

CHAPTER SIX   *The Reformist Wave Crests*

1. Shigemitsu, *Japan and Her Destiny*, p. 180.

2. See reminiscences of Yatsugi Kazuo (who was involved in the cabinet's set-up), in Nakamura, Itō, and Hara, *Gendai shi o tsukuru hitobito* 4:112. Also, Yatsugi Kazuo, interview with author, Tokyo, April 16, 1979.

3. Matsumura, *Machida Chūji-ō den*, p. 349; "Nagai Ryūtarō" hensankai, *Nagai Ryūtarō*, pp. 428–29.

4. Yatsugi, *Shōwa dōran shishi* 2:84–126 passim; Yatsugi, interview with author.

5. Berger, *Parties Out of Power*, p. 222.

6. Harada, *Saionji-kō to seikyoku* 8:63.

7. Itō Takashi, "The Role of Right-Wing Organizations in Japan," trans. Shumpei Okamoto, in Borg and Okamoto, *Pearl Harbor as History*, pp. 507–508.

8. Nagai R., "Rūzuberuto daitōryō ni tou," in his *Sekai o senku suru Nihon*, pp. 71–73.

9. Harada, *Saionji-kō to seikyoku* 8:68.

10. Ibid., 81.

11. Coox, *Anatomy of a Small War.*

12. Harada, *Saionji-kō to seikyoku* 8:75.

13. Berger, *Parties Out of Power,* p. 222.

14. Adachi, *Adachi Kenzō jijoden,* pp. 198–99.

15. Berger, *Parties Out of Power,* p. 253.

16. Arima Y., *Seikai dōchūki,* pp. 180–211; Kazami, *Konoe naikaku,* pp. 197–226; and Harada, *Saionji-kō to seikyoku* 8:256–72.

17. Kazami, *Konoe naikaku,* pp. 201–202.

18. "Nagai Ryūtarō" hensankai, *Nagai Ryūtarō,* pp. 459–63; Duus, "Nagai Ryūtarō: Tactical Dilemmas," p. 420–21; and Nagai's 1941 speech, "Shin seiji taisei no tōgōsei to sono taishūsei" (The unity and popular nature of the New Political Order), in his *Nagai Ryūtarō shi kō-A yūbenshū,* pp. 301–336.

19. Yatsugi Kazuo stressed this point in our conversation on April 16, 1979. Also "Nagai Ryūtarō" hensankai, *Nagai Ryūtarō,* p. 458; Berger, *Parties Out of Power,* p. 250; and Kido, *Kido Kōichi nikki* 2:778, entry of March 30, 1940, wherein appears mention of Nagai's connection with Kaya Okinori, an official who had ties with the army.

20. Baba, *Konoe naikaku shiron,* pp. 67–68.

21. "Nagai Ryūtarō" hensankai, *Nagai Ryūtarō,* pp. 451–53, though dealing with Nagai's activities in August 1940, presents a clear idea of his general thinking at this time.

22. Harada, *Saionji-kō to seikyoku* 8:256, 259, 261.

23. Matsumura, *Machida Chūji-ō den,* pp. 372–73; Yabe, *Konoe Fumimaro* 2:83; "Nagai Ryūtarō" hensankai, *Nagai Ryūtarō,* pp. 443–45.

24. Matsumura, *Machida Chūji-ō den,* pp. 372–73.

25. "Nagai Ryūtarō" hensankai, *Nagai Ryūtarō,* pp. 445–51; Yatsugi, *Shōwa dōran shishi* 2:307.

26. Correspondence of Nagai to Arima Yoriyasu, July 29, 1940; I am grateful to Mrs. Arima for making this correspondence available. One wonders about the intensity of outside pressures on Nagai in addition to his own self-imposed pressures.

27. Berger, *Parties Out of Power,* p. 257.

28. "Nagai Ryūtarō" hensankai, *Nagai Ryūtarō,* pp. 451–52; Yokusan undō shi kankōkai, *Yokusan kokumin undō shi* (hereafter abbreviated as *YKUS*), pp. 97–101, 110–111; and Yabe, *Konoe Fumimaro* 2:141.

29. Nagai R., "Seitō saiken no aki."

30. Yokusan undō shi kankōkai, *YKUS,* pp. 120, 122.

31. Ibid., pp. 130, 132.

32. Correspondence of Nagai to Arima, October 2, 1940.

33. Yokusan undō shi kankōkai, *YKUS,* p. 136. Correspondence of Kazami Akira to Arima, undated note suggesting the possibility of Nagai's becoming *sōmuchō* (general manager) should there be no one else to fill the position.

34. Tolischus, *Tokyo Record,* p. 83.

35. Berger, *Parties Out of Power,* p. 318. Also useful for understanding this problem is his analysis of the "political/public" distinction on pp. 176–84.

36. Nakamura Takafusa and Hara Akira, "Keizai shintaisei" (The new economic order), in Nihon seiji gakkai, *Nempō seijigaku, 1972: "Konoe shintaisei,"* pp. 71–133.

37. Yabe, *Konoe Fumimaro* 2:201.

38. Tolischus, *Tokyo Record,* p. 84; Kamei Kan'ichirō Papers.

39. An example would be the way in which prefectural governors became the heads of the prefectural branches.

40. Fairbank, Reischauer, and Craig, *East Asia,* p. 603.

41. Yokusan undō shi kankōkai, *YKUS,* p. 99.

42. Yatsugi, *Shōwa dōran shishi* 2:13.

43. Yabe, *Konoe Fumimaro* 2:156–58. Konoe commented later when recounting the incident that although politicians had a dark side, such show of emotion (by Nagai, Maeda Yonezō, Nakano Seigō, Kanemitsu Tsuneo, etc.) gave witness to a rather "pure" side in their makeup—especially when contrasted with the dispassionate, austere countenance of bureaucrats like Gotō Fumio under the same circumstances.

44. Nagai R., "Shin seiji taisei no tōgōsei to sono taishūsei," pp. 325–26.

45. Tolischus, *Tokyo Record,* pp. 247–49.

46. The second had resigned so that the prime minister could replace his foreign minister, Matsuoka Yōsuke. The third Konoe cabinet was set up on July 18.

47. "Nagai Ryūtarō" hensankai, *Nagai Ryūtarō,* pp. 479–80. Gaylord Kubota, in his "Arita Hachirō," has stressed the importance of a "China-centered foreign relations perspective framework" for Japanese (p. 8).

48. Drea, *1942 Japanese General Election,* p. 22, and pp. 25–90 passim.

49. Yokusan undō shi kankōkai, *YKUS,* pp. 453–57; "Nagai Ryūtarō" hensankai, *Nagai Ryūtarō,* pp. 474–75.

50. Nagai's activities in education during his last years are described in "Nagai Ryūtarō" hensankai, *Nagai Ryūtarō,* pp. 481–88. See also Nagai R., *Kō-A kyōiku no yōtei.*

51. Yokusan undō shi kankōkai, *YKUS,* pp. 408, 952.

52. Tsutsumi, *Taiheiyō no kakehashi,* p. 321.

53. Kido nikki kenkyūkai, *Kido Kōichi kankei monjo,* p. 612.

54. Yokusan undō shi kankōkai, *YKUS,* pp. 461–67; Ōki, *Ōki nikki,* pp. 59, 87, 103; "Nagai Ryūtarō" hensankai, *Nagai Ryūtarō,* p. 475.

55. "Nagai Ryūtarō" hensankai, *Nagai Ryūtarō,* pp. 490–94; Tsutsumi, *Taiheiyō no kakehashi,* pp. 328–29; Nagai T., *Isshō-kenmei ikimashō,* pp. 267–68; and conversations with Nagai family.

56. "Nagai Ryūtarō" hensankai, *Nagai Ryūtarō,* pp. 495–96; and Kido, *Kido Kōichi nikki* 2:1156.

57. *Shūgiin giji sokkiroku* 86, no. 2 (Dec. 28, 1944): 10–11.

58. Duus, "Nagai Ryūtarō and the 'White Peril,' " p. 42.

CHAPTER SEVEN   *Conclusion*

1. Katayama, interview with author, June 27, 1972.
2. Itō T., *Taishō ki 'kakushin' ha no seiritsu,* pp. 10–11, 299–300.
3. See discussion of Richard Hofstadter's ideas in Levine, "The Historian and the Culture Gap," p. 323.
4. Mikuriya, "Taishō demokurashii kara Shintaisei e," p. 49. Most commentators on Nagai emphasize that it was the English political system rather than the American presidential system that served as his Western model.
5. Najita, *Hara Kei,* p. 5. Ishida deals with the traditional tie between emperor and people in *Kindai Nihon seiji kōzō,* pp. 44–45.
6. Nagai R., *Zampan,* p. 196.
7. Peter Duus, "Ōyama Ikuo and the Search for Democracy," in Morley, *Dilemmas of Growth,* p. 445. For Ōyama's more liberal views during the days of Taishō democracy, see his "Shakai kaizō no kompon seishin" (The fundamental spirit of social reconstruction), in *Ōyama Ikuo zenshū* 4:128–38. This article first appeared in the journal *Warera* (We) in August 1919.
8. "Nagai Ryūtarō" hensankai, *Nagai Ryūtarō,* p. 44.
9. Azuma Shun'ei recorded that because of Nagai's love for drama, his son Michio had given serious consideration to having an author like Ozaki Shirō write a play about Ryūtarō's life as a memorial rather than the usual biography (*Omitsusa,* pp. 125–26).
10. A prime example would be the reformist Constitutional Young Men's party centering on Nagai and his causes, as reflected in the organ of that group, *Shinshimei* (inaugural issue, Oct. 1924).
11. Ideas discussed with Sakai Yukichi on November 9, 1973; also Sakai's "Dai-ichiji goken undō ni tsuite," esp. pp. 73–75.
12. Tetsuo Najita, "Some Reflections on Idealism in the Political Thought of Yoshino Sakuzō," in Silberman and Harootunian, *Japan in Crisis,* p. 47.
13. Maruyama, *Thought and Behavior,* p. 9.
14. Bellah, "Values and Social Change," pp. 32–52.

Select Bibliography

Works by Nagai Ryūtarō

Ajia saiken no gisen (Crusade for the rebuilding of Asia). Tokyo, 1937.

"Atarashiki 'ware' to atarashiki seiji" (A new "self" and new politics). *Shin Nippon* (New Japan) 7, no. 6 (June 1917): 9–12.

"Beikoku gakusha no Ajia imin haiseki ron o hyōsu" (A discussion of the exclusion argument of American scholars against Asian immigrants). *Waseda gakuhō* (Waseda school news), no. 147 (May 1907), pp. 12–21, no. 148 (June 1907), pp. 12–22.

"Bensei—seiji jihyō" (Crack of the whip!—editorial comment on politics). *Shin Nippon* 5, no. 5 (May 1915): 13–18.

"Bisumaruku ni kawatte, Kaizeru o azakeru bun" (Ridicule of the Kaiser instead of Bismarck). *Chūō kōron* (Central review) 29, no. 11 (Oct. 1914): 99–106.

"Chokugen—jiji hyōron" (Speaking frankly—a review of current events). *Shin Nippon* 6, no. 12 (Dec. 1916): 14–20; 7, no. 2 (Feb. 1917): 15–19; 7, no. 7 (July 1917): 13–17.

"Chōsen tōchi no kompon seisaku" (Fundamental policy for the rule of Korea). *Kensei* (Constitutional government) 6, no. 2 (Feb. 1923): 19–23.

"Chōshūjin no Nihon ka Nihonjin no Nihon ka" (A Japan of the people of Chōshū or a Japan of the Japanese?) *Shin Nippon* 7, no. 4 (Apr. 1917): 19–25.

"Daisan tō no muigi to yūigi" (The insignificance and significance of third parties). *Chūō kōron* 37, no. 6 (June 1922): 115–26.

"Daitōryō Rincorun ni kawatte, daitōryō Uirusun ni atau" (On behalf of President Lincoln, I present this to President Wilson). *Shin Nippon* 3, no. 5 (May 1913): 33–40.

"Doitsu no shōnin" (The merchants of Germany). *Shin Nippon* 1, no. 9 (Nov. 1911): 10–14.

"Ei-Bei no sekaiteki shidō to Nihon" (British-American international leadership and Japan). *Tōhō jiron* (Comments on Eastern affairs) 4, no. 8 (Aug. 1919): 74–79.

Eijin kishitsu omoide no ki (Recollections of the English people). Tokyo, 1910.

"Gikai seiji no shimei no tame ni" (For the fulfillment of parliamentary government). *Chūō kōron* 35, no. 9 (Aug. 1920): 53–57.

"Gikai shukusei yori mitaru dai ittō kyōsō" (Competition for first party from the standpoint of Diet regulation). *Chūgai shōgyō shimpō* (Domestic and foreign trade news), July 25–26, 1935.

Guraddosuton (Gladstone). Tokyo, 1922.

"Han-Amerikashugi no bō o haisu" (Defying the force of Pan-Americanism). *Tōhō jiron* 4, no. 10 (Oct. 1919): 53–60.

"Heiekizei okosubeshi" (The need for setting up a military service tax). *Shin Nippon* 2, no. 10 (Oct. 1912): 129–33.

"Hi-Monrōshugi ron" (The argument against Monroe-doctrinism). *Shin Nippon* 4, no. 7 (June 1914): 40–43.

"Hi-tenka taihei ron" (All's not right with the world!). *Shin Nippon* 2, no. 1 (Jan. 1912): 30–35.

"Iki'n ga tame no sensō yori iki'n ga tame no heiwa e" (From war to live to peace to live). *Chūō kōron* 37, no. 8 (July 1922): 115–27.

"Innai no gikai to ingai no gikai" (Deliberative assembly within the Diet and deliberative assembly outside the Diet). *Chūō kōron* 29, no. 4 (Apr. 1914): 122–26.

"Jisatsu zenin subeki ka hinin subeki ka—joron" (Should there be approval or disapproval of suicide?—an introduction). *Shin Nippon* 2, no. 11 (Nov. 1912): 78–81.

"Jōin tai minshū no mondai" (The problem of the upper house versus the people). *Kaizō* (Reconstruction), no. 12 (1923), pp. 167–71.

"Judōteki Nihon yori hatsudōteki Nihon e" (From a passive Japan to an active Japan). *Shin Nippon* 5, no. 11 (Nov. 1915): 150–56.

"Kaigai ijū wa yūeki-mugai ka mueki-yūgai ka mueki-mugai ka hatamata yūeki-yūgai ka" (Is foreign emigration profitable and harmless, futile and harmful, futile and harmless, or then again, profitable and harmful?). *Shin Nippon* 7, no. 9 (Sept. 1917): 13–18.

"Kaikyū seiji ka heimin seiji ka" (Class politics or democratic politics?). *Shin Nippon* 5, no. 3 (Mar. 1915): 71–74.

Kaizō no risō (The ideal of reconstruction). Tokyo, 1920.

"Kanryō seiji" (Bureaucratic government). *Shin Nippon* 2, no. 2 (Feb. 1912): 23–24.

"Katsura kō o toburau" (Mourning Marquis Katsura). *Shin Nippon* 3, no. 12 (Dec. 1913): 20–23.

"Keishichō no katsudō han'i o narubeku shōkyokuteki ni" (The necessity of a limited sphere of activity for the Metropolitan Police). *Chūō kōron* 38, no. 3 (Mar. 1923): 82–84.

Kō-A kyōiku no yōtei (The main principle of education for Asian development). Tokyo, 1944.

"Kōki shihai no shakaiteki shinriteki kōsatsu" (Social and psychological considerations concerning the relaxation of law and order). *Chūō kōron* 36, no. 7 (July 1921): 67–76.

"Kokka hijōji ni chokumen shite" (Confronting a national crisis). *Chūō kōron* 48, no. 1 (Jan. 1933): 44–47.

"Kokkashugi to kokusaishugi wa mujun sezu" (Nationalism and internationalism are not contradictory). *Chūō kōron* 36, no. 2 (Feb. 1921): 59–64.

"Kokumintō ni atau" (To the Kokumintō). *Shin Nippon* 2, no. 7 (July 1912): 15–18.

"Minseitō wa kokkashugi taishū tō" (The Minseitō is the party of the nationalist masses). *Chūō kōron* 43, no. 2 (Feb. 1928): 75–77.

"Minshū no yōkyū o taigen suru no michi wa tada seinen minshutō no sōzō aru nomi" (The creation of a young men's democratic party is the only way to embody the demands of the people). *Chūō kōron* 37, no. 13 (Dec. 1922): 65–75.

"Musan seitō no bunkai" (A disintegration of the proletarian parties). *Chūō kōron* 42, no. 11 (Nov. 1927): 84.

"Myōnichi no Manshū" (The Manchuria of tomorrow). *Shin Nippon* 1, no. 3 (June 1911): 9–14.

Nagai Ryūtarō shi daienzetsushū (The collected speeches of Nagai Ryūtarō). 2 vols. Tokyo, 1924–1930.

Nagai Ryūtarō shi kō-A yūbenshū (The collected speeches of Nagai Ryūtarō on the development of Asia). Tokyo, 1944.

"Naikaku shokō oyobi kishū ryōin giin ni ataete takushokumushō saikō no kyūmu o ronzu" (Speaking to the gentlemen of the cabinet and the members of both houses of the urgent business of reviving the Ministry of Colonial Affairs). *Chūō kōron* 31, no. 1 (Jan. 1916): 131–48.

"Nichi-Bei kyōshō ron" (Japanese-American agreement). *Shin Nippon* 1, no. 2 (May 1911): 9–16.

"Nisshi kyōdō—busōteki sangyō ron" (Japanese-Chinese cooperation—a discussion of the armaments industry). *Shin Nippon* 6, no. 7 (July 1916): 14–18; 6, no. 8 (Aug. 1916): 10–17.

"Nōsei no hon'i o aratamuru jidai—ōjinushi hon'i yori kosakunin hon'i e" (Era of revising the farm policy standard—from that of the large landowner to that of the tenant). *Chūō kōron* 36, no. 8 (July 1921): 81–90.

"Nyoze-gakan" (Thus I see). *Shin Nippon* 1, no. 5 (Aug. 1911): 12–16; 1, no. 7 (Oct. 1911): 30–32; 3, no. 1 (Jan. 1913): 9–17.

Ōkuma Shigenobu: Gikyoku (Ōkuma Shigenobu: A play). Tokyo, 1932.

"Ōshū no tairan o omou" (Thinking about the great disturbance in Europe). *Shin Nippon* 2, no. 12 (Dec. 1912): 32–41.

"Reigo netsugo" (Cold words, heated words). *Shin Nippon* 3, no. 2 (Feb. 1913): 26–30; 3, no. 3 (Mar. 1913): 23–26; 3, no. 4 (Apr. 1913): 36–38; 3, no. 6 (June 1913): 34–36; 4, no. 6 (May 1914): 62–65; 4, no. 7 (June 1914): 44–49 (including "Inukai Tsuyoshi kun ni atau" [To Inukai Tsuyoshi]); 4, no. 8 (July 1914): 53–60; 4, no. 9 (Aug. 1914): 50–56; 4, no. 10 (Sept. 1914): 36–40; 4, no. 12 (Oct. 1914): 44–49.

"Rōdō kumiai ron" (A discussion on labor unions). *Shin Nippon* 2, no. 5 (May 1912): 17–22.

"Ro-Doku o shite sono risō o jitsugen seshime yo" (Having Russia and Germany realize their ideal). *Chūō kōron* 37, no. 11 (Oct. 1922): 80–86.

"Rōdō sōgi no kaiketsu hōhō—1" (The means of resolving labor disputes—part 1). *Shin Nippon* 7, no. 11 (Nov. 1917): 31–38.

"Roshia haken'in o okuru" (Dispatching a representative to Russia). *Chūō kōron* 46, no. 4 (Apr. 1931): 378.

"Sawayanagi, Katō ryōhakushi no kokutei kyōkasho ron o yomu" (On reading the arguments of Drs. Sawayanagi and Katō on state textbooks). *Shin Nippon* 5, no. 1 (Jan. 1915): 37–39.

"Seitō saiken no aki" (Autumn of the rebuilding of the parties). *Hokkoku shimbun* (Hokkoku news), Jan. 1, 1935.

"Seiyūkai ni atau" (To the Seiyūkai). *Shin Nippon* 2, no. 10 (Oct. 1912): 124–28.

"Sekai no hammon" (The anguish of the world). *Shin Nippon* 1, no. 1 (Apr. 1911): 8–13.

"Sekai no ni-daiseiryoku yori obiyakasaruru Nihon" (Japan, threatened by two world trends). *Chūō kōron* 34, no. 9 (Aug. 1919): 40–46.

Sekai o senku suru Nihon (Japan taking the lead in the world).1942. Reprint. Tokyo, 1943.

Sekai seisaku jikkō (Diplomatic policy: Ten lectures). Tokyo, 1925.

"Senkyoken kakuchō ron" (Discussion on extending the suffrage). *Shin Nippon* 3, no. 3 (Mar. 1913): 19–22.

"Shakai kyōson no rinri to rinji gikai" (The moral of social coexistence and the special Diet). *Kaizō*, no. 8 (1920), pp. 73–77.

"Shakai mondai" (Social problems). *Waseda gakuhō*, no. 196 (June 1911), p. 508.

"Shakaishugi no Beikoku ni furuwazaru yuen o ronjite Nihon seifu no imin seisaku ni oyobu" (A discussion of the reasons for socialism's failure to flourish in America, and the emigration policy of the Japanese government). *Shin Nippon* 2, no. 4 (Apr. 1912): 85–89.

"Shakaiteki jiyū o ronzu" (On social freedom). *Waseda gakuhō*, no. 153 (Oct. 1907), pp. 40–45; no. 154 (Dec. 1907), pp. 45–51.

"Shidehara gaikō no honryō" (Characteristics of Shidehara diplomacy). *Chūō kōron* 42, no. 3 (Mar. 1927): 91–95.

Shikisha no mitaru futsū senkyo (Intellectuals look at universal suffrage). Tokyo, 1921. (Nagai, ed.)

"Shina taikan" (A general view of China). Parts 1–5. *Shin Nippon* 6, nos. 1–5 (Jan.–May 1916): 18–30, 15–22, 12–17, 16–22, 15–20.

"*Shin Nippon* no geki" (The manifesto of *Shin Nippon*). *Shin Nippon* 5, no. 2 (Feb. 1915): 19–25.

"Shisō-jō no jūjiro ni samayoeru Beikoku—sekai bummei no shidōsha ka ikakusha ka" (America, wavering intellectually at the crossroads—a leader of or threat to world civilization?). *Chūō kōron* 34, no. 10 (Sept. 1919): 89–100.

Shokumin seisaku (Colonization policy). Tokyo, 1916.

"Shokumin seisaku no kompon hōshin o ronjite Man-Sen tōitsu ni oyobu" (Discussing the basic line of colonization policy—including the consolidation of Manchuria and Korea). *Chūō kōron* 32, no. 10 (Sept. 1917): 128–38.

"Shokumin shisō no kakumei ki" (Revolutionary period in ideas of colonization). *Chūō kōron* 38, no. 1 (Jan. 1923): 106–119.

"Shushō oyobi naishō ni ataete shokumin kyōiku kikan setsuritsu no kyūmu o ronzu" (Speaking to the prime minister and home minister of the urgent business of establishing an agency for education on colonization). *Shin Nippon* 7, no. 3 (Mar. 1917): 18–22.

"Taikan ni atatte" (Retiring from office). *Shin kokusaku* (New national policy) 3, no. 2 (Jan. 25, 1939): 12.

"Tai-Shi gaikō no kompon hōshin (The basic policy of diplomacy toward China). Parts 1, 2. *Shin Nippon* 4, nos. 1, 2 (Jan., Feb. 1914): 49–53, 53–57.

"Tai-Shi gaikō no shippai doko ni ari ya" (Where is the blunder in foreign policy toward China!). *Shin Nippon* 5, no. 6 (June 1915): 69–76.

"Taishō ishin no jitsu o age yo" (Let's bring about the Taishō Restoration). *Chūō kōron* 28, no. 3 (Mar. 1913): 23–27.

"Taishō ishin o dankō se yo" (Let's carry out the Taishō Restoration). *Kensei* 5, no. 5 (Aug. 1922): 19–32.

"Taishū no hitori to shite" (As one of the masses). *Chūō kōron* 50, special anniversary issue (Nov. 1935): 347–56.

"Tanaka tai-Shi gaikō hihan—onozukara anadoru nakare" (Criticism of Tanaka diplomacy toward China—it should not merely be taken lightly). *Chūō kōron* 43, no. 9 (Sept. 1928): 53–57.

"Tenka no guron" (The most foolish views in the empire). Parts 1, 2. *Shin Nippon* 1, nos. 5, 6 (Aug., Sept. 1911): 9–12, 17–21.

"Tenka sambun ron" (The three sections of the realm). *Shin Nippon* 3, no. 7 (July 1913): 25–31.

"Tokutomi Soho shi no 'Jimu ikkagen' o yomu" (On reading Tokutomi Sohō's "Personal view of current affairs"), part 1, and "Sohō-sensei no 'Jimu ikkagen' o yomu" (On reading Sohō-sensei's "Personal view of current affairs"), parts 2, 3. *Shin Nippon* 4, nos. 2–4 (Feb.–Apr. 1914): 58–59, 68–71, 60–62.

"Tō-Ō no fūun—rekkyō no keikai" (The state of affairs in East Europe—a warning for the great powers). *Shin Nippon* 2, no. 11 (Nov. 1912): 17–29.

"Tōtaku kaisha no kaiaku" (Deterioration of the Oriental Development Company). *Shin Nippon* 2, no. 4 (Apr. 1912): 90–91.

"Tōyō takushoku kaisha bokumetsu ron" (Eradication of the Oriental Development Company). *Shin Nippon* 3, no. 8 (Aug., 1913): 24–31; 3, no. 9 (Sept. 1913): 18–25; 3, no. 10 (Oct. 1913): 24–29; 3, no. 12 (Nov. 1913): 12–19; 3, no. 13 (Dec. 1913): 22–29.

"Tsuyoku tadashiku akaruki Nihon no kensetsu" (The building of a strong, just, clean Japan). *Watakushi wa ikite iru* (I am alive). Nippon Columbia Co., Tokyo, 1960. Sound recording.

Uiruson kara Mussorīni made—Kōenshū (From Wilson to Mussolini—a collection of lectures). Osaka, 1927.
"Uttauru atawazaru mono ni kawarite uttau" (In place of those who have no recourse, I appeal). *Shin Nippon* 2, no. 8 (Aug. 1912): 18–25; 5, no. 6 (June 1915): 24–28; 5, no. 7 (July 1915): 18–22.
" 'Uttauru atawazaru mono ni kawarite uttau' no rombun o chūshi suru ni tsukite" (Regarding discontinuing the 'Uttauru' essay). *Shin Nippon* 5, no. 8 (Aug. 1915): 22.
Watakushi no shinnen to taiken (My beliefs and experiences). Tokyo, 1938.
Yasei (Voice of the opposition). Tokyo, 1916.
"Yo no fujin kan" (My views on women). *Fujin mondai kōenshū* (Collection of speeches on the woman problem). Tokyo, 1920.
Zampan (Leftovers). Tokyo, 1914.
Zeniya Gohee: Gikyoku (Zeniya Gohee: A play). Tokyo, 1939.

Primary Unpublished Documents

"Gotō Shimpei monjo" (Gotō Shimpei documents). National Diet Library, Tokyo.
Ishikawa Hanzan. Papers. University of Tokyo, Faculty of Law.
Kamei Kan'ichirō. Papers.
SCAP Files of the Government Section. Biographical File of Kodama Yoshio. Case file 194. National Archives, Washington, D.C.
"Terauchi Masatake kankei monjo" (Documents related to Terauchi Masatake). National Diet Library, Tokyo.

Sources in Japanese

Adachi Kenzō. *Adachi Kenzō jijoden* (The autobiography of Adachi Kenzō). Edited by Izu Tomihito. Tokyo, 1960.
Akegarasu Haya. *Akegarasu Haya zenshū* (The complete works of Akegarasu Haya). Mattō-shi, Ishikawa, 1954.
Arima Manabu. "Takabatake Motoyuki to kokka shakaishugi ha no tenkai —Taishō chūki shakai undō no ichimen" (Takabatake Motoyuki and the movement of the state socialism group—one phase of the socialist movement in mid-Taishō). *Shigaku zasshi* (Historical studies) 83, no. 10 (Oct. 20, 1974): 1–28.
Arima Manabu and Itō Takashi. Review of recent works on Taishō. *Shigaku zasshi* 84, no. 3 (Mar. 1975): 60–72.
Arima Yoriyasu. *Seikai dōchūki* (A traveler's journal of the political world). Tokyo, 1951.
———. *Yūjin Konoe* (My friend Konoe). Tokyo, 1948.
Asahi jānaru (Asahi journal), ed. *Shōwa shi no shunkan* (Moments in Shōwa history). Vol. 1. Tokyo, 1974.
Asano Saigawa. "Kanazawa seisen no tsuioku" (Reminiscences of the

Kanazawa political campaign). *Shin Nippon* 7, no. 6 (June 1917): 72-77.

Asukai Masamichi. "Taishō demokurashii to wareware" (Taishō democracy and us). *Asahi shimbun* (Asahi news), Feb. 17, 1975, p. 11.

Azuma Shun'ei. *Omitsusa* (These three things). Tokyo, 1968.

Baba Tsunego. *Gikai seiji ron* (On parliamentary politics). Tokyo, 1933.

———. *Konoe naikaku shiron—sensō kaishi no shinsō* (A historical essay on the Konoe cabinets—the truth on the beginning of the war). Tokyo, 1946.

———. "Nagai Ryūtarō ron" (Nagai Ryūtarō). *Chūō kōron* 47, no. 11 (Nov. 1932): 153-61.

———. *Seikai jimbutsu fūkei* (Views on figures in the political world). Tokyo, 1931.

Chūgai shōgyō shimpo henshūkyoku (Domestic and foreign trade news editorial office), ed. *Seijika gunzō* (A group of politicians). Tokyo, 1932.

Edgerton, H. E. *Eikoku shokumin hatten shi* (Origin and growth of the English colonies). Translated by Nagai Ryūtarō. Tokyo, 1909.

Eguchi Keiichi, chmn. *Taishō demokurashii* (Taishō democracy). Shimposiumu—Nihon rekishi, 20 (Symposium on Japanese history series, no. 20). Tokyo, 1969.

Enomoto hōreikan henshūbu (Enomoto regulations office), ed. *Kare wa ika ni shite konnichi no chii o eta ka* (How did he come to attain the position he holds today?). Tokyo, 1928.

Fujimura Michio. "Taishō ki no kyōka o megutte" (Concerning valuations of the Taishō period). *Rekishi to jimbutsu* (History and personalities), Sept. 1974, pp. 177-83.

Fujiwara Akira et al. *Kindai Nihon shi no kiso chishiki* (Basic knowledge concerning modern Japanese history). Tokyo, 1972.

Fukuzawa Yukichi zenshū (The complete works of Fukuzawa Yukichi). 2d ed. 21 vols. Tokyo, 1969-1971.

Harada Kumao. *Saionji-kō to seikyoku* (Prince Saionji and the political situation). 9 vols. Tokyo, 1950-1956.

Hara Keiichirō, ed. *Hara Kei nikki* (The diary of Hara Kei). 9 vols. Tokyo, 1950.

Hatoyama Ichirō. *Watakushi no jijoden* (My autobiography). Tokyo, 1951.

Hayashi Shigeru et al. *Ni/ni-roku jiken hiroku* (Secret documents of the 2/26 Incident). 4 vols. Tokyo, 1971-1972.

Heimin shimbun (Commoners' news), 1903-1905. Tokyo.

Hirano Yoshitarō. *Nakamura Tahachirō den* (The biography of Nakamura Tahachirō). Tokyo, 1938.

Hōchi shimbun (Hōchi news), 1917-1920. Tokyo.

Hokkoku shimbunsha henshūkyoku (Hokkoku news editorial office). *Fūsetsu no hi—gendai shi o kizanda Ishikawa kenjin-tachi* (A monument of the storm—people of Ishikawa Prefecture who have carved out modern history). Kanazawa, 1968.

Horibe Kyūtarō, ed. *Ōkuma Kumako fujin genkoroku* (Memoirs of Ōkuma Kumako). Tokyo, 1933.

Ichijima Kenkichi, ed. *Ōkuma kō hachijūgo-nen shi* (Eighty-five-year history of Marquis Ōkuma). 3 vols. Tokyo, 1926.

Imai Seiichi. *Taishō demokurashii* (Taishō democracy). Nihon no rekishi, 23 (Japanese history series, no. 23). Tokyo, 1966.

Imai Seiichi and Itō Takashi, eds. *Gendai shi shiryō* 44, *Kokka sōdōin* 2 (Modern history resources 44, National mobilization 2). Tokyo, 1974.

Inoue Kiyoshi, ed. *Taishō ki no seiji to shakai* (Politics and society in the Taishō period). Tokyo, 1969.

Inoue Kiyoshi and Watanabe Tōru, eds. *Taishō ki no kyūshinteki jiyūshugi—Tōyō keizai shimpō o chūshin to shite* (Radical liberalism of the Taishō period—Centering on the *Tōyō keizai shimpō*). Tokyo, 1972.

Ishida Takeshi. *Kindai Nihon seiji kōzō no kenkyū* (A study of the political structure of modern Japan). Tokyo, 1956.

Ishikawa kenchō (Ishikawa prefectural office), ed. *Ishikawa ken shi: Gendai hen* (History of Ishikawa Prefecture: Modern period). Vol. 1. Kanazawa, 1962.

Ishikawa Sanshirō. *Jijoden* (Autobiography). 2 vols. Tokyo, 1956.

Itō Kinjirō. *Washi ga kuni sa* (My country!). Tokyo, 1926.

Itō Masanori, ed. *Katō Takaaki*. 2 vols. 1929. Reprint. Tokyo, 1970.

Itō Takashi. "Nihon 'kakushin' ha no seiritsu" (The formation of the Japanese "reformists"). *Rekishi to jimbutsu*, Dec. 1972, pp. 28–53.

———. *Shōwa jū nendai shi danshō* (Literary fragments of Shōwa history, 1935–1945). Tokyo, 1981.

———. "Shōwa seiji shi kenkyū e no ichi shikaku" (One view on the research of Shōwa political history). *Shisō* (Thought), no. 624 (June 1976), pp. 215–28.

———. *Shōwa shoki seiji shi kenkyū* (Research into the political history of the early Shōwa period). Tokyo, 1969.

———. *Taishō ki 'kakushin' ha no seiritsu* (The formation of the "reformists" of the Taishō era). Tokyo, 1978.

——— et al. *Kataritsugu Shōwa shi—gekido no hanseiki* (Shōwa history handed down—a half century of upheaval). Vol. 1. Tokyo, 1975.

Itō Takashi and Sasaki Takashi. "Suzuki Tei-ichi nikki, Shōwa 8 nen" (The diary of Suzuki Tei-ichi, 1933). *Shigaku zasshi* 87, no. 1 (Jan. 1978: 68–95.

———. "Suzuki Tei-ichi nikki, Shōwa 9 nen" (The diary of Suzuki Tei-ichi, 1934). *Shigaku zasshi* 87, no. 4 (Apr. 1978): 57–82.

Iwasaki Yoshikatsu. "Sempai onshi no hen'ei" (A glimpse of respected teachers). *Yanagi* (Willow) 7, no. 12 (Aug. 1961): 1; 9, no. 2 (Feb. 1963): 1.

Kanechika Yasushi. *Konoe naikaku no shimei* (Mission of the Konoe cabinet). Tokyo, 1937.

Kano Masanao. *Taishō demokurashii no teiryū* (The undercurrents of Taishō democracy). Tokyo, 1973.

Katō Nihei. *Wakon kansai setsu* (Japanese ethics and Chinese knowledge). Tokyo, 1926.

Katō Shisen. *Shin daigishi meikan* (Directory of new members of the House of Representatives). Tokyo, 1924.

Katō Takaaki den kankōkai (Publication society for the biography of Katō Takaaki), ed. *Katō Takaaki den* (The biography of Katō Takaaki). Tokyo, 1928.

Kawasaki Hideji. *Waseda no seijika-tachi* (Politicians of Waseda). Tokyo, 1975.

Kazami Akira. *Konoe naikaku* (The Konoe cabinets). Tokyo, 1951.

Kensei (Constitutional government), 1918–1925. Tokyo.

Kensei kōron (Constitutional government review), 1924–1932. Tokyo.

Kido Kōichi. *Kido Kōichi nikki* (The diary of Kido Kōichi). 2 vols. Tokyo, 1966.

Kido nikki kenkyūkai (Research association for the Kido diary), ed. *Kido Kōichi kankei monjo* (Documents relating to Kido Kōichi). Tokyo, 1966.

Kimbara Samon. *Taishō demokurashii no shakaiteki keisei* (The social structure of Taishō democracy). Tokyo, 1967.

————. "Taishō demokurashii to gendai mimshushugi" (Taishō democracy and contemporary democracy). *Kagaku to shisō* (Science and thought), no. 13 (July 1974), pp. 19–29.

————. *Taishō ki no seitō to kokumin* (Political parties and the people during the Taishō period). Tokyo, 1973.

Kisaka Jun'ichirō. "Taishō ki mimponshugisha no kokusai ninshiki" (The Taishō democrats' understanding of international politics). *Kokusai seiji* (International relations), no. 51 (Jan. 1974), pp. 59–86.

Kisaki Masaru. *Kisaki nikki—Takita Choin to sono jidai* (Kisaki diary—Takita Choin and his times). Tokyo, 1965.

Kiyosawa Kiyoshi. *Ankoku nikki* (Diary of darkness). 3 vols. Tokyo, 1975.

Kobayashi Akio. "Taishō ki ni okeru shimin seisha no dōkō—Ishikawa ken Rikken seinentō ni tsuite" (Trends in citizens' political associations of the Taishō era—with reference to the Ishikawa Constitutional Young Men's party). Master's thesis, Kanazawa University, 1974.

Koizumi Matajirō. *Fusen undō hishi* (A secret history of the universal suffrage movement). Tokyo, 1928.

Kojima Naoki. "Makaritōru" (Pushing through!). *Sandee Mainichi* (Sunday Mainichi). Apr. 29, 1973, pp. 84–85.

Kokumin shimbun (Kokumin news), 1917–1920. Tokyo.

Kokusaku kenkyūkai (National policy research association). *Shōwa jūyonen-do jigyō jimu oyobi kaikei hōkoku* (Work, operations, and financial reports for 1939). Tokyo, 1940.

Komaki Ōmi. *Tanemaku hitobito* (Sowers). Kamakura, 1978.

Kondō Masao. *Katō Takaaki*. Tokyo, 1959.

Makino Ryōzō kankōkai (Makino Ryōzō publication society), ed. *Makino Ryōzō*. Tokyo, 1962.

Masumi Junnosuke. *Nihon seitō shi ron* (A history of Japanese political parties). 7 vols. Tokyo, 1965–1980.

Matsumoto Shigeharu. "Seian jihen no chūkan hōkoku" (Interim report on the Sian Incident). *Kaizō* 19, no. 2 (Feb. 1937): 76–92.

———. *Shanghai jidai—jānarisuto no kaizō* (The Shanghai era—recollections of a journalist). 3 vols. Tokyo, 1974–1975.

Matsumura Kenzō. *Machida Chūji-ō den* (Machida Chūji). Tokyo, 1950.

———. *Sandai kaikoroku* (Reminiscences of three eras). Tokyo, 1964.

Matsuo Takayoshi. *Chōsen ron—Yoshino Sakuzō* (Views on Korea—Yoshino Sakuzō). Tokyo, 1970.

———. "Natsume Sōseki to denshachin neage hantai undō" (Natsume Sōseki and the opposition movement to the rise in streetcar fares). *Tosho* (Books), no. 27 (May 1974), pp. 41–45.

———. *Taishō demokurashii* (Taishō democracy). Tokyo, 1974.

———. *Taishō demokurashii no kenkyū* (Research on Taishō democracy). Tokyo, 1966.

Mikuriya Takashi. "Nagai Ryūtarō—1920 nendai to 1930 nendai" (Nagai Ryūtarō—the twenties and thirties). Seminar paper. University of Tokyo, 1973.

———. "Taishō demokurashii kara Shintaisei e—Nagai Ryūtarō to Nakano Seigō" (From Taishō democracy to the New Political Order—Nagai Ryūtarō and Nakano Seigō). Assistant's thesis. University of Tokyo, Faculty of Law, 1974.

Mitani Taichirō. *Nihon seitō seiji no keisei: Hara Kei no seiji shidō no tenkai* (The formation of party politics in Japan: The development of the political leadership of Hara Kei). Tokyo, 1967.

———. *Taishō demokurashii ron* (Taishō democracy). Tokyo, 1974.

———, ed. *Yoshino Sakuzō ronshū* (A collection of essays of Yoshino Sakuzō). Tokyo, 1975.

Mitsukawa Kametarō. "Rōsōkai no ki" (Account of the Rōsōkai). Parts 1, 2. *Dai Nippon* (Great Japan), April, June 1919, pp. 102–103, 99.

———. *Sangoku kanshō igo* (After the Triple Intervention). 1935. Reprint. Tokyo, 1977.

———. *Ubawareteru Ajia* (Plundered Asia). Tokyo, 1921.

Miwa Kimitada. *Kyōdōtai ishiki no dochakusei* (Nativism in the idea of a cooperative body). Tokyo, 1978.

Miyaji Masato. *Nichi-Ro sengo seiji shi no kenkyū* (A study of political history after the Russo-Japanese War). Tokyo, 1973.

Miyamoto Matahisa. "Mimponshugisha to shite Nagai Ryūtarō—Sōdaikyōju jidai" (The democrat Nagai Ryūtarō, while a professor at Waseda). Okayama daigaku kyōyōbu (Liberal arts faculty of Okayama University), *Kiyō* (Annals), no. 2 (Mar. 31, 1966), pp. 1–23.

Miyatake Gaikotsu. *Meiji enzetsu shi* (A history of Meiji oratory). Tokyo, 1926.

Nagai Michio. "Bikko to seiji" (Lameness and politics). *Asahi jānaru*, Feb. 9, 1964, pp. 59–61.

———. *Ishoku no ningen zō* (Novel personalities). Tokyo, 1965.

"Nagai Ryūtarō" hensankai ("Nagai Ryūtarō" editing society), Matsumura Kenzō, ed. *Nagai Ryūtarō*. Tokyo, 1959.

Nagai Tsuguyo. *Isshō-kenmei ikimashō* (Let's live to the fullest!). Edited by Nagai Michio. Tokyo, 1982.

Nagaoka Shinjirō. "Katō Takaaki ron" (Katō Takaaki). *Kokusai seiji,* no. 1 (1966), pp. 27–40.

Nagashima Ryūji. *Seikai hiwa* (Secret tales of the political world). Tokyo, 1928.

Nakamura Takafusa, Itō Takashi, and Hara Akira, eds. *Gendai shi o tsukuru hitobito* (People who have made modern history). 4 vols. Tokyo, 1971–1972.

Nakanishi Keijirō. *Waseda daigaku hachijū-nen shi* (Eighty-year history of Waseda University). Tokyo, 1962.

Nakano Seigō. "Kaizō dōmei ron" (The Kaizō dōmei). *Tōhō jiron* 4, no. 9 (Sept. 1919): 7–15.

Nakano Yasuo. *Seijika Nakano Seigō* (The politician Nakano Seigō). 2 vols. Tokyo, 1971.

Nihon kokusai seiji gakkai—Taiheiyō sensō gen'in kenkyū-bu (Japanese association of international relations—Research division on the causes of the Pacific War), ed. *Taiheiyō sensō e no michi* (The road to the Pacific War). 8 vols. Tokyo, 1962–1963.

Nihon seiji gakkai (The Japanese political science association), ed. *Nempō seijigaku, 1972: Konoe Shintaisei no kenkyū* (Political Science annual bulletin, 1972: Studies on Prince Konoe's New Order). Tokyo, 1972.

Nozaki Masasuke. *Wakatsuki dainaikaku* (The great Wakatsuki cabinet). Tokyo, 1931.

Oka Yoshitake. *Konoe Fumimaro.* Tokyo, 1972.

———. *Tenkanki no Taishō* (Taishō, a turning point). Nihon kindai shi taikei, 5 (Outline of modern Japanese history series, no. 5). Tokyo, 1969.

Ōki Misao. *Ōki nikki—shūsenji no Teikoku gikai* (The Ōki diary—the Imperial Diet at the end of the war). Tokyo, 1969.

Ōkuma Shigenobu. *Ōkuma haku shakai gan* (Count Ōkuma's social views). Tokyo, 1910.

———. "Shin Nippon ron" (New Japan). *Shin Nippon* 1, no. 1 (Apr. 1911): 1–7.

———. "Tōzai no bummei" (The civilization of East and West). *Shin Nippon* 1, no. 2 (May 1911): 1–8.

Ōta Masao. "Ōyama Ikuo no mimponshugi ron" (Ōyama Ikuo's thoughts on democracy). *Dōshisha hōgaku* (Dōshisha law review), no. 100 (Jan. 1967), pp. 27–74.

———. *Taishō demokurashii kenkyū* (Research on Taishō democracy). Tokyo, 1975.

Ōyama Ikuo. *Ōyama Ikuo zenshū* (The complete works of Ōyama Ikuo). 5 vols. Tokyo, 1947–1949.

Ozaki Shirō. *Waseda daigaku* (Waseda University). Tokyo, 1953.

Rikken minseitō shi (History of the Constitutional Democratic party). 2 vols. Tokyo, 1973.

Saitō Eiko, ed. *Kikuchi Shigeru chosakushū, dai-ikkan: Yanakamura mondai to gakusei undō* (The collected writings of Kikuchi Shigeru, Volume I: The Yanakamura problem and the students' movement). Tokyo, 1977.

Sakai Yukichi. "Dai-ichiji goken undō ni tsuite" (The first movement to protect the Constitution). Unpublished paper. Tokyo, 1967.

Sakuma Shōzan. Nihon shisō taikei 55 (An outline of Japanese thought no. 55). Tokyo, 1971.

Sasaki Takashi. "Kyokoku-itchi naikaku ki no seitō—Rikken seiyūkai to Saitō naikaku" (Political parties in the "National Government" period—the Seiyūkai and the Saitō cabinet). *Shigaku zasshi* 86, no. 9 (Sept. 1977): 43–77.

Satō Seizaburō. "Kyōchō to jiritsu no aida" (Between association and autonomy). *Nempō seijigaku* (Annals of the Political Science association [Japan, 1969]). Tokyo, 1970.

Sekishun. Ibaraki Prefecture, 1923.

Shidehara heiwa zaidan (Shidehara peace foundation), ed. *Shidehara Kijūrō.* Tokyo, 1955.

Shinobu Seizaburō. *Taishō demokurashii shi* (A history of Taishō democracy). 3 vols. Tokyo, 1954–1959.

———. *Taishō seiji shi* (A political history of the Taishō period). 4 vols. 1952. Reprint (4 vols. in 1). Tokyo, 1968.

Shinshimei (New mission), 1924–1926. Tokyo.

Shisō no kagaku kenkyūkai (Research society for the science of thought), ed. *Tenkō* (Conversion). 3 vols. Tokyo, 1959–1962.

Shūgiin giji sokkiroku (Records of the House of Representatives proceedings). Vols. 43–89. Tokyo (Teikoku gikai [Imperial Diet]), 1920–1945.

Shūgiin jimukyoku (Secretariat of the House of Representatives), ed. *Shūgiin giin sōsenkyo ichiran* (A summary of the general election for members of the House of Representatives). Tokyo, 1928–1932.

Sumiya Etsuji et al. *Niijima Jō shokanshū* (Collected letters of Niijima Jō), Iwanami bunko (Iwanami library) 5310–5312. Tokyo, 1954.

Suzuki Umeshirō. *Nihon kaizō no dōgi oyobi sono kōryō* (The morality and essential principles of the reconstruction of Japan). Tokyo, 1919.

Takahashi Masao. *Shimada Saburō—Nihon seikai ni okeru jindō-shugisha no shōgai* (Shimada Saburō—the life of a humanitarian in the Japanese political world). Yokohama, 1954.

Takano Zen'ichi, ed. *Nihon shakaishugi no chichi Abe Isoo* (The father of Japanese socialism—Abe Isoo). Tokyo, 1970.

Takeda Taijun, ed. *Seijika no bunshō* (Writings of politicians). Tokyo, 1960.

Tanaka Sōgorō. *Kita Ikki: Nihon fuashisuto no shōchō* (Kita Ikki: Symbol of a Japanese fascist). Tokyo, 1959.

———. *Kōtoku Shūsui.* Tokyo, 1971.

Tokikoyama Tsunesaburō. *Waseda seikatsu hanseiki* (A half-century of the life of Waseda). Tokyo, 1973.

Tokyo Asahi shimbun (Tokyo Asahi news). Tokyo.

Tokyo Nichinichi shimbun (Tokyo Nichinichi news). Tokyo.

Tokyo Nichinichi shimbunsha and Osaka Mainichi shimbunsha, (Tokyo Nichinichi news and Osaka Mainichi news), eds. *Meiji, Taishō, Shōwa gikai seiji rimen shi* (An inside history of Meiji, Taishō, Shōwa parliamentary politics). Tokyo and Osaka, 1937.

Tomita Nobuo. "Hoshu shihai no kōzō to minshū ishiki—Shōwa ki sōsenkyo no shiteki kōsatsu" (The structure of conservative control and mass consciousness—a historical study of Shōwa general elections). *Kindai kokka no shisō* (Thought of the modern nation). Edited by Joseph Pittau. Nihon no shakai bunka shi, 6 (Social-cultural history of Japan series, no. 6). Tokyo, 1974.

——— et al. *Nihon seiji no jitsuryokusha-tachi* (Men of ability in Japanese politics). Vol. 3. Tokyo, 1981.

Tōyama Shigeki and Adachi Shizuko. *Kindai Nihon seiji hikkei* (A handbook of modern Japanese politics). Tokyo, 1961.

Tsuda Sōkichi. *Shisō, bungei, Nihongo* (Thought, literature, the Japanese language). Tokyo, 1961.

Tsutsumi Kōjirō. *Taiheiyō no kakehashi* (Bridge across the Pacific). Tokyo, 1963.

Ueda Sotoo. *Sōsenkyo ki—fu-Waikaku senkyo kanshō seikirara kan* (An open view of government interference in the election at the time of the Ōkuma cabinet). Tokyo, 1917.

Uehara Etsujirō. *Demokurashii to Nihon no kaizō* (Democracy and the reconstruction of Japan). Tokyo, 1919.

Wakatsuki Reijirō. *Kofūan kaikoroku* (The reminiscences of Wakatsuki Reijirō). Rev. ed. Tokyo, 1975.

Waseda daigaku shuppanbu (Waseda University publications department), ed. *Meiji bummei shi ni okeru Ōkuma Shigenobu* (Ōkuma Shigenobu in the history of Meiji civilization). Tokyo, 1962.

Watanabe Ikujirō. *Ōkuma Shigenobu.* Tokyo, 1958.

Yabe Teiji. *Konoe Fumimaro.* 2 vols. Tokyo, 1952.

Yabe Teiji nikki kankōkai (Publication society for the diary of Yabe Teiji). *Yabe Teiji nikki: Ichō no maki* (The diary of Yabe Teiji: Ginkgo volume). Tokyo, 1974.

Yamamoto Shirō. *Taishō seihen no kisoteki kenkyū* (Fundamental research on Taishō political change). Tokyo, 1970.

Yamaura Kan'ichi. "Kaiso Yokusankai no hitobito" (Personnel of the reorganized Yokusankai). *Kaizō* 23, no. 9 (May 1941): 210–217.

——. "Kakushin seijika ron" (Reformist politicians). *Kaizō* 20, no. 6 (June 1938): 93-1.

——. "Nagai Ryūtarō to Nakajima Chikuhei" (Nagai Ryūtarō and Nakajima Chikuhei). *Nippon hyōron* (Japan review), Mar. 3, 1937, pp. 159-63.

——. *Seikyoku o meguru hitobito* (People moving in political circles). Tokyo, 1926.

Yamazaki Kōichi. " 'Genron no buki' migaite—Abareta Nihon shi-jō no shishitachi" (With the "weapon of speech" polished—patriots of the restive history of Japan). *Rondan Hokkaidō* (The world of criticism in Hokkaido), no. 145 (Sept. 1973), pp. 82–84.

Yanagi (Willow). Tokyo, 1961–1963.

Yatsugi Kazuo. *Shōwa dōran shishi* (A private history of Shōwa in upheaval). 3 vols. Tokyo, 1971–1973.

Yokusan undō shi kankōkai (Publication society for the history of the Yokusan movement), Shimonaka Yasaburō, ed. *Yokusan kokumin undō shi* (History of the Yokusan national movement). Tokyo, 1954.

Yomiuri shimbun (Yomiuri news). Tokyo.

Yoshino Sakuzō. "Kensei no hongi o toite sono yūshū no bi o nasu no michi o ronzu" (The cardinal principle of constitutional government and the way to its achievement). *Chūō kōron* 30, no. 1 (Jan. 1916): 17–114.

——. "Kokka seikatsu no isshin" (Reformation of national life). *Chūō kōron* 35, no. 1 (Jan. 1920): 117–56.

——. "Minshūteki jii undō o ronzu" (Discussing democratic demonstrations). *Chūō kōron* 29, no. 4 (Apr. 1914): 87–114.

Sources in English

Akita, George. *The Foundations of Constitutional Government in Modern Japan, 1868-1900.* Cambridge, Mass., 1967.

Allardyce, Gilbert. "What Fascism Is Not: Thoughts on the Deflation of a Concept." *American Historical Review* 84, no. 2 (Apr. 1979): 367–88.

Andrew, Nancy. "The Seitōsha: An Early Japanese Women's Organization, 1911-1916." In *Papers on Japan* 6:45–69. Harvard University, East Asian Research Center, Cambridge, 1972.

Arima, Tatsuo. *The Failure of Freedom: A Portrait of Modern Japanese Intellectuals.* Cambridge, Mass. 1969.

Ayusawa, Iwao F. *A History of Labor in Modern Japan.* Honolulu, 1966.

Bamba, Nobuya. *Japanese Diplomacy in a Dilemma: New Light on Japan's Foreign Policy, 1924-1929.* Vancouver, 1972.

Beasley, W. G. *The Modern History of Japan.* New York, 1963.

Beckmann, George M. and Okubo Genji. *The Japanese Communist Party 1922-1945.* Stanford, 1969.

Bellah, Robert N. "Japan's Cultural Identity: Some Reflections on the

Work of Watsuji Tetsuro." *Journal of Asian Studies* 24, no. 4 (Aug. 1965): 573–594.

———. "Values and Social Change in Modern Japan." *Asian Cultural Studies*, no. 3, pp. 13–56.

Bergamini, David. *Japan's Imperial Conspiracy.* New York, 1971.

Berger, Gordon M. "Japan's Young Prince: Konoe Fumimaro's Early Political Career, 1916–1931." *Monumenta Nipponica* 29, no. 4 (Winter 1974): 451–75.

———. *Parties Out of Power in Japan, 1931–1941.* Princeton, 1977.

———. "The Search for a New Political Order: Konoe Fumimaro, the Political Parties, and Japanese Politics During the Early Shōwa Era." Ph.D. diss., Yale University, 1972.

Bernstein, Gail Lee. *Japanese Marxist: A Portrait of Kawakami Hajime 1879–1946.* Cambridge, Mass., and London, 1976.

Borg, Dorothy and Shumpei Okamoto, eds. *Pearl Harbor as History: Japanese-American Relations 1931–1941.* New York and London, 1973.

Boyle, John Hunter. *China and Japan at War, 1937–1945: The Politics of Collaboration.* Stanford, 1972.

Brown, Delmer M. *Nationalism in Japan.* Berkeley, 1955.

Bryan, J. Ingram. *Japan from Within: An Inquiry into the Political, Industrial, Commercial, Financial, Agricultural, Armamental and Educational Conditions of Modern Japan.* London, 1924.

Burkman, Thomas Wesley. "Japan, the League of Nations, and the New World Order, 1918–1920." Ph.D. diss., University of Michigan, 1975.

Chang, Richard T. *Historians and Taisho Statesmen.* Washington, D.C., 1977.

Clarke, Joseph I. C. *Japan at First Hand: Her Islands, Their People, the Picturesque, the Real with Latest Facts and Figures on Their War-time Trade Expansion and Commercial Outreach.* 1918. Reprint. Wilmington, Del., 1973.

Colgrove, Kenneth. "The Japanese Privy Council." *American Political Science Review* 25 (Aug., Nov. 1931): 589–614, 881–905.

Coox, Alvin D. *The Anatomy of a Small War: The Soviet-Japanese Struggle for Changkufeng-Khasan, 1938.* Westport, Conn., 1977.

———. "Evidences of Antimilitarism in Prewar and Wartime Japan." *Pacific Affairs* 46, no. 4 (Winter 1973–1974): 502–514.

Craig, Albert M., ed. *Japan: A Comparative View.* Princeton, 1979.

Craig, Albert M. and Donald H. Shively, eds. *Personality in Japanese History.* Berkeley, 1970.

Crowley, James B. "Japan's Military Foreign Policies." In *Japan's Foreign Policy 1868–1941: A Research Guide,* edited by James William Morley, pp. 3–117. New York and London, 1974.

———. *Japan's Quest for Autonomy: National Security and Foreign Policy 1930–1938.* Princeton, 1966.

———, ed. *Modern East Asia: Essays in Interpretation.* New York, 1970.

Davis, Sandra T. W. *Intellectual Change and Political Development in Early Modern Japan: Ono Azusa, A Case Study.* London and Toronto, 1980.

de Bary, Wm. Theodore, Ryusaku Tsunoda, and Donald Keene, comp. *Sources of Japanese Tradition.* 1958. Reprint (text ed. in 2 vols). New York and London, 1964.

De Vos, George E. et al. *Socialization for Achievement: Essays on the Cultural Psychology of the Japanese.* Berkeley, Los Angeles, and London, 1973.

Drea, Edward J. *The 1942 Japanese General Election: Political Mobilization in Wartime Japan.* East Asian Series Research Publication, no. 11. Center for East Asian Studies, The University of Kansas. Lawrence, Kans., 1979.

Dull, Paul S. "Count Kato Komei and the Twenty-one Demands." *Pacific Historical Review* 19, no. 2 (May 1950): 151–61.

Duus, Peter. "Nagai Ryūtarō and the 'White Peril,' 1905–1944." Included in "A Symposium on Japanese Nationalism." *Journal of Asian Studies* 31, no. 1 (Nov. 1971): 41–48.

———. "Nagai Ryūtarō: The Tactical Dilemmas of Reform." In *Personality in Japanese History,* edited by Albert M. Craig and Donald H. Shively, pp. 399–424. Berkeley and Los Angeles, 1970.

———. *Party Rivalry and Political Change in Taishō Japan.* Cambridge, Mass., 1968.

———. Review of *The Japanese Oligarchy and the Russo-Japanese War,* by Okamoto Shumpei. *Journal of Asian Studies* 30, no. 4 (Aug. 1971): 897–98.

———. "Whig History, Japanese Style: The Min'yūsha Historians and the Meiji Restoration." *Journal of Asian Studies* 33, no. 3 (May 1974): 415–36.

Duus, Peter and Daniel I. Okimoto. "Fascism and the History of Pre-War Japan: The Failure of a Concept." *Journal of Asian Studies* 39, no. 1 (Nov. 1979): 65–76.

Fahs, Charles B. "Political Groups in the Japanese House of Peers." *American Political Science Review* 34 (Oct. 1940): 896–919.

Fairbank, John K., Edwin O. Reischauer, and Albert M. Craig. *East Asia: The Modern Transformation.* Boston, 1965.

Falconeri, G. Ralph. Review of *Revolt in Japan: The Young Officers and the February 26, 1936 Incident,* by Ben-Ami Shillony. *Journal of Asian Studies* 33, no. 4 (Aug. 1974): 710–12.

Fletcher, William M., III. "Ideologies of Political and Economic Reform and Fascism in Prewar Japan: Ryū Shintarō, Rōyama Masamichi, and the Shōwa Research Association." Ph.D. diss., Yale University, 1975.

———. "Intellectuals and Fascism in Early Shōwa Japan." *Journal of Asian Studies* 39, no. 1 (Nov. 1979): 39–63.

Fresno Republican, 1920. Fresno, Calif.

Fukuzawa, Yukichi. *The Autobiography of Yukichi Fukuzawa.* Translated by Eiichi Kiyooka. New York and London, 1966.

Gay, Peter. "Peter Gay on 'Voltaire's Politics.'" *Times Literary Supplement* (London), June 12, 1981, pp. 673–74.

———. "Weimar Culture: The Outsider as Insider." In *The Intellectual Migration, Europe and America, 1930–1960,* edited by Donald Fleming and Bernard Bailyn, pp. 11–93. Cambridge, Mass., 1969.

Goodman, Grant K., comp. *Imperial Japan and Asia: A Reassessment.* Occasional Papers of the East Asian Institute, Columbia University. New York, 1967.

Greene, Nathanael, ed. *Fascism: An Anthology.* New York, 1968.

Griffin, Edward G. "The Universal Suffrage Issue in Japanese Politics, 1918–25." *Journal of Asian Studies* 31, no. 2 (Feb. 1972): 275–90.

Grilli, Peter M. "Abe Jirō and Santarō no nikki." In *Papers on Japan* 4:64–94. Harvard University, East Asian Research Center. Cambridge, 1967.

Hackett, Roger F. *Yamagata Aritomo in the Rise of Modern Japan, 1838–1922.* Cambridge, Mass., 1971.

Hall, John Whitney. *Japan: From Prehistory to Modern Times.* New York, 1970.

Hane, Mikiso. *Japan: A Historical Survey.* New York, 1972.

Havens, Thomas R. H. *Valley of Darkness: The Japanese People and World War II.* New York, 1978.

Hershey, Amos S. and Susanne W. Hershey. *Modern Japan: Social—Industrial —Political.* Indianapolis, 1919.

Hofstadter, Richard. *The Age of Reform: From Bryan to FDR.* New York, 1955.

———. *The American Political Tradition and the Men Who Made It.* New York, 1948.

Ike, Nobutaka. *The Beginnings of Political Democracy in Japan.* Baltimore, 1950.

International Encyclopedia of the Social Sciences. Edited by David L. Sills. New York and London, 1968.

Iriye, Akira. *Pacific Estrangement: Japanese and American Expansion, 1897–1911.* Cambridge, Mass., 1972.

The Japan Biographical Encyclopedia and Who's Who. 3d ed. Tokyo, 1964–1965.

Jansen, Marius B. *Japan and China: From War to Peace, 1894–1972.* Chicago, 1975.

———. *The Japanese and Sun Yat-sen.* Cambridge, Mass., 1954.

———, ed. *Changing Japanese Attitudes Toward Modernization.* Princeton, 1965.

Kublin, Hyman. *Asian Revolutionary: The Life of Sen Katayama.* Princeton, 1964.

Kubota, Gaylord C. "Arita Hachirō and the Anti-Comintern Pact of November 1936: A Case Study in 'Thin Ink' Diplomacy." Translation of article published in Japanese as "Arita Hachirō: Nichi-Doku bōkyō kyōtei ni okeru usuzumi iro gaikō no tenkai." *Kokusai seiji,* no. 56 (1976), pp. 46–64.

Large, Stephen S. *The Yūaikai, 1912–19: The Rise of Labor in Japan.* Tokyo, 1972.

Lebra, Joyce C. "Ōkuma Shigenobu, Modernization and the West." In

Japan's Modern Century, edited by Edmund Skrzypczak, pp. 27–40. Tokyo and Rutland, Vt., 1968.

———. *Ōkuma Shigenobu: Statesman of Meiji Japan.* Canberra, 1973.

Lensen, George Alexander. *Japanese Recognition of the USSR: Soviet-Japanese Relations 1921–1930.* Tokyo, 1970.

Levine, Lawrence W. "The Historian and the Culture Gap." In *The Historian's Workshop: Original Essays by Sixteen Historians,* edited by L. P. Curtis, Jr., pp. 307–326. New York, 1970.

Lockwood, William W. *The Economic Development of Japan: Growth and Structural Change, 1863–1938.* Princeton, 1954.

———, ed. *The State and Economic Enterprise in Modern Japan.* Princeton, 1965.

Lu, David J. *From the Marco Polo Bridge to Pearl Harbor: Japan's Entry into World War II.* Washington, D.C., 1961.

———, comp. *Sources of Japanese History.* 2 vols. New York, 1974.

Maruyama, Masao. *Thought and Behaviour in Modern Japanese Politics.* Edited by Ivan Morris. London, 1963.

Mason, R. H. P. *Japan's First General Election.* Cambridge, 1969.

Masumi, Junnosuke. "The Present Condition of Japanese Political Studies." Parts 1, 2. *Asian Forum* 2, nos. 2, 3 (Apr.–June, July–Sept. 1970): 88–103, 152–67.

Matsumoto, Sannosuke. "The Significance of Nationalism in Modern Japanese Thought: Some Theoretical Problems." Included in "A Symposium on Japanese Nationalism." *Journal of Asian Studies* 31, no. 1 (Nov. 1971): 49–56.

Matsumoto, Shigeharu. "The New Labor Movement in Japan." *Nation,* Mar. 25, 1925, p. 313.

Matsuo, Takayoshi. "The Development of Democracy in Japan—Taishō Democracy: Its Flowering and Breakdown." *Developing Economies* 4, no. 4 (Dec. 1966): 612–37.

———. "Profile of Asian Minded Man 6: Sakuzō Yoshino." *Developing Economies* 5, no. 2 (June 1967): 388–404.

Maxon, Yale Candee. *Control of Japanese Foreign Policy: A Study of Civil-Military Rivalry 1930–1945.* Berkeley and Los Angeles, 1957.

Mayo, Marlene, ed. *The Emergence of Imperial Japan: Self-Defense or Calculated Aggression?* Problems in Asian Civilizations Series. Lexington, Mass., 1970.

Miller, Frank O. *Minobe Tatsukichi: Interpreter of Constitutionalism in Japan.* Berkeley and Los Angeles, 1965.

Mitchell, Richard H. "Japan's Peace Preservation Law of 1925: Its Origins and Significance." *Monumenta Nipponica* 28, no. 3 (Autumn 1973): 317–45.

———. "The Peace Preservation Law." Paper read at Association for Asian Studies Meeting, Boston, April 1, 1974.

———. *Thought Control in Prewar Japan.* Ithaca and London, 1976.

Morley, James W., ed. *Dilemmas of Growth in Prewar Japan.* Princeton, 1971.

Morris, Ivan. *Nationalism and the Right Wing in Japan: A Study of Post-War Trends.* London, 1960.

———, ed. *Japan 1931–1945: Militarism, Fascism, Japanism?* Problems in Asian Civilizations Series. Boston, 1963.

Morton, William Fitch. "The Tanaka Cabinet's China Policy, 1927–1929." Ph.D. diss., Columbia University, 1969.

———. *Tanaka Giichi and Japan's China Policy.* New York, 1980.

Moskowitz, Karl. "The Creation of the Oriental Development Company: Japanese Illusions Meet Korean Reality." *Occasional Papers on Korea,* no. 2 (Mar. 1974), pp. 73–121.

Nagai, Michio. "Herbert Spencer in Early Meiji Japan." *Far Eastern Quarterly* 14, no. 1 (Nov. 1954): 55–64.

———. "Westernization and Japanization: The Early Meiji Transformation of Education." In *Tradition and Modernization in Japanese Culture.* Edited by Donald H. Shively, pp. 35–76. Princeton, 1971.

Najita, Tetsuo. *Hara Kei in the Politics of Compromise, 1905–1915.* Cambridge, Mass., 1967.

———. *Japan.* Englewood Cliffs, N.J., 1974.

Nakane, Chie. *Japanese Society.* Berkeley and Los Angeles, 1970.

Notehelfer, F. G. "Japan's First Pollution Incident." Included in "Symposium: The Ashio Copper Mine Pollution Incident." *Journal of Japanese Studies* 1, no. 2 (Spring 1975): 351–83.

———. *Kōtoku Shūsui: Portrait of a Japanese Radical.* Cambridge, 1971.

Ogata, Sadako N. *Defiance in Manchuria: The Making of Japanese Foreign Policy, 1931–1932.* Berkeley and Los Angeles, 1964.

Okamoto, Shumpei. *The Japanese Oligarchy and the Russo-Japanese War.* New York and London, 1970.

Okudaira, Yasuhiro. "Some Preparatory Notes for the Study of the Peace Preservation Law in Pre-War Japan." *Annals of the Institute of Social Science,* no. 14, pp. 49–69. University of Tokyo. Tokyo, 1973.

Ōkuma, Shigenobu, ed. *Fifty Years of New Japan.* Vol. 1, *History of Political Parties.* Tokyo, 1910.

Payne, Stanley G. *Fascism: Comparison and Definition.* Madison, 1980.

Peattie, Mark R. *Ishiwara Kanji and Japan's Confrontation with the West.* Princeton, 1975.

Pierson, John D. "The Early Liberal Thought of Tokutomi Sohō: Some Problems of Western Social Theory in Meiji Japan." *Monumenta Nipponica* 29, no. 2 (Summer 1974): 199–224.

———. *Tokutomi Sohō, 1863–1957: A Journalist for Modern Japan.* Princeton, 1980.

Pyle, Kenneth B. *The New Generation in Meiji Japan: Problems of Cultural Identity, 1885–1895.* Stanford, 1969.

———. "The Technology of Japanese Nationalism: The Local Improvement Movement 1900–1918." *Journal of Asian Studies* 33, no. 1 (Nov. 1973): 51–65.

Reischauer, Edwin O. *The United States and Japan*. 3d ed. New York, 1965.
Reischauer, Robert Karl. *Japan: Government—Politics*. New York, 1939.
Rōyama, Masamichi. *Foreign Policy of Japan, 1914–1939*. 1941. Reprint. Westport, Conn., 1973.
Ruggiero, Guido de. *The History of European Liberalism*. Translated by R. G. Collingwood. [London], 1927. Reprint. Boston, Beacon Paperback, 1959.
Scalapino, Robert A. *Democracy and the Party Movement in Prewar Japan: The Failure of the First Attempt*. Berkeley and Los Angeles, 1953.
Shigemitsu, Mamoru. *Japan and Her Destiny*. Edited by Major-General F. S. G. Piggott, translated by Oswald White. New York, 1958.
Shillony, Ben-Ami, *Politics and Culture in Wartime Japan*. London, 1981.
———. *Revolt in Japan: The Young Officers and the February 26, 1936, Incident*. Princeton, 1973.
———. "The Showa Restoration, Elements in the Ideology of the Rebel Young Officers in Japan in the 1930's." Paper read at the Midwest Japan Seminar, Milwaukee, May 15, 1971.
Silberman, Bernard S. "The Political Theory and Program of Yoshino Sakuzō." *Journal of Modern History* 31, no. 4 (Dec. 1959): 310–24.
Silberman, Bernard S. and H. D. Harootunian, eds. *Japan in Crisis: Essays on Taishō Democracy*. Princeton, 1974.
Smethurst, Richard J. *A Social Basis for Prewar Japanese Militarism: The Army and the Rural Community*. Berkeley, 1974.
Smith, Henry Dewitt, II. *Japan's First Student Radicals*. Cambridge, Mass., 1972.
Steinhoff, Patricia G. "The Legal Control of Ideology in Pre-war Japan." Paper read at the Twenty-eighth International Congress of Orientalists, Canberra, Jan. 6–12, 1971.
———. "Tenkō: An Analysis of Defection from the Pre-war Japanese Communist Party." Paper read at the Pacific Sociological Association Meeting, April 16–19, 1970.
———. "Tenkō: Ideology and Societal Integration in Pre-war Japan." Ph.D. diss., Harvard University, 1969.
Storry, Richard. *A History of Modern Japan: An Account of an Early Decision by an Asian Nation to Come to Terms with the Economic and Political Patterns of the West*. London, 1960.
———. *The Double Patriots*. Boston, 1957.
Strong, Kenneth. *Ox Against the Storm: A Biography of Tanaka Shozo, Japan's Conservationalist Pioneer*. [Victoria], 1977.
Takahashi, Makoto. "The Development of War-time Economic Controls." *Developing Economies* 5, no. 4 (Dec. 1967): 648–65.
Takeda, Kiyoko. "Pioneers of Modern Japan: 8, Yoshino Sakuzō." *Japan Quarterly* 12, no. 4 (Oct.–Dec. 1965): 515–24.
Takemoto, Toru. *Failure of Liberalism in Japan: Shidehara Kijuro's Encounter with Anti-liberals*. Washington, D.C., 1978.

Tanin, O. and E. Yohan [pseuds.]. *Militarism and Fascism in Japan.* London, 1934.

Teilhard de Chardin, Pierre. *Human Energy.* Translated by J. M. Cohen. London, 1969.

Titus, David Anson. *Palace and Politics in Prewar Japan.* New York and London, 1974.

Tolischus, Otto D. *Tokyo Record.* New York, 1943.

Totten, George O. *The Social Democratic Movement in Prewar Japan.* New Haven, Conn., 1966.

———, ed. *Democracy in Prewar Japan: Groundwork or Facade?* Problems in Asian Civilizations Series. Boston, 1965.

Tsurumi, Kazuko. *Social Change and the Individual: Japan Before and After Defeat in World War II.* Princeton, 1970.

Valliant, Robert B. "The Selling of Japan: Japanese Manipulation of Western Opinion, 1900–1905." *Monumenta Nipponica* 29, no. 4 (Winter 1974): 415–38.

Wainwright, S. H. "Educational Results and Prospects." *The Japan Weekly Mail,* Nov. 3, 1900, pp. 478–81.

Ward, Robert Edward. "Party Government in Japan: A Preliminary Survey of Its Development and Electoral Record, 1928–1937." Ph.D. diss., University of California at Berkeley, 1948.

———, ed. *Political Development in Modern Japan.* Princeton, 1968.

Ward, Robert and Dankwart Rustow. *Political Modernization in Japan and Turkey.* Princeton, 1964.

Wheeler, John K. "Rōyama Masamichi and the Search for a Middle Ground, 1932–1940." In *Papers on Japan* 6:70–101. Harvard University, East Asian Research Center. Cambridge, 1972.

Wilson, George Macklin. "Kita Ikki's Theory of Revolution." *Journal of Asian Studies* 26, no. 1 (Nov. 1966): 89–99.

———. "A New Look at the Problem of 'Japanese Fascism.' " *Comparative Studies in Society and History* 10, no. 4 (July 1968): 401–412.

———. *Radical Nationalist in Japan: Kita Ikki 1883–1937.* Cambridge, Mass., 1969.

———, ed. *Crisis Politics in Prewar Japan.* Tokyo, 1970.

Wray, Harold J. "A Study in Contrasts: Japanese School Textbooks of 1903 and 1941–5." *Monumenta Nipponica* 28, no. 1 (Spring 1973): 69–86.

Yoshino, Sakuzō. "Fascism in Japan." *Contemporary Japan* 1 (Sept. 1932): 185–97.

Young, A. Morgan. *Japan in Recent Times: 1912–26.* 1929. Reprint. Westport, Conn., 1973.

Index

About the Author

Sharon Minichiello received an M.A. and Ph.D. in history from the University of Hawaii. Her doctoral studies concentrated on modern Japanese political history, and subsequent research has focused on the interaction of Western and Japanese political thought. She has served as a visiting scholar on both the Faculty of Letters and Faculty of Law at the University of Tokyo and at Harvard University's Japan Institute. Since joining the history faculty of Loyola Marymount University, Los Angeles, in 1975, Professor Minichiello has received that institution's Outstanding Teacher of the Year Award six times.

Production Notes

This book was designed by Roger Eggers. Reverend Eijo Ikenaga provided the cover calligraphy. Composition and paging were done on the Quadex Composing System and typesetting on the Compugraphic 8400 by the design and production staff of University of Hawaii Press.

The text typeface is Baskerville II and the display typeface is Compugraphic Palatino.

Offset presswork and binding were done by Vail-Ballou Press, Inc. Text paper is Writers R Offset, basis 50.